RETURN *to the* RIVERS

Dearest Villi, Jasmine & Lamaar,

May a new pilgrimage of
flavors begin with this book.
Love
Vikas Khanna

RETURN
to the
RIVERS

RECIPES *and* MEMORIES
of the **HIMALAYAN RIVER VALLEYS**

VIKAS KHANNA

with *Andrew Blackmore-Dobbyn*

LAKE ISLE PRESS
New York

Published by:
Lake Isle Press, Inc.
2095 Broadway, Suite 301
New York, NY 10023
(212) 273-0796
E-mail: info@lakeislepress.com

Distributed to the trade by:
National Book Network, Inc.
4501 Forbes Boulevard, Suite 200
Lanham, MD 20706
1(800) 462-6420
www.nbnbooks.com

Library of Congress Control Number: 2013951725
ISBN-13: 978-1-891105-53-1
ISBN-10: 1-891105-53-1

Editor: Jennifer Sit

Book design: Ellen Swandiak
Production design: Liz Trovato
Cover design: Polo Black Golde

This book is available at special sales discounts for bulk purchases as premiums or
special editions, including customized covers. For more information, contact the
publisher at (212) 273-0796 or by e-mail: info@lakeislepress.com

First edition

Printed in the United States of America

10 9 8 7 6 5 4 3 2 1

BUDDHIST MEALTIME PRAYER

This food is the gift of the whole universe,

Each morsel is a sacrifice of life,

May I be worthy to receive it.

May the energy in this food,

Give me the strength,

To transform my unwholesome qualities

into wholesome ones.

I am grateful for this food.

TOO MANY PEOPLE TO THANK

To write a cookbook is an enormous undertaking and one person cannot do it alone. There is research to be done, recipes to be tested, photographs to be taken, and the hard work of writing.
I have tried my best to credit all of the generous individuals who shared their knowledge with me, and if I have forgotten someone, I apologize and thank you deeply for your help. I could never have written this book without the cooks who shared their wisdom and recipes.

In testing recipes, I am grateful for the help of Lindsay Chapman. For transcribing recipes from my hard-to-understand notebooks, I thank Niriti Nagpal, who also helped immeasurably with arranging travel and itineraries, organizing documents and photos, keeping me organized and focused on the job at hand, and providing enormous assistance with the initial concept of this book. For assistance with food photography, my thanks to Ronnie Bhardwaj. For ongoing consultation, especially with respect to culture and recipes from Tibet, my thanks to Tashi Chodron, the Momo Maven of New York City and the driving force behind VoicesofTibet.org, an organization that works to preserve the stories of Tibet's rich cultural heritage. Also, Tashi's brother, Lama Ugen Palden Rongdrol, professional Tibetan opera singer and dancer, master of "Cham" Lama dance, for his help with the momos and the meat chapter. The chapter on bread benefited greatly from the contributions of Tashi's mother, Cho Lhamo, one of the last of Tibet's great warrior horsewomen and a wonderful baker. Tsering Wangmo, author of the *Lhasa Moon Tibetan Cookbook*, a well-known classic, contributed wonderful advice. Elizabeth Esther Kelly, author of *Tibetan Cooking*, was supportive and informative. Mr. Lobsang Nyandak Zayul from Office of Tibet inspired me greatly. Professor Robert Thurman was instrumental in bolstering my faith in this project. I thank Shelley and Don Rubin from the Rubin Museum of Art for their ongoing moral support and belief in this project. Rajesh Bhardwaj from Junoon Hospitality provided encouragement and support. Thanks also to Hiroko Kiiffner and her staff at Lake Isle Press, especially Jennifer Sit, for her belief in this project. It is unlikely this book would have been finished without their patient advice and support through the long process of writing this book. Thank you to Ellen Swandiak for her beautiful design.

Finally, for taking my stories, words, and ideas and turning them into this book, along with countless hours of research, writing and rewriting the recipes, help with recipe testing, and encouragement when the end of this book seemed so far away, thanks to my friend and collaborator in all my creative ventures, Andrew Blackmore-Dobbyn.

I have one special person to thank for his inspiration in finishing this project because I had begun to think it was just too big a job. When I mentioned this project to His Holiness, the Dalai Lama, he encouraged me with kind words to document a way of life that is fast disappearing. He knows this better than most. Thanks to him I was moved to keep writing in honor of the beautiful spirit that inhabits the roof of the world. Thank you, Your Holiness.

The last person I have to thank is a woman in Tibet whose name I do not know. Much that is contained in this book was in a laptop computer I was carrying throughout the Himalayas and at one point I left the laptop in a café when I ran to catch a bus out of Lhasa to Kathmandu. There was no backup copy. This woman ran up the side of a mountain to catch up to the bus and made sure that I got it back. She shrugged it off as though it were no big deal and refused to accept any reward, insisting that anyone would have done the same. I don't know how much I would have been able to reconstruct if I had not gotten the laptop back. There were many photographs that I would have lost permanently. Bless you a thousand times, wherever you are.

THE DALAI LAMA

FOREWORD

The Himalayas are truly the roof of our world. This mountain range defines our existence in terms of who we are and where we belong. It speaks to our lofty aspirations as well as our profound spiritual beliefs.

The cultures, cuisines, and spiritual foundations of the Himalayan people are as deeply rooted as the skies in this region are soaring in their reach and grandeur.

The cuisine of this region also reflects the richness of the unique culture of the people of the Himalayas, and Mr. Vikas Khanna presents a whole new celebration of their life. I am pleased to say the simple foods of the Himalayan people are well captured in this book.

June 23rd, 2009

Preface

Himalayas. One word. It conjures up a forbidding and remote place, as far from humanity as one can get and still be on the planet. And yet the high peaks are so very warm and close to my heart, and have been since I was a boy. The Himalayas have always represented freedom to me. I have long felt that if I could just roam through those rugged mountains and breathe their pure air, my life would be complete. It took great effort for me to finally reach those peaks and today, I carry their spirit with me wherever I go. Indeed, it is the Himalayas' spiritual power that has helped make me into the person—and the chef—I am today.

I am from Amritsar in Punjab, an area in northwestern India to the south of the Himalayas. From an early age, I was aware that the rivers that flow around my hometown began their journey in those mountains. In fact, Punjab means "five rivers," and those rivers—the Jhelum, Ravi, Chenab, Beas, and Sutlej—are the reason that since the ancient Indus Valley civilization, the land around Amritsar has always been such a fertile region.

When I was young, I dreamt of the Himalayas— vast, limitless peaks where gods were born and great birds soared. Perhaps I dreamt of them because I was born with clubfeet and therefore could not run or climb trees like other children. But as so often happens, my misfortune turned into

a gift. Because I couldn't play like other children, I learned to cook. I would spend hours at my grandmother Biji's side, absorbing her large store of family recipes and taking in all her wisdom about cooking and its connection to our culture.

Back then, most Indian children with my condition would not have been treated, but luckily for me, I was the son of Bindu Khanna. We rode all around the region of Amritsar on her moped. I hung onto the back for dear life as she searched for a doctor who would agree to take installment payments for treating me. Our relatives advised her not to bother to seek out medical care—she already had another son who was perfectly healthy. Luckily for me, she did not listen to their naysaying.

My grandfather was yet another pillar of my childhood, the single most important source of my deep spiritual connection to the Himalayas. He was a very tall man and when he looked over my head, he always appeared to be dreaming of something unimaginably distant—he taught me about religion, spirituality, and poetry, and about the awe-inspiring power of the Himalayas.

When I was growing up, there was a picture in my house of the pilgrimage site, Vaishno Devi Temple, a sacred place in the Jammu and Kashmir regions of northern India. As a child, my grandfather would

BORDER ROADS ORGANISATION
FOTULA TOP
HT-13479FT
4091 MT
HIGHEST POINT THE
SRINAGAR LEH ROAD
55RCC

tell me stories about how during his life he had made many pilgrimages there. He was losing all hope that he would get to see this sacred place again before he died. No one in our family would agree to make the trip with him, and he knew that he could not do it alone.

So when I was only seven years old, I solemnly promised him that I would take him to the temple one day and he accepted this without comment. As it turned out, my vow to my grandfather also became a promise to myself—that one day, when my feet were treated, I would be able to run free. The place that symbolized that freedom for me was the Himalayas.

It turned out that my grandfather proved to be even stronger than I had realized. When I was 14 years old and my feet were finally straightened—my mother did eventually find a doctor to treat me— my grandfather and I took a trip to Vaishno Devi Temple together, just the two of us. The ascent to the shrine from Jammu takes about seven hours. First, you embark on a two-hour bus ride (providing the bus doesn't break down) from Jammu to Katra. From Katra you proceed on foot for 13.5 kilometers. We tied the customary red headbands that indicate a person is on a pilgrimage around our heads and joined the other pilgrims who were chanting "Jai Mata di," which means "Hail the Divine Mother," as we made our way up to the shrine. There are no shortcuts to reach the temple. While I trotted back and forth on my newly straightened legs, feeling like a colt in his first spring, my grandfather walked slowly and with patience.

When the two of us finally reached the temple, I was exhausted and complaining bitterly about the

long trek. But not my grandfather. At age 74, he was still going strong and smiling as we made our offerings to Shakti, the Hindu Mother Goddess.

Since that first pilgrimage to Vaishno Devi Mandir, a sacred place representing all that I believe about the essential nature of the Himalayas, I have made more trips to the tall peaks than I can begin to count. The Himalayas are where I held my first job after cooking school. There were family trips to the region, weddings, visits to friends, vacations in the foothills, not to mention many longer adventures with a backpack to find recipes for this book.

Thus, the course of my professional life was set. Along the way, I absorbed many important lessons about life that I still carry with me today. My mother taught me that with persistence all things are possible. Because of that faith, she is the person who is most responsible for any success I can claim for myself as a chef. My Biji instilled in me her love of food. And my grandfather? He gave me the gift of freedom—the spirit and determination to explore these mountains whenever the spirit moves me.

So, for nearly thirty years I have traveled to this area at the top of the world, and every time I return I am newly awed by the kindness and hospitality of the people I've met during my journeys. Along the way, during these trips, I have collected recipes from many of the Himalayan people I encountered, as well as from family and friends who supported my quest to find and document authentic Himalayan food and culture. I've taken liberties by not adhering to a strict chronology of my many visits to the mountains. I believe the timing is less significant to my story of the Himalayas than the fall of a single snowflake.

Lhasa, Tibet.

Introduction

Why *Return to the Rivers*? Why not *Roof of the World* for a title? Among the Himalayan people, these daunting peaks are known as Bam-i-dunia, or "the roof of the world." We tend to think of the Himalayas almost exclusively as a group of very high peaks, the highest in the world. A place of dangerous adventures. A place of awesome beauty, but also of unforgiving terrain, of hostile weather, and treacherous ascents.

SACRED WATERS

What the Himalayas really are, though, is a source of life. The rivers of this region, even more than the mountains, are profoundly sacred. They are the very lifeblood of more than three billion people, over half the world's population, who live not in the mountains themselves, but along the rivers that flow from them. These rivers, which nourish and replenish fertile valleys, flow down through the Indian subcontinent, and into China, Southeast Asia, South Asia, and Pakistan. The Himalayas are not only a watershed of unimaginably vast proportions that nurture half the world's population; they are a place of great spirituality. Deeply sacred to the people who inhabit these parts of Asia, the Himalayas also figure largely in the Hindu religion. Many representations of Hindu gods show them positioned in the mountains or by a sacred river. For instance, the sacred Ganges that begins in the Himalayas, flows from the head of the god Shiva, one of the holiest of Hindu deities.

Originating in the western Himalayas, the Ganges flows south then east until it completes its journey in the Bay of Bengal. The Bay of Bengal is where the cycle of life ends and the process of reincarnation begins. Whether one is cremated in Kolkata or far up the river in the sacred city of Benares, the ashes of the dead are carried to the end and they are bathed in the river of forgetfulness to begin life again. It is also the end of the water cycle. The snows of the Himalayas that begin to melt in the spring are carried down the river, watering the fertile valleys before ending up in the bay where they can evaporate and be carried back up to the mountains in the form of clouds.

THE THREADS THAT TIE US

When I think about the Himalayas and the rivers that flow from them, I recall the invisible threads that tie us to one another and to the world around us. These threads are essential elements that allow us to feel that our very lives have meaning and substance, to feel that our actions do in fact matter. My life in New York is rich and fulfilling, but there are times when I miss life back home in India where I am closely connected to my beloved Himalayas and to other aspects of the natural world.

Guru Padmasambhava Rinpoche
sculpture. Near Thimphu. Bhutan.

My latest stay in Bhutan in 2011 reminded me of how much my life in New York was disconnected from that world. When I am living and traveling in the Himalayas I feel intimately tied to nature in a way that I don't anywhere else. When in Bhutan, I often stay with my dear friend Tenzin Dorji, who is also a travel guide. He lives in a beautiful traditional home in Balakha Village just on the outskirts of Paro, the major city of Bhutan and one of the few cities in the world where there is only one traffic light. The people's connection to the Gods in Heaven and life on earth is very close. I often find the urge to visit Paro to find my center of gravity. During this stay, I taught English to 8-10 year old children at a small school run by Tenzin's sister in the backyard of her home.

To get to Tenzin's home, I had to walk through a rice field in front of the house. On my left was the Bhutanese red rice and on my right, white basmati rice. On the east side of the house sat an apple orchard. Using those apples, I taught some neighbors how to make an American apple pie and their favorite American apple dessert, an apple crisp. The milk, butter, and cheese I consumed came from a cow whose head I rubbed every day on my way home from the school. I ate vegetables that were farmed behind the house in a gently sloping field that supplied all the produce Tenzin's family ate and also dried, preserved, and stored for the long Himalayan winters. A farm just down the road, visible from my bedroom window, supplied the wool from its sheep that was used to weave the blanket that covered my bed. In town, there was a farmers' market where people sometimes bartered with one another, trading handmade goods such as yak cheese, prayer wheels, and woolen clothes for produce or meat.

Whatever you consume in Bhutan, you have a fairly direct relationship with the person who produced it. The lack of anonymity allows people to feel proud of their work and conversely holds them accountable for anything subpar. When you know the person who is going to use what you've just produced, you try harder not to disappoint them. In this way, you come to form close relationships with your neighbors and townspeople.

Everything you do is not merely for your own benefit, but rather for the benefit of all. If you have to trade your rice for your neighbor's wool, the community is obliged to become deeply interdependent. This is how you get to live a life of deep spiritual meaning. Indeed, the people of Bhutan work hard to maintain this spiritual connectedness—even at the cost of slowing the country's economic development. Very few people leave Bhutan without feelings of deep regret. Yet when I returned to New York after living for one and half months in Paro, I felt that I was bringing a bit of that sense of connectedness home with me.

During my travels through the region, I have been overwhelmed by people's generosity, even more so because the people of the Himalayas live very simple lives in which food is a precious and limited commodity. Providing hospitality, serving guests food and drink, is costly and therefore takes on great importance. Moreover, offering hospitality is much more than the preparation and serving of food to guests. Each gesture of welcome is as important to the host as it is to the recipient.

Namgyal Tsemo Gompa Monastery. Leh, Ladakh.

Swayambhunath Temple, Nepal.

Dechen Phodrang Monastery.
Thimphu, Bhutan.

THE SILK ROAD

In ancient times, the Silk Road passed through the Himalayas and was a vital link between China, South Asia, Central Asia, the Middle East, North and East Africa, and Europe. The Silk Road was how goods travelled from China to Europe for many centuries before speedier sea routes overtook land routes. With all the movement up and down the Silk Road, it is nearly impossible to say authoritatively that a dish originated in one specific place or time. Many of these dishes could lay claim to a home in several different places with only minor adjustments in technique or ingredients. They have evolved over countless generations and been handed down through nomadic people, traders and the local populations of all these places. While there is a certain popular image of an idyllic Himalayan Shangri-La as an isolated paradise, it simply isn't true. Though traveling in the Himalayas can be difficult—current conflicts may make it forbidding—there have always been people coming and going, now more than ever.

PRESERVING TRADITIONS

This cookbook covers Bhutan, Nepal, Tibet, and northern India—all regions in the Himalayas that I've traveled to in search of recipes for this book. Most of these recipes have crossed and recrossed borders numerous times throughout their history. Suffice it to say that where I say a recipe is from Nepal, it could just as easily come from Tibet or Kashmir or any other Himalayan region for that matter. The current borders are not what they were a thousand years ago, nor will they be the same a thousand years from now. If you remember that the mountains were there before there were people or borders or nations and they will be there long after we are all gone, then this culinary mixing starts to make a great deal of sense.

For me, the fact that the region is modernizing drove my desire to write this book to help preserve what I can about its foodways and culture. It was this passion for food, aided by hours spent in the kitchen with my grandmother Biji, that ultimately led to my quest for authentic Himalayan recipes. My goal has been to document what the average person eats on a daily basis and to describe the culture and traditions—especially the Himalayans' gracious hospitality—surrounding the serving and eating of food.

The difference in regional cuisines within the Himalayas can be attributed to the availability of ingredients. Very little grows at high elevations and some aspects of Himalayan cuisine reflect the limited variety of foods available to ordinary cooks. However, in areas in northern India, such as my hometown of Amritsar in the Punjab region, ingredients may be much more varied.

Jokhang Protector Chapel, Tibet.

Dechen Phodrang Monastery.
Thimphu. Bhutan.

Dal Lake, Srinagar.

LIVELY MARKETS

Most people in this part of the world lack the luxury of refrigeration. Because few people own refrigerators or freezers, people do their marketing daily. What's on the table at home directly reflects what's for sale or has been bartered for at the local market. Foods bought at local markets are often heavily seasoned, dried, or pickled to prolong shelf life, allowing them to be stored through the long winter months.

Beyond being places to buy, sell, and trade foods, markets are also where social bonds are forged. My favorite market in the world is the floating vegetable market in Srinagar's Dal Lake where the boats congregate in the early morning in beautiful, sparkling waters surrounded by tall peaks. In Thimphu, Bhutan, I enjoyed sitting and drinking tea while people bartered goods; more than an hour could go by before any money actually changed hands. Once people have what they need, they sit and enjoy the rest of the morning in each other's company. Indeed, markets—the shoppers, the food vendors, the people I met there—were the source for many of the recipes in this book.

VEGETABLES

There are only so many vegetables that can grow at elevations over 10,000 feet. Moreover, the growing season is very short, typically lasting from June to October. In most of Tibet, there is only time for planting and harvesting one crop. Tibetans must therefore put aside vegetables for the long winter months by preserving them. I've included several recipes in this book for preserved vegetable dishes.

MEAT

Other than Nepal, where abundant pastureland allows people to raise goats and lamb, there are few areas in the higher reaches of the Himalayas to graze animals. Typically, only after an animal's useful life has ended is it then slaughtered and used as meat. One example of this practice is the sturdy and sure-footed yak, the Himalayas' work horse, that carries heavy loads over the area's narrow and treacherous paths. During their productive years, yaks provide milk and wool. But inevitably they end up, once they're old and no longer useful on the trail, in the stew pot. There is a popular saying among the desert people of Morocco: "Little by little the camel goes into the pot." The same might be said of the yak of the Himalayas. Remember though, a yak that very nearly dies of old age before it's turned into a meal is not a tender animal and needs a good deal of time to cook. As yak meat is difficult to find outside of the region, I have used lamb in recipes that traditionally call for yak.

Despite the difficulty of raising animals, there are very few vegetarians in the Himalayas because people need to consume vast amounts of protein to survive in the region's harsh climate and meat, though it is expensive, provides a much-needed source of protein.

Kathmandu. Nepal.

Amdo, Tibet.

NOTES ON THE RECIPES

I have attributed these recipes to specific countries on the basis of where I learned the recipe, and not their point of origin, which, as previously noted, is often difficult to determine. In some sections of this book, one country or another may be more heavily represented, based on the extent of my travels and the availability of ingredients.

Since much of this region lives simply and frugally, people of this region structure their daily meals around what is available; they do not use recipes per se. They don't go out looking for beef when they still have a goat leg to finish up. For the most part, the recipes as you see them here are derived from talking, watching, and working with cooks from all over the Himalayas and have been translated into measurements for the American home kitchen.

In the interest of authenticity, I have tried to preserve most of the recipes I include in this book just the way I found them and have only made minor adjustments so that they can easily be prepared in a Western kitchen. Most of the dishes contain relatively few ingredients and are not heavily seasoned though the exception would be the strongly flavored condiments. The general simplicity of the Himalayan diet lends itself to the addition of many condiments. Himalayans use quite a lot of them, stirring them into simpler soups, stews, and main dishes to provide a flavor boost.

This book is intended to be a record of what the average person eats and does not include much fancy food. However, whenever I'm in the mountains I do get invited to weddings and other special occasions. I've also attended numerous religious festivals as the people of the Himalayas are deeply spiritual. Thus, some special occasion dishes are represented here as well.

I hope that you will enjoy my Himalayan culinary adventures. The Himalayan people possess a deeply mindful way of living in which the gift of food is acknowledged daily—a model for all of us. I hope that I have done some small justice to the immeasurable kindness I received as I struggled to translate the native foodways of a culture so steeped in generosity and spirituality.

CHINA

TIBET

• Amdo

Town of Bayi

Shigatse • Lhasa ◎

Kongpo •

• Gyantse

ARUNACHAL
PRADESH

Jasbir •

Mustang •

BHUTAN

• Pokhara

SIKKIM

• Trongsa

Kathmandu ◎

Paro • ◎

• Bhaktapur

Gangtok • Thimphu

Ilam • Darjeeling

Phuentsholing

Janakpur •

• Siliguri

Jaigaon

ASSAM

NAGALAND

BURMA

MEGHALAYA

BIHAR

MANIPUR

BANGLADESH

TRIPURA

WEST
BENGAL

MIZORAM

Kolkatta
◎

Cooking in a
Bhutanese home.

Himalayan Flavors

Though some parts of the Himalayas use few spices in their cooking, many regions use rich, soothing spices to keep warm during the harsh winters. Throughout my travels, spices have come to mean much more to me than added flavorings.

The use of spices varies from region to region, but a very strong memory for me was seeing a spice shop at Jokhang Temple in Tibet. As I wandered searching for handmade *thangkas*, embroidered silk paintings, I discovered a spice shop, which turned out to also be an herbalist store filled with jars of pomegranate seeds, turmeric, and many other spices. I was amazed to discover that here, as in India, spices were also commonly used for medicinal purposes.

I consider myself very fortunate to have plucked the stigma of the crocus flower in the saffron fields of the Pampore Valley. Turmeric, with its bright yellow color, is not only used in creating the great curries of Nepal, but is an important part of many sacred rituals. One of the greatest reminiscences of my visits in Nepal is a bowl of golden colored lentils flavored with mild delicate *jimbu*, while in Kashmir, I found the the liquorice flavors of fennel seeds to be addictive.

Szechuan peppercorns are an intricate part of Tibetan and Bhutanese cuisines. I remember seeing a woman selling Szechuan peppercorns, locally known as *thingay*, in Bhutan. She was sitting on the roadside by a beautiful bridge decorated with prayer flags fluttering in a light breeze. The wind carried with it not just prayers, but the intoxicating fragrance of her aromatic peppercorns.

These ingredients are the soul of Himalayan cooking. Every time I pick up a jar of the Himalayan pink salt in the pantry at my restaurant Junoon or a grocery store anywhere in the world, the light reflecting off the pink gem-like crystals transports me to the translucent clouds and the crystal clear, crisp air of the Himalayas.

WORKING WITH SPICES

Grinding Spices If spices such as peppercorns need only be coarsely crushed, a mortar and pestle or the bottom of a heavy pan works fine. To grind aromatics such as garlic, ginger, and chiles into a fine paste, we traditionally use a mortar and pestle, but a mini food processor would work as well. For grinding spices finely, a spice or coffee grinder is the easiest way.

Dry-Roasting The essence of many recipes lies in dry-roasting, a method that accentuates and rounds out the taste and aroma of many spices. The process releases the essential oils, adding a fuller character and a deeper, nuttier flavor.

To dry-roast: Heat a heavy-bottomed pan, such as a cast iron skillet, over medium heat until hot. Spices of similar size can be roasted together. Add the whole spices or nuts and roast until very fragrant and lightly browned, stirring constantly with a wooden spoon to prevent burning, 2 to 5 minutes, depending on the size of the spice. Only roast as much as you need for the recipe you are making to preserve the freshness of your spices.

Woman making ginger paste in Kolkata.

Spice blends

CHAAT MASALA

This sweet, spicy and tangy combination is used in a variety of ways in Indian cooking. It is most commonly used to flavor the fresh salads and snacks that are sold on the streets. It can be sprinkled on fresh fruit or vegetables in addition to being used for the recipes in this book.

makes about 3/4 cup

2 tablespoons cumin seeds

1 tablespoon fennel seeds

1 tablespoon coriander seeds

1 1/2 teaspoons black peppercorns

1 teaspoon cayenne pepper

1 tablespoon carom seeds

1 tablespoon whole green cardamom pods

1 teaspoon chile flakes

8 to 10 whole cloves

1 tablespoon mango powder (see page 45)

1 dried red chile

Place a heavy-bottomed pan, such as a cast-iron skillet, over medium-high heat. Add the cumin, fennel, coriander, and peppercorns, and dry-roast until the aroma becomes highly fragrant, about 2 minutes. Let the spices cool and combine with the rest of the ingredients. Grind to a fine powder in a spice grinder. Store in a jar with a tight-fitting lid for up to 3 months.

GARAM MASALA

The most important spice blend in North Indian cuisine, there are as many varieties of garam masala as there are cooks who blend their own spices. I have included three varieties here and encourage you to come up with your own blend to suit your taste. Adding a little pinch of garam masala at the end of cooking or right before serving adds more flavor to the dish.

Indian Garam Masala

makes about 1/2 cup

3 tablespoons whole green cardamom pods

2 black cardamom pods

1 tablespoon black peppercorns

1 tablespoon whole cloves

1 teaspoon ground ginger

1 teaspoon coriander seeds

2 tablespoons ground cinnamon

1/4 teaspoon mace flakes

2 dried bay leaves

Kashmiri Garam Masala

makes about 1/2 cup

Two 2-inch cinnamon sticks

1/4 cup black cumin seeds

2 or 3 bay leaves

2 tablespoons whole green cardamom pods

1/4 cup black peppercorns

1 1/2 teaspoons whole cloves

1 tablespoon fennel seeds

1/2 teaspoon mace flakes

Pinch of freshly grated nutmeg

Pakistani Garam Masala

makes about 1/2 cup

1 tablespoon black peppercorns

1/4 cup black cumin seeds

1 tablespoon black cardamom seeds (removed from pods)

1 teaspoon whole cloves

1 tablespoon green cardamom seeds (removed from pods)

Heat a heavy skillet, preferably cast iron, over medium heat. Lightly roast all the spices, stirring continuously until all are darker in color and very fragrant, 1 to 2 minutes. Remove from the skillet and cool. (Alternatively, place all of the spices on a large rimmed baking sheet and roast in a 300°F oven until very fragrant, about 5 minutes.) Transfer to a spice grinder in batches and grind to a fine powder. Store in an airtight container in a cool, dark place. This masala will keep well for up to 3 months.

SPICES

Asafetida Generally used in Indian vegetarian cooking, this strong smelling spice adds a deep, garlic-like flavor to recipes. Because of its strong, distinctive odor and flavor, asafetida should be used in small amounts. Look for ground asafetida, which mixes in rice flour and turmeric to cut the intensity, instead of the more potent lump form. Although not widely distributed, asafetida is often sold in South Asian groceries. Be sure to store in an airtight container.

Bay Leaves Also known as bay laurel, bay leaves are sold both fresh and dry. I use dry leaves in my recipes, which have a more distinctive, less bitter taste. Bay leaves should be removed from the dish

before serving. Dry, the leaves will keep for up to a year. If they lose their olive green color and start to turn brown or yellowish, it's time to replace them. Bay leaves can be found in the spice section of most grocery stores.

Black Cardamom The robust aroma of black cardamom can improve nearly any curry or meat dish. It is excellent in biryani (a rice dish). Black cardamom pods can be used in soups, chowders, casseroles, and marinades for smoky flavor. It is one of the ingredients in the recipe for garam masala (see page 39), a very extensively used spice blend in India.

Black Cumin Seeds The black variety of cumin seeds has a mellower flavor than regular cumin and is used to delicately flavor lentils and curries. The seeds are believed to increase heat in the body, making metabolism more efficient, and were used for medicinal purposes in ancient Egypt. It is important to note that black cumin seeds differ from nigella, or kalonji, another very small, very black seed.

Black Salt or Kala Namak Contrary to its name, black salt ranges from pale purple to salmon pink in color when it is ground. It is an unrefined table salt with a very strong and sulfurous taste. I have to warn you that this salt is an acquired taste. It is available in lump or ground form. Its distinctive flavor and aroma helps to bring out the flavor in relishes, salads, and raitas.

Cardamom Cardamom, one of the most ancient and expensive spices, grows in small pods and comes in three different colors: black, white, and pale green. The pale green is the most common and flavorful. The black seeds inside the pod hold the fragrance and are used in almost every part of Indian cuisine, from savory dishes like curries to desserts such as rice pudding. The sharp and bitter taste mellows and sweetens as it cooks. The seeds are also known as "grains of heaven" for their exceptional flavor. When we call for ground cardamom it is best to buy the pods whole and grind them yourself. Cardamom pods may be crushed open by rolling them under a rolling pin, flattening them with a small frying pan or saucepan, or by using the flat edge of a knife blade if you don't have a mortar and pestle in your kitchen. If you can't find whole pods or don't want to go to the trouble, use the ground cardamom sold at your local grocery.

Carom Seeds These tiny black seeds of the carom plant, called ajwain in India, resemble cumin seeds, but they are somewhat smaller. They are also known as owa or omam. They are pungent in aroma and have a sharp taste, reminiscent of thyme. I use this spice in small quantities, as it has a very strong and distinctive flavor. Normally it is dry-roasted or fried in ghee before use.

Cayenne Pepper Not a native ingredient to Indian cooking, cayenne pepper is a good substitute for Indian "chilly powder," a blend of several different dried chile peppers. I call for cayenne pepper throughout as it's more widely available. It adds a clean, clear heat to dishes without imparting much flavor of its own.

Cinnamon Cinnamon, the dried inner bark of a laurel tree, plays an important role in Indian cuisine, flavoring everything from meats and curries to desserts and teas. Traditionally, whole cinnamon sticks are used in Indian cooking, but

Spice cart at Jokhang Monastery in Lhasa.

I use ground cinnamon in a few of my recipes. Ground cinnamon is available at most grocery stores, but grinding your own from cinnamon sticks ensures you the freshest ground cinnamon possible.

Cloves Cloves are the dried unopened buds of a tropical tree. Deep reddish-brown cloves add a strong fragrance to rice and grain recipes and are often lightly fried in hot oil, perfuming the food that is to be cooked. Cloves also serve more practical purposes: a whole clove can be used as a local anesthetic for a toothache or chewed on to freshen your breath.

Coriander Seeds Coriander seeds are spherical, pale-green-to-beige-brown and about the size of a peppercorn. The seeds are aromatic, with a spicy hint of lemon. Keep the seeds in small quantities in airtight containers--they lose their flavor quickly with exposure and age. Coriander seeds can also be purchased already ground (simply called ground coriander in most groceries), but as with all spices, buy whole seeds if you can, and grind as needed for best results.

Cumin Seeds Varying in color from beige to nearly black, cumin seeds are essential to Indian cooking. With a strong, earthy taste and warm aroma, cumin seeds are used somewhat sparingly. Often, the seeds are fried in oil at the start of the dish. Frying cumin seeds is one of the scents that most reminds me of my Biji, as she started many meals that way. If whole seeds aren't available to you, feel free to buy ground cumin.

Curry Leaves Curry leaves are an integral part of Indian cooking. Mainly used as an aromatic flavoring for curries and soups, curry leaves release a fresh citrus aroma when cooked. Fresh curry leaves, which I use exclusively in these recipes, are often first fried in oil, which enhances the flavor of both the leaves and the oil. Dried curry leaves are used much like bay leaves. Fresh curry leaves can be found in the fruit section of Indian specialty food stores.

Dried Red Chiles These are whole dried red-hot chiles that are usually added to hot oil to infuse the oil with their strong flavor. Quick contact with hot oil enhances and intensifies the flavor of the skins.

Fennel Seeds These are oval, pale greenish-yellow seeds of the common fennel plant. They are sweetly aromatic and have a light anise flavor. They are used in both sweet and savory dishes. Roasted fennel seeds are often chewed as a digestive and mouth freshener after Indian meals.

Fenugreek Leaves Called kasoori methi, this dried leaf lends a rich, pleasantly bitter flavor to curries. Fresh leaves are available in season and frozen leaves are also sometimes available, but I prefer the taste of the dried leaves and use them throughout. Fenugreek leaves can be found at Indian specialty food stores.

Fenugreek Seeds Fenugreek seeds come from the same plant as fenugreek leaves. These small seeds have a powerful, bitter taste and are used in small amounts. When frying or dry-roasting these seeds, take care not to overcook—the seeds will become excessively bitter and inedible.

Himalayan Pink Salt Salt is the world's oldest known food additive. Himalayan salt has been a part of my pantry ever since I spent time in Nepal. It adds a wonderful aroma and earthy taste to food and can be found at many specialty stores. Most Himalayan salt actually comes from salt mines in Pakistan.

Jimbu Jimbu is a delicate herb commonly used in Nepali cuisine. It grows in a harsh, dry climate like that in Mustang, Nepal and is commonly used to flavor, meats, vegetables, lentils, and even pickles. Before adding to a dish, jimbu herb is briefly fried in oil to enhance its flavor. Once fried, it tastes of garlic and onion. Care must be taken that it doesn't burn.

Mace Mace, the dried, amber-colored covering of the nutmeg seed, tastes similar to nutmeg, but with a more intense flavor. Mace is available as whole flakes or blades and ground—buy the flakes or blades for the best flavor.

Mustard Seeds Mustard seeds are the tiny round, hot, and pungent seeds of an annual plant from which cabbages, broccoli, and other vegetables are derived. They come in white, yellow, brown, and black varieties. The large white seeds are used to make commercial mustards in the United States; the yellow and brown ones are used for European mustards and for pickling; the black seeds are commonly used in Indian cuisine. They are used in both whole and ground forms. The whole seeds are used to season vegetables, curries, appetizers, salads, and legumes, while the powder is used to steam fish, in curries, and for making pickles. The black seeds are also the source of mustard oil. Note that prepared Western mustards are not an effective substitute for mustard seeds in any of these recipes.

Nutmeg The rich brown seed of the fruit of a tropical evergreen, nutmeg has a warm, sweetly spicy flavor used to season both savory and sweet dishes. It is available in whole and ground forms. For best results, I always prefer buying it whole and then freshly grating or grinding it according to the recipe. A microplane grater works well for this task.

Paprika, Kashmiri A spice made by grinding dried mild chiles, paprika is used in many different cuisines. The Indian variety is called Kashmiri mirch; mild Hungarian paprika also works well in these recipes.

Jimbu.

Peppercorns These small berries of a pepper plant are picked at various stages of ripeness and dried to varying degrees, which creates different varieties and flavors, from very hot and a little plain-tasting to sweet, complex, and aromatic. I prefer black peppercorns in most of my dishes for their deep, mellow flavor. For chutneys, I often use pickled green peppercorns, which have a lighter, more ethereal taste.

Saffron Saffron is the world's most expensive spice and with good reason: one pound of saffron requires almost seventy-five thousand handpicked blossoms of the Crocus Sativus. From those blossoms, the stigmas are removed and dried. Saffron has a distinctively warm, rich, powerful, and intense flavor. It can be purchased in strands or ground. I recommend strands for the sake of quality. My grandmother kept a private supply of saffron that she used to mark special occasions. On my birthday, she would mix a little saffron with water and mark my forehead with it. Eventually that saffron always ended up in my mouth.

Star Anise These star-shaped pods have a pronounced liquorice flavor, stronger than fennel or anise seed. I add whole star anise to dishes like curries to add dimension to the flavor. Star anise can also be used to flavor sweet dishes.

Szechuan Peppercorns An aromatic spice used commonly in Tibetan and Bhutanese cuisine. It adds a lot of flavor and a heat that is not pungent, but leaves a tingly sensation in the mouth, along with a lemony aftertaste. It is known as emma in Tibet, timur in Nepal, and thingay in Bhutan. Frying or dry-roasting releases its oils, enhancing the woody flavor and aromas.

Turmeric Turmeric is what gives curry powder its characteristic bright yellow color. Related to ginger, this root is used in ground form. It has a deep, astringent flavor, indispensible to Indian cuisine. While traveling in Tibet, I was surprised to learn

Sunflower seeds, a Tibetan favorite.

that turmeric is primarily used there as a medicine and must be purchased in a natural remedy pharmacy.

PANTRY

Chickpea Flour Chickpea flour, also known as gram or besan flour, is used in many Indian recipes, *dosas* (an Indian kind of crepe) especially. It is simply ground, dried chickpeas and can be found in Indian groceries, health food stores, and some gourmet shops.

Ghee (Clarified Butter) Also known as clarified butter, ghee is butter that has been melted down to separate the milk solids and water from the butterfat. After melting and sitting over low heat, the water evaporates, and a few milk solids float to the surface (and are skimmed off), while the remainder of the heavier milk solids sink to the bottom. The butterfat, clear and yellow, is poured off the top and preserved, leaving the whey to be discarded. Ghee can be purchased in jars from Indian groceries but is not difficult to make. Allow for about 25% loss to the skimming process when calculating how much you need to make. Ghee keeps well in the refrigerator, up to six months, but it will absorb refrigerator odors if not properly sealed. Ghee gives a clean butter flavor and burns at a much higher temperature than whole butter. It also can be kept for a time at room temperature, which is preferable in a warm climate where refrigeration is a luxury.

Jaggery Jaggery is natural, unrefined brown sugar that may be made from dates, cane juice, or palm sap that is boiled down. It is purchased in large, circular blocks and is rock hard. For use, the jaggery must be broken off in pieces or grated.

Mango Powder The dried pulp of green (unripe) mangoes is ground to make mango or amchoor powder. It is beige in color, slightly fibrous in appearance, and sweet-and-sour in taste. It is used particularly to add tartness to a dish such as a salad or chaat. It is available in South Asian grocery stores.

Mustard Oil My preferred brand of mustard oil is Tez, which has a pungent and spicy aroma. Mustard oil adds a nice spiciness to food when used as a cooking oil. The use of mustard oil for cooking purposes is somewhat controversial due to its erucic acid content. We have been using it in India for more than a thousand years without ill effects. In fact, many would tout its various health benefits. If you have any reservations, just substitute a plain vegetable oil in any recipe where it is listed as an ingredient.

Poha (Pressed Rice) Poha, also known as cheura, is made from parboiled rice that is rolled flat and dried. There are two types: thick and thin. The thinner variety has more applications in the kitchen and is more costly. The appeal of poha is that it can absorb hot or cold liquid and softens quickly to be eaten as a porridge. It can also be fried and turned into a crispy snack.

Rose Water Rose water, essentially rose petals cooked in water, is sometimes distilled to give it a purer, more concentrated floral flavor. It imparts an intoxicating scent of roses to rice dishes, desserts, and drinks. When using rose water for the first time, use a light hand until you are familiar with the

floral flavor. I recommend buying rose water rather than making your own: store-bought roses are often sprayed with pesticides. Rose water is available at Indian groceries.

Tamarind The sticky, sour pulp from the tamarind bean pod is used in chutneys and assorted preserves. Available both as a pressed slab (which still contains the seeds from the tamarind pod) and bottled concentrate, I recommend the bottled concentrate which is sold as tamarind paste in Indian groceries, for ease of use.

If purchased as a slab that includes seeds, the pulp will need to be removed and softened. Place the slab in a heavy-bottomed saucepan and cover it with cold water. Bring to a boil over medium-high heat. Reduce heat and let simmer until the pulp is softened, about half an hour. Let cool before pressing and scraping the pulp through a strainer or sieve.

Tsampa Tsampa is an important Tibetan staple made by roasting and grinding barley into a flour. It is also used in Nepal where it can be made from any kind of toasted grain. In the Himalayan region of India, it is known as sattu and comes from barley or wheat. In Tibet, tsampa is available in two varieties: the coarser Amdo tsampa and the more finely textured, regular tsampa. To enjoy tsampa at home, you can either buy it (www.tibetantsampa.com) or make it in your own kitchen. You can toast whole barley and then grind it in your spice grinder, which will give you the coarser Amdo tsampa. You can also buy already milled barley flour and toast it in a dry skillet over medium heat, which will result in a finer tsampa.

FRESH INGREDIENTS

Cilantro In India, most street vendors include a complimentary bunch of cilantro and a handful of green chiles when you purchase groceries—these two ingredients are used extensively in our cuisine. Cilantro is used fresh and added to a dish at the last minute to preserve its fresh flavor. It keeps best refrigerated, wrapped in moist paper towels.

Dill Fresh dill has a very distinctive flavor and is often paired with fish, cucumbers, or potatoes, or added to dips, salad dressings, and cream sauces. Dill loses its flavor when heated, so always add it to cooked dishes at the last minute.

Ginger Ginger is used frequently for its rich, pungent aroma and peppery bite. Fresh ginger is best when the roots are firm and the knobs snap when broken. Dried, ground ginger should have an intense gingery aroma.

Green Chile Peppers Chiles are one of the most important ingredients for pungency and heat in Himalayan cuisine. In most regions, they are served raw on the side as an accompaniment to the meal. To reduce the heat of the peppers, remove the seeds and ribs and only use the green outer flesh. Thai chiles, the very small, very hot, pointed chiles we generally use in Indian cuisine are not typically available in grocery stores, but you may be able to find them in Asian groceries. I often suggest serrano peppers as a substitute, as they are readily available, though they're not as hot.

Be careful when handling any hot pepper. Wash your hands immediately after touching as the oils in the pepper can burn your skin. If you're working with a particularly hot pepper, wear gloves to be safe.

Kathmandu, Nepal.

The highest point en route from Srinagar to Leh.

Kulfi vender in Kolkata.

STREET FOODS

Roadside snacks are an important part of Himalayan culture and everyone eats them all day long. When you ride a bus or a train anywhere in the region, you stop frequently as the bus picks up and discharges passengers. And at each and every stop there are people selling street snacks made from local ingredients. Part of the reason that people eat so many snacks in the Himalayas is that it takes a lot more calories to get through the day at high elevations.

Most of the snacks are fairly simple and made with low-cost, readily available ingredients. Himalayans are highly entrepreneurial and all you need to start a street food business is a little cart or even just a basket. As always, there are people who are more enterprising and competitive and their snacks are a little better than average, a little more complex. It pays to wait and see who is doing the most business. If a vendor has a line, there's probably a good reason for it, and you should head in that direction.

There are so many street foods in the Himalayas that I could only include a sampling in this cookbook. You will also find street foods, such as noodles or some sweets, featured elsewhere in this book. Tibetan momos, for example, are often sold by street vendors, but as they are so iconic of the Himalayas and also serve as important religious festival foods, I thought they deserved special attention.

Split Chickpea Chaat

SERVES 6 TO 8 AS A SNACK

1 cup split chickpeas

1 teaspoon ground turmeric

1 teaspoon salt

4 cups water

1 red onion, finely chopped

1 tomato, seeded and finely chopped

3 tablespoons finely chopped fresh cilantro

Juice of 1 lemon

Pinch of cayenne pepper

1 fresh green chile (such as serrano), finely chopped

Traveling in the remote Ladakh region means you should be mindful of your nutritional needs. A beautiful but austere place, Ladakh is 10,000 feet above sea level, which places extra demands on your body requiring additional amounts of protein and carbohydrates. This chickpea chaat, popular in Ladakh, is one of my favorites snacks that I enjoyed while climbing the hills of the region. Even by the end of the trek, I didn't tire of the snack. Of course, chickpea chaat is equally delicious at sea level.

An alternative way to prepare chickpea chaat is to soak the chickpeas overnight, then drain and dry them well on paper towels. Fry in 350°F oil before mixing them with the other ingredients in the recipe. When finished, they are crunchy and make a great party snack.

In a pot, combine the chickpeas, turmeric, salt, and water and bring to a boil over high heat. Lower the heat to medium and cook, stirring occasionally until the chickpeas are cooked, but still firm, 20 to 25 minutes. Drain and cool.

In a bowl, combine the onion, tomato, cilantro, lemon juice, cayenne, and chile and mix well. Add the chickpeas and toss well to evenly coat. If necessary, season with additional salt before serving.

Fried Ginger Eggplant

SERVES 6 TO 8 AS A SNACK

2 large Japanese or Chinese eggplants (about 1 1/2 pounds)

Salt

1 teaspoon ground turmeric

1/2 teaspoon cayenne pepper

1-inch piece fresh ginger, peeled and coarsely chopped

2 cloves garlic, coarsely chopped

1 fresh green chile (such as serrano), coarsely chopped

1 cup chickpea flour (see page 44)

Pinch of asafetida (see page 40)

2 tablespoons finely chopped fresh cilantro

1/2 cup water

Vegetable oil, for frying

Nepalese Tomato Chutney (page 370), for serving

When traveling in Nepal, you frequently come across food carts strung along the roadsides. People line up for snacks like this fried eggplant rolled up in newspapers or served in small bowls made of compressed, dried leaves.

The spicy chickpea flour batter is easy to prepare, and it can be kept in the refrigerator for several days and used as needed. Just about any vegetable can be fried in this batter, but one of my favorite treats is frying battered slices of bread. My sister Radhika loves it and always checks my refrigerator when she comes to visit to see if I have any of the batter lying around.

The batter tends to thicken as it sits, so thin it by adding a few tablespoons of water to bring it back to the correct consistency.

Trim the eggplants and slice them 1/4 inch thick on the diagonal. Transfer to a nonreactive (glass or stainless-steel) bowl and sprinkle with 1/2 teaspoon salt, the turmeric, and cayenne. Using your hands, mix to evenly coat them. Let rest for at least 15 minutes.

Using a mortar and pestle or mini food processor, grind the ginger, garlic, and chile to a fine paste. Add a tablespoon of water if necessary.

In a bowl, combine the chickpea flour, asafetida, cilantro, a pinch of salt, and the ginger paste and gradually add the water. Use a wooden spoon to mix it to a smooth mixture of pancake batter consistency.

Line a baking sheet with paper towels. Heat at least 3 inches of oil in a deep, heavy pot to 350°F. Gently dip the eggplant slices into the batter a few at a time, coating them with a thin layer of the batter. Fry until crisp, turning with a slotted spoon to ensure even cooking.

Remove with a skimmer or slotted spoon and drain the excess oil on the paper towels. Serve hot with tomato chutney.

Mini Chickpea Dumplings in Cumin Yogurt

SERVES 6 TO 8 AS A SNACK

1 cup chickpea flour
(see page 44)

1/2 teaspoon ground turmeric

1 1/2 teaspoons salt

1/2 teaspoon cayenne pepper

3/4 cup water

Vegetable oil, for frying

2 cups low-fat plain yogurt

1 tablespoon sugar

1 tablespoon cumin seeds, dry-
roasted and coarsely ground

A couple of years ago I ate a contemporary version of this dish, famous throughout India, at the wonderful now-closed Tabla restaurant in New York City. Chef Floyd Cardoz, with his inventive cooking at Tabla, has done more than any Indian chef in the United States to bring Indian cuisine into the American culinary mainstream. When I tasted these dumplings, his version transported me back to my aunt's house in Jammu. Since she didn't much care for eating yogurt by itself, this dish was a must-have at her home for nearly every meal.

Make sure to serve the chickpea dumplings immediately once they're added to the yogurt as they get soggy fairly quickly.

Mix together the chickpea flour, turmeric, 1/2 teaspoon of the salt, and the cayenne in a bowl. Gradually add the water and whisk it to a smooth paste, stirring continuously to avoid any lumps.

Line a baking sheet with paper towels. Heat 4 inches of oil in a wok over medium-high heat to 350°F. With one hand, hold a perforated skimmer 4 to 5 inches above the oil. Gently pour 1/4 cup of the batter over the skimmer and spread it in a circular motion with your fingertips. The batter will drop into the oil in thick droplets. Fry until golden brown and crisp. Remove with a clean skimmer or slotted spoon and drain on the paper towels. Repeat with the remaining batter.

Whisk the yogurt, sugar, cumin, and the remaining 1 teaspoon of salt until smooth. Stir in the dumplings and serve immediately.

108 Caves of Meditation, Drak Yerpa.
Lhasa, Tibet.

108 Caves of Meditation Spicy Potatoes

SERVES 4 TO 6 AS A SNACK

1 pound russet potatoes or other white potato

Salt

2 teaspoons cayenne pepper

You're going to need a little something to keep your energy up while climbing up to Drak Yerpa in Tibet, the famous monastery and meditation caves near Lhasa that sit perched on the mountain side at well over 10,000 feet. Sold in small plastic bags along the route up to the caves, these potatoes make a perfect snack for the climb.

Wash the potatoes and cut into 1-inch cubes, leaving the skin on. Fill a saucepan with salted water, add the potatoes, and bring to a boil. Boil until the potatoes are cooked through, 10 to 12 minutes. Drain. Mix together a 1/2 teaspoon salt and the cayenne and toss with the potatoes. Serve warm or at room temperature.

Durbar Square Chaat Piti

SERVES 4 TO 6 AS A SNACK

2 cups puffed rice

1 russet potato, peeled, boiled until tender, and cubed

1/4 cup cooked fresh peas or thawed frozen peas

1/2 red onion, finely chopped

1 fresh green chile (such as serrano), chopped

1 tablespoon Tabasco or other hot sauce

1 teaspoon cumin seeds, lightly toasted and crushed

I enjoyed this rice snack in Durbar Square across from the old royal palace in Kathmandu, but I could have easily found it in other Himalayan cities. Chaats (a savory salad or snack) are made with puffed or flattened rice. They are among the most popular roadside snacks throughout the Himalayas and form the base for a seemingly infinite variety of small treats. Depending on what is available seasonally, I often make these piti at home with fruit and tamarind chutney in the summer or small cubes of pumpkin in the fall.

Puffed rice is par-cooked rice that is baked in an oven until puffed. It is similar to "Rice Krispies" and can be purchased in South Asian groceries.

Combine all of the ingredients in a large bowl and mix well. Serve immediately.

Channa Dal and Peanut Chaat

SERVES 4 AS A SNACK

1/2 cup channa dal
(split chickpeas)

Pinch of ground turmeric

1 teaspoon salt

2 cups water

1 peeled, cooked russet potato,
cubed

1/4 cup unsalted roasted peanuts,
with or without skin

1/2 red onion, finely chopped

1 fresh green chile (such as
serrano), chopped

1/2 teaspoon Chaat Masala
(page 39)

The equivalent of popcorn in the Himalayas, this snack is much loved by people throughout the region and can be enjoyed almost any time. The combination of crunchy peanuts with pan-roasted chickpeas is addictive and delicious. On the menu at my restaurant Junoon, we add cooked basmati rice and serve it as an accompaniment to mint-marinated chicken tikka.

In a medium-sized pot, combine the chickpeas, turmeric, salt, and water; bring to a boil over high heat. Lower the heat to medium and cook, stirring occasionally, until the chickpeas are cooked but still firm, 20 to 25 minutes. Drain and let cool.

Heat a heavy-bottomed nonstick skillet over medium heat. Cook the drained chickpeas, stirring continuously, until dry and crisp.

Transfer to a bowl and toss with the potato, peanuts, onion, chile, and chaat masala until well coated. Serve warm or at room temperature.

Cucumbers with Lime and Chaat Masala

SERVES 4 AS A SNACK

3 cucumbers (about 2 pounds)

Juice of 1/2 lime

2 tablespoons Chaat Masala
(page 39)

Summer salads are common all over the Indian subcontinent and this nice little snack is tangy and refreshing during those hot months. In Nepal, I noticed many people eating this snack before their workday. For the dish's principal flavoring, some regions use tamarind for the tartness it lends, others use cilantro chutney for its herbal zip, and still others prefer chile paste for its heat. There are no fixed rules about the seasonings. If you're ambitious, you could try them all.

For people with sensitive stomachs, you could peel and seed the cucumbers. Instead of cucumber, you could also try blanched summer squash.

Trim the ends of the cucumbers and halve them lengthwise. Rub them gently with the lime and sprinkle liberally with the chaat masala. Serve immediately.

Spicy Fried Tofu

SERVES 4 AS A SNACK

1 pound extra firm tofu,
drained well

1 teaspoon cayenne pepper

1 teaspoon salt

2 tablespoons vegetable oil

Tibetan Chile-Garlic Paste
(page 374), for serving

There are a few pointers for this tofu dish I had in Nepal that will help you achieve excellent results. First, be sure to drain the tofu well and use only extra firm Chinese-style tofu. Use a nonstick or cast-iron pan when frying and don't overcrowd the pan. Most importantly, leave the tofu undisturbed while cooking; this allows that wonderful golden crust we all love to develop. The skewers are intended to make it easier to carry the tofu as a street snack. If you find the skewers cumbersome, you needn't bother with them at all.

Use paper towels to dry the moisture from the tofu, gently pressing it with your hands. Slice the tofu crosswise into slabs about 1/3 inch thick. Rub the tofu pieces with the cayenne and salt and individually thread them on 6-inch wooden skewers. If not cooking immediately, refrigerate until you are ready.

Line a baking sheet with paper towels. Heat the oil in a nonstick or cast-iron skillet over medium heat and swirl the pan to evenly coat the bottom. Gently cover the surface of the pan with the seasoned tofu in one layer, being careful not to overcrowd the pan. (Work in batches, if necessary.) Let the tofu cook until a golden crust begins to form around the edges, 4 to 5 minutes. Turn the tofu to the other side and fry until golden brown and crisp, about 3 minutes.

Remove from pan and drain on the paper towels to remove excess oil. Serve on the skewers with chile-garlic paste.

Spicy Mixed Fruit Chaat

SERVES 6 AS A SNACK

3 cups bite-size pieces mixed
seasonal fruits (such as apples,
watermelon, or papaya)

1/4 cup fresh pomegranate seeds

Juice of 1 lime

1/2 teaspoon cayenne pepper

1/2 teaspoon black salt
(see page 40)

This fruit chaat recipe comes from the Nepalese town of Bhaktapur where I watched a young boy selling it on the street. As each person placed an order, he would mix the chaat up quickly and serve it right away in a banana leaf. I asked him for three orders at once, but he was really not sure he wanted to do that and kept offering to make them one at a time so they would stay fresh. He didn't want the fruit to start releasing its juices when combined with the salt before I could eat them. I had to reassure him several times that I really wanted all three chaats at once so I could shoot them for a photo for this book. He finally relented, but with grave misgivings. After he handed me the chaats and I got my shot, I found two small children passing by and treated them to the extra two dishes of fruit.

Himalayan fruit chaats vary with the seasons, the region, and available fruits. Each variety has its own pungency and seasoning. In Kashmir, I ate sweet pineapple with just a sprinkle of chiles; in Assam, a spicy chaat of oranges; in Bhutan, apples are the fruit of choice.

Combine all of the ingredients in a large bowl and mix well. Serve immediately.

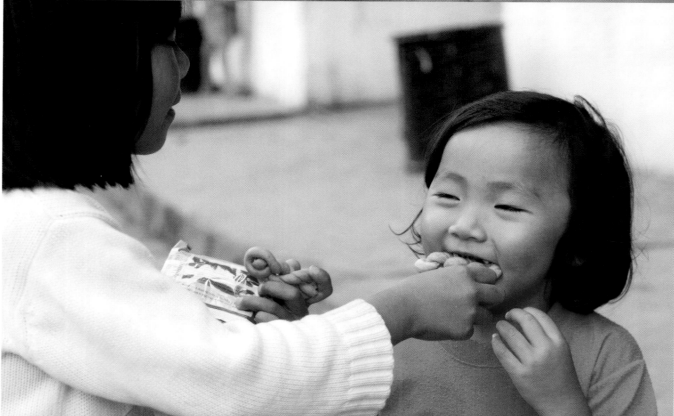

Kabzays

One day, I bought several of these pastries at a bakery in Bhutan to photograph for this book. It wasn't long before I was joined by two young girls who watched me with hungry eyes. The little one poked her older sister who then came up to me and demanded to know if I was going to eat all of the kabzays. I explained that I was taking pictures and certainly wouldn't be able to consume all of them. That was enough of an answer for her, and in the midst of my attempting to take the picture, she helped herself to two kabzays and delivered the third to her sister. Her toothless smile and the joy on their faces gave me more delight than the taste of the dish itself. What good is the food if it doesn't bring joy to people's lives, even if it is just a simple smile?

Bhutanese Breakfast Pastries ⇒

Bhutanese Breakfast Pastries [Kabzays]

Learning to roll the kabzay takes a little time to master, but just keep at it and you will soon get the hang of it.

MAKES 4 PASTRIES

2 cups all-purpose flour, plus more for dusting

1/2 cup sugar

1/2 teaspoon salt

1 teaspoon baking soda

About 1 cup warm water

Vegetable oil or peanut oil for frying, plus more for rolling

Combine the flour, sugar, salt, and baking soda in a large bowl. Gradually add the water and mix with your hands until well-combined. Knead in the bowl until you have a firm, but pliable dough. Turn the dough out onto a lightly floured surface, and knead it until very elastic, 4 to 5 minutes. Cover with plastic wrap and let stand for at least an hour.

Divide the dough into four portions. Roll each piece on a lightly floured surface into an even long rope, about 1/4 inch thick. Hold the end of a rope in one hand and using your other hand, twist the rope, holding it gently between thumb and forefingers. The twists have to be very even and sometimes require a little more practice. When it is twisted all the way to the end, bring the two ends together to form an oval, sticking the two ends together with a dab of water.

Carefully twist the oval to form a figure eight, set aside, and cover with a damp kitchen towel. Repeat with the remaining dough, keeping the twists covered until ready to fry.

Line a baking sheet with paper towels. Heat about 2 inches of oil in a wok over medium heat to 325°F. Carefully transfer the twists into the oil and fry, turning for even cooking, until golden, 2 to 3 minutes.

Remove with a skimmer or slotted spoon and drain on the paper towels to remove excess oil. Serve warm.

Bhutanese Rose Pastries [Kaptas]

MAKES 40 TO 50 PASTRIES

2 large eggs

1 teaspoon salt

1 cup milk

1 cup all-purpose flour

Vegetable oil, for frying

I was really surprised when I saw these beautiful deep-fried pastries being sold by street vendors in Thimphu, Bhutan. They looked very similar to Scandinavian rosette cookies and make a great tea-time snack. The Bhutanese use an iron mold similar to the ones used for Scandinavian cookies that can be easily found at a restaurant supply store.

In a large bowl, beat the eggs with a whisk until frothy. Add the salt and milk and whisk until creamy. Gradually whisk in the flour just until the batter is smooth and free of lumps. It should have the consistency of thick pancake batter.

Line a baking sheet with paper towels. Heat at least 4 inches of oil in a Dutch oven over medium-high heat to 375°F.

Preheat the iron by letting it sit in the oil for 5 minutes. Dip the heated iron into the batter, being sure to hold the iron straight as you dip it, and return to the oil without touching the bottom of the Dutch oven. Let fry until lightly browned, 20 to 35 seconds. Lift out the iron and let the excess oil drain back into the pot for a few seconds. Use a sharp knife or a fork to remove the kapta and place on the paper towels.

Reheat the iron by briefly dipping it in the oil, then resume dipping it in the batter and frying. Let the kaptas cool to room temperature before serving.

Hazratbal Shrine

Hazratbal Shrine is one of the most sacred sites for Muslims in Srinagar. During the month of Ramadan, these very popular, prized fritters are available outside the mosque in huge quantities.

Lotus roots are available throughout Dal Lake in Kashmir in abundance, and the vendors who make lotus root fritters are among the most fascinating street food cooks you can observe in the area. First, the cooks heat oil in a huge, heavy metal wok and fill it with battered lotus roots, 2 to 3 inches deep. They then evenly pour more hot oil over the frying lotus and add another layer of battered lotus. The process of layering the battered lotus with hot oil is repeated until the lotus roots reach the top of the wok. The lotus roots form one big, fried cluster, shaped to the form of the wok, and is removed with large spoons when almost, but not quite, done. From this single mass of fried lotus, individual portions are pulled off by the handful, fried further, and served to hungry customers anxiously waiting to break the Ramadan fast. In this recipe for the home kitchen, the fritters are fried individually, but don't worry, they are just as delicious.

Hazratbal Lotus Root Fritters

Hazratbal Lotus Root Fritters

SERVES 6

8 to 10 ounces fresh lotus root (available at Asian groceries), washed and peeled

4 cups water

3/4 cup chickpea flour (see page 44)

1 teaspoon cayenne pepper

1 teaspoon salt

1 teaspoon ground turmeric

1 1/2 teaspoons Kashmiri or Hungarian paprika (see page 43)

1/4 teaspoon carom seeds (see page 41)

1 tablespoon vegetable oil, plus more for frying

Cut the lotus root into 1/2-inch-thick slices and wash them thoroughly with warm water to remove any particles of sand. In a pot, combine them with the water and bring to a boil over high heat. Boil until tender, 6 to 8 minutes. Drain and cool to room temperature.

In a bowl, combine the chickpea flour, cayenne, salt, turmeric, paprika, carom seeds, and 1 tablespoon vegetable oil. Gradually stir in about 1/2 cup water, a little at a time until it has the consistency of thick pancake batter; mix well to avoid any lumps.

Line a baking sheet with paper towels. Heat 4 inches of oil in a wok or deep-fryer over medium heat to 350°F.

Fold the lotus root into the batter and mix well to evenly coat. Fry a few pieces at a time, turning them once, until golden and crisp, 4 to 5 minutes. Remove with a skimmer or slotted spoon, drain on the paper towels, and serve hot. Repeat with the remaining lotus root pieces.

Fried Nepalese Doughnuts

MAKES 16 TO 18 DOUGHNUTS

2 cups all-purpose flour, plus more for dusting

2 teaspoons baking powder

1/2 teaspoon salt

1 medium egg

1/2 cup sugar

1 tablespoon unsalted butter, melted

1 cup whole milk

Throughout Nepal, people love doughnuts with chai and eat them in the morning and in the afternoon as a snack. I once walked by a doughnut store in Kathmandu and saw people jumping off their motorbikes and out of their cars to run inside for handfuls of doughnuts. When I told the man making the doughnuts that I wanted to learn how to prepare them, he was suspicious and not particularly interested in bonding over recipes until I mentioned that the doughnuts I make in New York are very popular. Perhaps I exaggerated just a bit, but it is true that my sister dearly loves my spiced doughnuts. With that, the doughnut man and I finally negotiated an exchange of our secret recipes. I went first and showed him my version in which I use yeast, something he had never seen before, and many spices, which also surprised him. He quickly began selling my batch of doughnuts as soon as they were ready. In turn, he taught me his recipe, and it was a great trade.

Sift together the flour, baking powder, and salt into a bowl.

In another bowl, beat the egg with the sugar until lighter in color and frothy. Add the butter and milk and mix well. Fold in the dry ingredients and mix just until a soft dough is formed, without overmixing. Cover the dough and let rest while heating the oil for frying.

Line a baking sheet with paper towels. Heat 3 inches of oil in a wok over medium-high heat to 350°F.

On a lightly floured surface, roll the dough to 1/2 inch thick. Cut with a doughnut cutter. Fry a few doughnuts and holes at a time until golden on both sides, turning once, about 5 minutes total.

Remove with a slotted spoon and drain on the paper towels. Let cool before serving.

Ramadan Black Beans

SERVES 6 AS A SNACK

1 cup dried black beans

4 cups water

1 teaspoon salt, plus more
if desired

1 teaspoon cumin seeds

2 teaspoons cayenne pepper

1 teaspoon ground turmeric

Juice of 1 lemon

This is another street food that is popular during Ramadan for breaking the daily fast. The black beans in Kashmir are somewhat smaller than the ones I see in the stores here, but both are delicious.

Soak the black beans in the water overnight at room temperature.

Place the beans, soaking water, and 1 teaspoon salt in a large pot. The water should cover the beans by 2 inches; add more if necessary. Bring to a boil over high heat, and then lower the heat to medium-low. Cover and simmer, stirring occasionally, until the beans are tender, about 1 hour. Drain and transfer to a bowl.

In a cast-iron skillet or a frying pan, dry-roast the cumin over medium-low heat. Stir continuously until darker in color and fragrant, 1 to 2 minutes.

On a work surface, grind the cumin coarsely with a rolling pin and add to the drained beans. Stir in the cayenne, turmeric, and lemon juice and mix well. Season with additional salt if necessary. Serve warm or at room temperature.

Spicy Lemon Grilled Corn

MAKES 6 EARS CORN

6 tender ears corn

1 tablespoon vegetable oil

1 fresh green chile (such as serrano), seeded and minced

Juice of 1 lemon, plus 1 lemon, cut into 6 wedges

1 teaspoon black salt (see page 40)

1 tablespoon finely minced fresh ginger

1 tablespoon finely minced garlic

1/4 teaspoon cayenne pepper

1/8 teaspoon Szechuan peppercorns, finely ground with a mortar and pestle or in a spice grinder (see page 44)

1/2 teaspoon freshly ground black pepper

Sometimes a bus trip in the Himalayas can take considerably longer than you expect. Most travelers in the Himalayas expect this and carry along extra food just in case. On one occasion, I was on my way to Siliguri when the bus broke down on an empty stretch of road. We were stuck for hours waiting for repairs and by the time we got to Siliguri, I was famished. The first thing I saw when I got off the bus was a man selling this wonderfully grilled, spiced corn. I was in heaven as I ate three ears of it.

Heat a charcoal or gas grill to medium-high.

Remove and discard the husk and silk from the corn. Wash the corn to remove any dirt and pat dry with paper towels.

In a small bowl, combine all of the remaining ingredients (except for the lemon wedges) and mix well. Spread the spice mixture evenly over each ear of corn and rub the entire surface, making sure each kernel is covered. Set aside for about 10 minutes to allow the flavors to be absorbed.

Place the corn on the grill and roast, turning occasionally with tongs, until dotted with char marks. Transfer the corn to a platter, garnish with the lemon wedges, and serve warm.

Festival of Losar

Back in the late 1990s, I managed to arrive in the Bhutanese town of Paro about a week before the festival of Losar. Everyone was very busy getting ready for the big celebration. Before these festivals, people make pilgrimages, traveling long distances, to be with family members. Many ritual foods must be prepared and as usual, I was on the lookout for new recipes. Luckily for me, people engaged in big projects, such as making these tscho cookies, always welcome an extra pair of hands. The communal nature of these festivals is a big part of why I love them so much; I get to meet new people and see how their communities thrive. There is a well-established tradition of joking, singing, and trading stories while preparing various ritual foods and it's a great deal of fun. On top of that, there is the pleasure of sharing the fruits of your labor with the rest of the community.

Festival Lotus Blossom Cookies ⟹

Festival Lotus Blossom Cookies [Tscho Kapsey]

These cookies are meant to look like lotus blossoms, a highly auspicious symbol in Buddhism. The food coloring (something I don't normally use in my cooking), brushed in between the layers, helps to highlight the unique shape of the fried kapsey.

YIELD 6 COOKIES

1 teaspoon red food coloring (optional)

1 egg yolk, lightly whisked

12 egg roll skins

Vegetable oil, for frying

Confectioners' sugar, for sprinkling

If you decide to use food coloring, stir it into the egg yolk thoroughly. Using a brush, lightly color one side of an egg roll wrapper with the egg yolk and carefully place another wrapper. Make vertical cuts, 1/2 inch apart, from the bottom edge of the wrapper to 3/4 of the way to the top of the wrapper, leaving about 1 1/2 inches along the top uncut (it will look like thick fringe). Make sure you end up with an even number of strips all attached at the top.

To shape the petals, lift the first and third strip of the fringe and pinch the tips together over the second strip, using egg yolk to seal if needed. To form the second petal, pinch together the tips of the second and fourth under the first petal. Continue pinching alternate strips over and under to form the remaining petals. Cover the kapsey with a damp kitchen towel. Repeat with the remaining egg roll skins, keeping them covered until ready to fry.

To shape the flower, bring together both ends of the wrapper to form a circle and pinch tips together to seal. The petals should fan out from the circle like a flower.

Line a baking sheet with paper towels. Heat 3 inches of oil in a wok or Dutch oven over medium heat to 350°F. Fry the shaped cookies without overcrowding, a few at a time, until golden, crisp, and cooked through, about 3 minutes on each side. Remove with a skimmer or slotted spoon and drain on the paper towels. Let cool slightly and sprinkle with confectioners' sugar while still warm.

Ilam Fried Zucchini Blossoms

MAKES 10 TO 12 FRITTERS

10 to 12 zucchini blossoms

1 1/2 cups chickpea flour (see page 44)

1/2 cup all-purpose flour

1 teaspoon salt

1/2 teaspoon cayenne pepper

1/2 teaspoon ground turmeric

1 fresh green chile (such as serrano), minced

1 teaspoon cumin seeds

1/2 to 1/3 cup water

Vegetable oil, for frying

Nepalese Tomato Chutney (page 370), for serving

In 1993, during my culinary training at the Soaltee Hotel in Kathmandu, I met a French woman who was on her way back to her job at a public health service camp in far eastern Nepal. She had been in the town of Ilam and told me how beautiful it was with so much feeling that I resolved to go there the very next chance I got.

The name Ilam means "twisted road" and you must travel a very long and winding road indeed to get there. It took nineteen and a half hours by bus from Kathmandu and my body was aching, but the town is, without a doubt, transcendentally beautiful. In addition to tea, the surrounding area is also known for growing cardamom, potatoes, and rice, and for its dairy products. On my first day in Ilam, I stopped at a roadside stand and ate fried zucchini blossoms, a snack that's very popular not only in Ilam, but throughout Nepal.

These fried blossoms will seem familiar to anyone who has tried the Italian version, but are more heavily spiced. This is a delicious spring treat, especially when served with the tomato chutney.

Remove any squash attached to the flowers and make sure the blossoms are free of insects.

Sift together the flours, salt, cayenne, and turmeric into a bowl. Add the chile and cumin. Gradually whisk in the water until the batter reaches the consistency of heavy cream; whisk continuously to prevent lumps. Cover and set aside for 10 minutes at room temperature.

Line a platter with paper towels. Heat 3 inches of oil in a deep, heavy-bottomed saucepan over medium-high heat to 375°F.

Stir the batter again and add a little water if it has thickened up. One at a time, dip a blossom in the batter to evenly coat it and gently shake off the excess batter. The blossom should only be lightly coated with batter. Carefully transfer it to the oil. Repeat with the remaining blossoms (being careful not to overcrowd the pot) and fry in batches for about 2 minutes, turning occasionally to ensure they are evenly golden brown. Remove with a slotted spoon and transfer to the platter to drain.

Serve hot with tomato chutney.

Divine momos

Momos are one of the best-known foods in Tibet and Nepal and are much loved as a religious festival food, a street food, and as restaurant fare. There are numerous ways to fold them and some difference of opinion (as I discovered) about the names of the various shapes. To avoid the controversy and stick with essentials, I have included directions for making the two most prevalent shapes of momos—the circular pouch and the crescent. For the fillings, I have included recipes for meat, mixed vegetables, and spinach and cheese. You can fill momos with pretty much anything you like as long as you make sure the filling is well seasoned and not too wet.

When I first read *Lhasa Moon Tibetan Cookbook*, written by my friend and wonderful Tibetan cookbook author Tsering Wangmo, I was captivated by a Tibetan saying: "Making momos is too much work; eat too much and your stomach will hurt." I was still smiling the next day whenever I thought of that saying. Though nearly every culture can lay claim to some form of dough filled with meat or vegetables—and they happen to be among my favorite foods wherever I go—if there is one food that is emblematic of the Himalayas, momos are it.

To learn about momos, I sought out my two favorite momo experts who taught me most of what I know: my good friend Tashi Chodron, who used to make the momos for the Rubin Museum Café in New York City and Tsering Wangmo. Tashi is known around New York as the Momo Queen. (It was Tashi's brother, Lama Ugen Palden Rongdrol, who helped me make the momos for the photos seen here.) There is no one set shape for a specific momo, but there are some general associations between individual shapes and particular fillings. The list that follows is by no means encyclopedic since there are many ways to fold momos and some people call the same shapes by different names. Just enjoy these tasty little bites for what they are—delicious morsels that can be enjoyed almost any time of day.

TIBETAN STOVES

In the past, momos were not steamed as they are today. They were slowly cooked by indirect heat in the ashes in the underpart of traditional Tibetan stoves constructed of brick and clay. As is typical in regions where fuel is scarce, the stoves had two functions—cooking the food and heating the home. Tibetans used dried yak dung, which admittedly took some getting used to but was not offensive since the yak was vegetarian and the dung was dried. The stove was constructed with a firebox in the middle, and the cooking pots went directly on top of the fire.

Today, these stoves are increasingly rare because most people, even the nomadic tribes, are gravitating toward metal stoves. The result is that momos are now steamed in the Chinese style. But even today, you can still find a couple of places in Lhasa where momos are prepared in the traditional manner.

This is something of a diversion from the topic, but there are three main gods of the traditional Tibetan kitchen. They are the gods of fire, water, and food. The god of wealth is an honorary member of this fraternity. This underscores the sacred nature of food in a place where it is sometimes scarce. Many people who live in rural areas have very little to eat until the spring harvest comes in. Because of this there are some rules and taboos about the stoves: One must never step over the stove. Never spit in the direction of the stove. Never urinate in, on, or around the stove. Never cook meat directly on the fire, nor bones, nor skin. When moving on and leaving the stove behind, one must add a little yak dung to the firebox and sprinkle a little tsampa as an offering. Failure to observe these rules could lead to disaster, so dare not risk angering the kitchen gods. Seen in this context, momos take on somewhat more importance as a food of ritual and are a typical celebratory food during religious festivals.

THE SHAPES

1. Shamomo is typically a non-vegetarian momo, mostly beef-filled.

2. Tsemomo is a round momo, usually made with a vegetable filling.

3. Langshamomo is the crescent-shaped momo, finely pleated and often filled with beef.

4. Jashamomo is a chicken momo. Tashi says you could call it the "namastemomo" as it resembles the traditional greeting of hands together at the top.

5. Hrihchusmomo and **motuk** are made for soup (much like wonton soup) and are smaller than the regular steamed momo on its own.

TO FOLD THE MOMOS

Round Momos, or Tsemomos Place 1 to 2 tablespoons of the filling in the center of the circle of dough. Use your thumb and forefinger to pinch a small fold in the edge of the circle. Then, leaving your thumb in the same position, gather another pinch of dough from the outside edge with your forefinger. Keep repeating this motion, occasionally using your other thumb to push the filling in toward the center. The pinched edge will form a spiral, gradually closing down to a tiny hole that you can pinch shut. When the shape is complete, press the sides lightly to puff up the momo.

Crescent Momos, or Langshamomos Place 1 to 2 tablespoons of the filling in the center of the circle of dough. Use your thumb and forefinger to pinch a small fold in the edge of the circle. Continue pinching the two opposite edges together, but with each pinch, fold a pleat in the outside edge. With your other thumb, keep pushing the filling in toward the center. You can leave the crescent shape as is, or pinch the two ends together to form a circle if you need another shape to distinguish different fillings.

TO COOK THE MOMOS

Momos may be steamed, deep-fried, pan-fried, or baked. Traditionally, momos were cooked by burying them in the hot ashes of the cooking fire in a mud-brick hearth, and you can still find them made this way in the villages and tents of rural Tibet. Cooking in steam is a fairly recent introduction, influenced by Chinese cooking and established first, as most new fashions are, in Lhasa. If you are purist enough to bury your momos in ashes, then you should also use authentically fatty cuts of meat for the filling and probably not bother with vegetable momos.

To steam, arrange the momos on a lightly oiled steamer tray. You can fit them as close together as you like, so long as they do not touch. Bring the water to a boil before placing the tray of momos in the steamer. A large wok works best for this.

Steam meat momos for 10 minutes at most, and vegetable momos for 5 to 7 minutes. Spinach momos need only 4 minutes, as the filling is precooked. Be careful not to overcook the momos. Test them by opening the steamer and touching the dough lightly with a fingertip. The dough will no longer be sticky when done.

You can make momos in advance and freeze them for later use. First freeze them on a tray and then place them in zip-locking plastic bags. When you want to cook them, do not thaw them; just place the frozen momos in the steamer. Allow 15 minutes for frozen meat momos, and 10 to 12 minutes for frozen vegetable momos. Serve with any chile sauce and soy sauce.

Basic Momo Dough

MAKES ABOUT 24-30 MOMOS

2 cups sifted all-purpose flour,
plus additional flour for
rolling dough

1 teaspoon salt

3/4 cup tepid water

Make sure that the water is tepid; too cold and the dough will be hard to work with.

Combine the flour and salt in a large bowl and mix well. Add 1/2 cup of the water to the bowl and mix well with your hands until well combined. Then add the rest of the water about 1 tablespoon at a time, kneading in between each addition, until the dough is smooth, firm, and elastic. Let the dough rest, covered with a damp cloth, for half an hour before proceeding.

To roll out the dough, pinch off pieces about 1 heaping tablespoon in size and shape into smooth, round balls. Remember to keep the dough covered with a damp cloth as you work to prevent it from drying out. When you have the dough portioned into balls, it's time to start rolling.

Roll each ball out into 3-inch circles on a lightly-floured smooth surface and fill as directed.

Lamb Momo Filling

FILLING FOR ABOUT 24 MOMOS

1 pound lamb shoulder, trimmed but with still enough fat to add flavor, chopped by hand or coarsely ground

1 red onion, finely chopped

1 scallion, white part only, coarsely chopped

1/3 cup finely chopped fresh cilantro

1 fresh green chile (such as serrano), minced

1-inch piece fresh ginger, peeled and minced

1 teaspoon ground cumin

2 cloves garlic, minced

1/4 teaspoon Szechuan peppercorns, lightly crushed with a mortar and pestle (see page 44)

1 teaspoon salt

2 tablespoons vegetable oil

1 teaspoon soy sauce

The city of Shigatse is the hub of the road network that links the western part of Tibet to Lhasa and Nepal. One of the best momos I have ever eaten was in Shigatse, where they were baked in the traditional way in the ashes of a hearth.

Most of the momos served in the Himalayan regions are made with hand-chopped meat. This creates a much better texture than using machine-ground meat. The most common meat used for momo filling in most of Tibet and Bhutan is yak meat, which can be replaced with lamb, pork, or beef. As a chef in Thimphu once advised me, always bring the refrigerated filling to room temperature before stuffing the dough.

Combine all the ingredients in a bowl and mix well with a fork or using the tips of your fingers. Once all the ingredients are well combined, add 1/4 cup water and mix again until the filling is uniformly blended.

At this point, you can either fill the dumplings or cover the mixture with plastic wrap and refrigerate for up to 2 days.

Vegetable Momo Filling

FILLING FOR ABOUT 36 MOMOS

1/2 head small green cabbage, tough outer leaves and inner core removed

1 small carrot, peeled and finely shredded

1 cup tightly packed chopped fresh spinach

1 tablespoon vegetable oil

1 large white onion, finely chopped

1 scallion, finely chopped

2 cloves garlic, finely chopped

1-inch piece fresh ginger, peeled and finely chopped

1/2 cup chopped fresh mushrooms (optional)

1/2 teaspoon cayenne pepper

1/4 teaspoon Szechuan peppercorns, coarsely ground with a mortar and pestle or in a spice grinder (see page 44)

1 tablespoon soy sauce

1 teaspoon salt

In Nepal and Eastern India, I noticed that ground spices such as cumin, coriander, and turmeric were more prevalent in the momo filling. Tibetan cooking in general does not use many spices, but it adapts as it travels the world. The momo is a perfect example of an enduring classic dish; as it travels, it incorporates regional ingredients and techniques and continues to be popular. Mushrooms are often added to this filling when they are in season and available.

Finely chop the cabbage and combine it with the carrot and spinach in a bowl.

In a skillet, heat the oil over medium heat and fry the onion, stirring continuously, until golden brown, 4 to 5 minutes. Add the scallion, garlic, and ginger and cook until fragrant, about 2 minutes. Add the cabbage, carrot, and spinach mixture and let cook, covered, until cabbage is softened, 5 to 8 minutes. If using the mushrooms, add them to the pan and cook for another 5 minutes or until the moisture released from the mushrooms evaporates. Add the cayenne, Szechuan pepper, soy sauce, and salt and mix well for another minute. Remove from the heat and let cool at room temperature for 10 minutes.

Cover and store in the refrigerator for at least 1 hour for flavors to marry before using.

Spinach and Cheese Momo Filling

FILLING FOR ABOUT 24 MOMOS

1/4 cup mustard oil (see page 45) or vegetable oil

1 1/2 yellow onions, chopped

3 cloves garlic, finely chopped

1-inch piece fresh ginger, peeled and finely chopped

1 pound fresh spinach, coarsely chopped

1/2 pound blue cheese, preferably Maytag or gorgonzola

In many parts of the Himalayas, people consume a lot of cheese. Yak milk is widely available and eating cheese guarantees people sufficient protein and calories to survive the severe winters. I tried a similar filling to this one in Paro except the cook used green chiles instead of spinach. You can certainly do the same for a much spicier filling.

Heat the oil in a skillet over medium-high heat until slightly smoky. Lower the heat to medium and fry the onions until translucent, about 2 minutes. Add the garlic, ginger, and spinach and cook, stirring continuously until fragrant, 2 to 3 minutes. Remove from the heat and let it come to room temperature before stirring in the cheese.

Traditional pasta machine in Bhutan.

SOUPS & NOODLES

The average person in the Himalayas does not sit down to a meal with a soup course. In fact, with some exceptions, there is little to differentiate a soup from a main dish. These hearty soups are authentic, everyday fare and can be meals in themselves. They are simple, sturdy, and always served with bread and hot sauces. As with everything else in the Himalayas, fuel is expensive and the fire that cooks foods must also heat the house, so frugality is important. Where possible, everything goes in the same pot. On a cold day, these soups will warm and energize you.

Noodles, of all shapes and made from a variety of ingredients, are such an important part of everyday meals in the Himalayas that legends have been created around them. In some regions, cutting the noodles is considered unlucky. I met a wonderful woman in Lhasa who told me that long noodles represent long life and respect for elders. While another noodle seller told me in Bhutan that a noodle represents continuation.

It still brings a smile to my face when I remember noodles being scraped out of a block of potato starch or extruded from a wonderful press like a giant lemon squeezer. But most of all, I cherish the patience, love, and trust with which people were willing to share with me their generations-old family secrets for making the perfect noodle.

Thenthuk

I first tasted this soup after a long trip from China to Lhasa. Two days of waiting for the weather to clear to be able to fly into Lhasa had jangled my nerves, and when I finally made it to the Brahmaputra Hotel near the Potala Palace, I was exhausted. The staff took one look at me and served me this soup. Immediately after, I collapsed into bed and the soup kept me warm all night. First thing in the morning, I went looking for the cook to get the recipe.

In Tibetan, "then" means pull and "thuk" means noodles. Thenthuk is a hearty soup, more like a whole meal. Later, during other journeys in Tibet, I had several different versions of this classic dish, some included meat as in this recipe. Most recipes do not use egg in the dough, though I did meet cooks who made egg noodles for this dish.

Lhasa Pulled Noodle Soup ⟹

Lhasa Pulled Noodle Soup [Thenthuk]

SERVES 4

NOODLES

1 1/2 cups all-purpose flour

1/2 cup water

SOUP

1 small daikon (about 1/2 pound), peeled and sliced thinly

3 tablespoons vegetable oil

1 large red onion, diced

2 cloves garlic, chopped

2 tablespoons chopped peeled fresh ginger

1 tomato, seeded and chopped

1/2 pound thinly sliced beef top round

1 quart water or vegetable broth

3 cups coarsely chopped fresh spinach

4 scallions, chopped

Salt

To make the noodles, place the flour in a mound on a work surface, make a well in the center, and pour in the water. Using a fork, gently incorporate the flour into the water a little at a time to form a firm, satiny dough. Knead well until smooth, flexible, and stretchy, but not sticky. Let the dough rest for 30 minutes, covered with a damp kitchen towel. Roll out to 1/8 inch thick. Cut into long strips, about 1 inch wide.

To make the soup while the noodle dough is resting, soak the daikon in cold salted water for 15 minutes. Drain and rinse the daikon.

Heat the oil in a large soup pot over medium-high heat. Add the onion, garlic, and ginger and cook, stirring occasionally, until softened. Add the tomato and cook until it is very soft. Push the vegetables to the far side of the pot. Add the beef a few slices at a time and brown. When all the beef is browned, add the water. Bring to a boil, then lower the heat and simmer for about 10 minutes. Add the daikon and cook for 2 minutes.

Bring the soup back to a boil. Take a strip of dough and flatten it with your fingers. Laying the long end over your wrist, use your thumb and forefinger to pinch off 1/2-inch sections into the boiling broth. Repeat with the remaining noodles. Cook for about 2 minutes, then stir in the spinach and scallions. When the noodles float, after 6 to 8 minutes, the soup is ready. Season with salt to taste and serve hot.

Himalayan Potato and Spinach Soup with Kopan Masala

SERVES 6 TO 8

1/4 cup (1/2 stick) unsalted butter

1 tablespoon minced, peeled fresh ginger

1 tablespoon minced garlic

1 cup diced red onion

1/2 teaspoon cayenne pepper

1/2 teaspoon Kopan Masala (recipe follows)

3 cups unseasoned mashed potatoes (about 4 russet potatoes)

4 cups water

1 cup chopped fresh spinach

1 pound fresh firm tofu, cut into 1-inch cubes

1 1/2 teaspoons white vinegar

1 tablespoon soy sauce (optional)

1/2 teaspoon freshly ground black pepper

Salt

2 tablespoons chopped scallion

In Dharamshala, the seat of government for Tibetans in exile, you can find the best Tibetan restaurant in India: Namgyal Café. Situated in His Holiness the Dalai Lama's main monastery complex, all of the café's proceeds support the temple and the monks. You wouldn't expect it, but they serve a really good thin-crust pizza. When I visited, I was lucky enough to meet a young cook named Losang who made me this off-the-menu soup despite the restaurant being crazy busy.

There is, no doubt, a version of this soup in every country of the Himalayas and in many countries around the world. The soothing sounds of chanted prayers that surrounded me while I ate made this one even more special to me.

Melt the butter in a large saucepan over medium heat. Add the ginger, garlic, and onion and cook for 2 to 3 minutes, until garlic is softened. Add the cayenne and masala and cook 1 minute more. Add the potato and mix well. Cook and stir for 3 minutes. Add the water 1 cup at a time, stirring continuously with a whisk until smooth. Add the spinach and tofu and bring to boil. Add the vinegar, soy sauce (if using), black pepper, and salt to taste and simmer 5 minutes. If soup is too thick, add a little water. Add the scallion and serve hot.

Kopan Masala

MAKES ABOUT 2/3 CUP

1/4 cup coriander seeds

1/4 cup cumin seeds

10 whole black cardamom pods

15 whole green cardamom pods

1 teaspoon whole cloves

Two 2-inch cinnamon sticks, broken up

1 teaspoon black peppercorns

1/4 teaspoon freshly grated nutmeg

The fragrance of this aromatic spice blend is the pure essence of the Kopan Monastery just north of the ancient Buddhist town of Bodnath in Nepal. This is my variation of the dried spice mixture from the kitchens of this legendary monastery.

Combine all of the ingredients and grind until fine, but not to a powder, with a spice grinder or food processor. Store in an airtight jar.

Paro Cheese and Tomato Soup

SERVES 4

2 tablespoons vegetable oil

1 white medium onion, chopped

1/4 teaspoon garlic, chopped

1 teaspoon minced, peeled fresh ginger

1/4 pound ground beef

1 tomato, seeded and finely chopped

2 tablespoons crumbled blue cheese, preferably Churu (page 268) or Maytag

1/4 teaspoon ground Szechuan peppercorns (see page 44)

5 1/4 cups water, divided

Salt

3 tablespoons cornstarch

2 scallions, chopped

On my first Sunday in Paro, I went to the weekly local market that sells a variety of foods, particularly vegetables and cheese. I developed a peculiar fascination with churu, a cheese made from yak's milk. The first bite I tasted was quite pungent, but the heady aroma got into me, and I wound up eating it again and again. Churu has an intense flavor and though loved by locals, may not be to everyone's taste. Regardless, I had this soup, popular in the Tibetan region of Kongpo, with tsampa dough almost every day for breakfast.

In this recipe, I use blue cheese, which yields the closest approximation to the real homemade churu (page 268).

Heat the oil in a heavy-bottomed pot over medium-high heat and add the onion, garlic, and ginger. Cook, stirring continuously, until the onion begins to brown, about 4 minutes. Add the beef and cook, stirring, 3 to 4 minutes. Add the tomato, cheese, Szechuan pepper, 5 cups of the water, and salt to taste and bring to a boil.

Lower the heat to low and simmer until the beef is cooked through and all the ingredients are well combined, 3 to 4 minutes.

Mix the cornstarch with the remaining 1/4 cup water and gently add it to the simmering soup, stirring continuously to avoid any lumps. Increase the heat to high, and bring to a boil, stirring until thickened.

Top with the scallions and serve hot.

Sikkim Nettle Soup [Sishnu]

SERVES 4

1 tablespoon vegetable oil

3 cloves garlic, minced

5 cups vegetable broth or water

2 teaspoons salt

1/2 cup tsampa (see page 46)

2 cups packed nettle leaves

Cooked rice, for serving

Sikkim, a mountainous state in northeast India, has a climate that varies from subtropical to tundra and has five seasons, the fifth being the monsoon. The powerful monsoons cause frequent landslides and leach nutrients from the soil, making it even more difficult to farm on the rocky terrain. Foraging for wild plants such as nettles is a way of life.

This quick and easy soup is prepared from the leaves of edible wild varieties of nettles available mainly in the months of April and early May at gourmet shops and farmers' markets here. They taste much like spinach and are similarly packed with iron, but have a great refreshing lemony flavor. A word of caution: nettles sting so wear gloves while handling the leaves.

This is a typical Himalayan spring soup often served with rice. Sometimes, I like to purée it for a smooth, velvety version.

In a heavy-bottomed pot, heat the oil over medium heat and cook the garlic, stirring, until fragrant, about 1 minute. Add the vegetable broth and salt and bring to a boil over high heat. Lower the heat to low and simmer, gradually stirring in the tsampa. Continue stirring until the soup is thickened, 3 to 4 minutes. Add the nettles and simmer until the nettles are cooked and tender, about 10 minutes. Add salt to taste.

The soup is ready to serve at this point, but can also be puréed in a blender. Serve hot with cooked rice.

Kashmiri Tomato and Almond Shorba

Shorba is one of those dishes that contains a good part of the world's history. It began as the word shorb or shorba in Arabic, meaning the verb, to drink, or the noun, a drink. The word made its way to Persia then to Turkey during the Ottoman Empire's reign, where the word became chorba and was a hearty soup. From there, it worked its way west into Europe, where the word evolved into sorbetto, sorbet, and sherbet, specifically referring to sweetened ices once made with snow or shaved ice and flavored syrup enjoyed by the ancient Persians and Arabs. As the word moved east again, it became ciorba, a sour soup, in Romania, and another soup, shurpa, in Russia. Then across North Africa and East Africa, it is shorba, any soup or drink. It's one very well-traveled word. So depending on where you are, this word refers to soup, a drink, or frozen sweetened fruit purée.

In Kashmir, it refers to this Moghul-influenced soup, as evidenced by the presence of nuts. Much of Kashmiri cuisine bears this imprint of history and is wonderfully complex and rich.

Shah-e-Hamdan Mosque in Srinagar, Kashmir.

SERVES 4

1 tablespoon ghee (clarified butter) or vegetable oil

1 onion finely chopped

4 green cardamom pods, crushed open

1-inch cinnamon stick, coarsely broken

3 tomatoes, peeled and chopped

1 teaspoon salt

5 cups water or vegetable broth

1 tablespoon tomato purée

1/2 cup sliced blanched almonds, divided

1/4 cup heavy cream

Freshly ground black pepper

Heat the ghee in a Dutch oven over medium heat and cook the onion, cardamom, and cinnamon until the spices become fragrant and the onion has softened, 2 to 3 minutes. Add the tomatoes and salt and cook, breaking up the tomatoes with the back of a wooden spoon, for 2 minutes.

Add the water, tomato purée, and half of the almonds and bring to a boil over high heat. Lower the heat to low and simmer until all of the flavors are well blended, 4 to 5 minutes.

Remove from heat. Working in batches, carefully purée soup in a blender until smooth.

Pour the blended soup back into the Dutch oven, add the cream, and bring to a boil over high heat. Lower heat to low and cook until thick, 10 minutes.

Season with salt and pepper to taste, top with the remaining almonds, and serve hot.

Bhutanese Red Rice and Chicken Soup

SERVES 4 TO 6

1/2 pound boneless, skinless chicken thighs, cut into thin strips

Salt

1/2 teaspoon sugar

1 teaspoon cornstarch

1 cup Bhutanese red rice, rinsed and drained

1/2 cup vegetable oil, divided

2 1/2 quarts cold water

Pretty much everyone who farms the land in Bhutan grows rice. Bhutanese red rice is similar to whole-grain brown rice in its chewy texture and nutty flavor. The first time I ever tried red rice was when I was in Kalustyan's, a shop on Lexington Avenue in Manhattan. For me, it is the Spice Store of All Spice Stores in Manhattan, and has one of the best selections of grains and legumes. On this occasion, I bought a small bag of red rice, but unfortunately overcooked it while dealing with a kitchen emergency at the Rubin Museum Café. In an effort not to waste food, I made it into a soup special. Hearty and comforting, it was well received and became a regular item on the menu. I burst out laughing when I was served a nearly identical soup in Bhutan.

In a bowl, combine the chicken, 1/2 teaspoon salt, the sugar, and cornstarch. Cover and refrigerate for at least 3 hours.

In a large heavy-bottomed pot, combine the rice, 1/2 teaspoon salt, 1/4 cup of the oil, and the water and bring to a boil over high heat, stirring occasionally. Lower the heat to low and simmer, stirring occasionally for even cooking, for 2 1/2 hours, until most of the rice breaks down and the soup thickens.

Heat the remaining 1/4 cup oil in a skillet over medium heat and fry the chicken, stirring gently, until cooked through, about 4 minutes.

Add the cooked chicken to the soup and cook for another 3 to 4 minutes, until well combined and thick. Salt to taste and serve hot.

Darjeeling Corn Soup

SERVES 4 TO 6

1 tablespoon unsalted butter or vegetable oil

1/2 Spanish onion, chopped

1/4 teaspoon Kashmiri or Hungarian paprika (see page 43)

1 clove garlic, finely chopped

1/2-inch piece fresh ginger, peeled and finely chopped

1 tomato, seeded and diced

One 14-ounce package firm tofu, cut into small cubes

1 teaspoon salt, or more to taste

4 cups water

Kernels cut from 3 ears fresh corn

1 tablespoon cornstarch

1 scallion, chopped

Darjeeling has long been known for its tea, but it has also always functioned as an important crossroads of Sikkim, Nepal, Bhutan, and Bengal. During its long history, Darjeeling has fallen under the control and influence of many rulers. This soup represents the cross-fertilization of several cultures and is a perfect example of how culinary traditions can overlap and blend.

Due south from Darjeeling is Kolkata, at the delta of the Ganges River, where historically, a large population of Chinese immigrants have lived. From this culture comes the addition of tofu and cornstarch. The New World influence is apparent from the use of corn and tomatoes, so much a part of Indian cuisine that Indians think of them as native ingredients. Then there is the typical Indian reliance on ginger, garlic, and onions as a flavor base. There are many restaurants in India specializing in this Indian-Chinese hybrid cuisine that has become very popular throughout the country.

In a heavy-bottomed soup pot, melt the butter over medium heat. Add the onion and cook, stirring occasionally, until browned and soft, about 2 to 3 minutes. Add the paprika, garlic, and ginger and cook until fragrant. Add the tomato, tofu, salt, and water and bring to a boil.

Add the corn. Mix the cornstarch with a little cold water and stir into the soup. Bring to a boil and simmer for about a minute, stirring until thickened.

Top each serving with chopped scallion and serve hot.

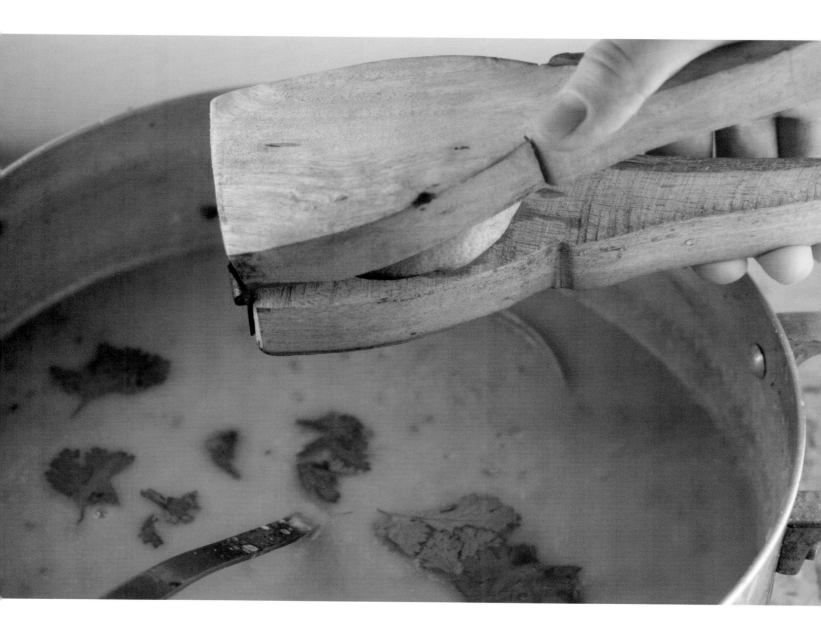

Mrs. Shreshta's Red Lentil Soup

SERVES 6 TO 8

1 tablespoon unsalted butter

2 tablespoons vegetable oil, divided

2 cups chopped red onion

1 tablespoon minced, peeled fresh ginger

1 tablespoon finely chopped, seeded green chile (such as serrano)

6 cups water

2 cups dried red lentils

1/2 teaspoon ground turmeric

2 teaspoons salt

1/2 teaspoon jimbu (see page 42)

1/3 cup chopped fresh cilantro

2 tablespoons fresh lemon juice

Whenever I talk about Nepal, I inevitably end up describing a close family friend, Mrs. Kamala Shreshta, and her cooking. Like my Biji, she was able to infuse her dishes with lots of love and generosity. People will forgive you a lot in your cooking if you display this kind of spirit, a point I always try to instill in the young cooks who work for me. No matter who you are, you will make mistakes. But if your basic intentions are pure, people will respond to that and offer you a second chance.

I am sure my Kamala Auntie would be proud of the way I teach cooks because that is how she taught me this soup. When I made this dish for the first time in Kamala Auntie's kitchen in Kathmandu, I used jimbu, the highlight of this dish, the same way I use cumin, cooking it for about a minute to bring out the flavor of the spice. This method turned out to be completely wrong and it destroyed the flavor of this delicate herb. Luckily for me, Kamala Auntie's heart was full of forgiveness, and she corrected me with such warmth that I actually didn't feel too badly about my botched dish. We started over and I managed to make a wonderful pot of lentils.

Turmeric gives this creamy soup a deep golden color, and the red lentils lend it a slightly sweeter flavor than the brown or green varieties would.

Melt the butter and one tablespoon of the oil in a saucepan over medium-high heat. Add the onion, ginger, and chile and cook until soft, about 4 minutes. Stir in the water, lentils, turmeric, and salt. Bring to a boil. Lower the heat and simmer until the lentils are well cooked and soft, skimming the scum continuously, 15 to 20 minutes.

Place one-third of the lentil mixture in a blender. Secure the blender lid, but remove its center piece to allow the steam to escape. Cover the open lid with a kitchen towel and blend the lentils to a fine purée. Add the purée back to the pot and keep warm over low heat.

Heat the remaining tablespoon oil in a small skillet, remove from heat, and stir in the jimbu. Add the jimbu, cilantro, and lemon juice to the soup and stir well. Serve warm.

Chicken and Garlic Soup with Tsampa

SERVES 4 TO 6

3 tablespoons vegetable oil

1 red onion, finely chopped

4 cloves garlic, minced

1/2 pound chicken or other meat, hand-chopped or ground

6 cups water or Basic Broth (see page 129), divided

1 tomato, finely chopped

1/2 cup finely ground tsampa (see page 46)

Salt

2 scallions, thinly sliced, for garnish

Traditionally, this soup is made with ground beef, but chicken works equally well. Feel free to experiment with different varieties of meat because that is often how people cook in the Himalayas. One day they may have chicken and not beef, or lamb and not goat. (My friend Dev, who helped out with recipe testing, says that he made the soup with lamb for his kids and they were crazy about it.)

If you are handy with a knife and have a good, heavy, sharp one, try chopping the meat by hand as cooks in the Himalayas do, stopping before it gets too fine. Tsampa adds an earthy undertone and also thickens the soup.

In a Dutch oven, heat the oil over medium heat and cook the onions and garlic, stirring continuously until golden brown, 5 to 6 minutes. Increase the heat to high, add the chicken and cook until lightly browned, pressing constantly with the back of a wooden spoon to separate the meat, 4 to 5 minutes.

Add 5 cups of the water and the tomato and bring to a boil.

In a small bowl, mix the tsampa with the remaining 1 cup water. Add the tsampa mixture to the stew, a little at a time, stirring continuously until well combined. Bring back to a boil and cook until the soup thickens to your desired consistency, 5 to 10 minutes. Season with salt to taste. Serve hot, topped with the scallions.

Tashi delek

On one trip I made to Tibet, I stayed at a hotel near the Potala Palace, Tibet's most important spiritual site and the hereditary seat of His Holiness the Dalai Lama. I enjoyed how close the hotel was to the very heart of Lhasa. I could walk everywhere easily—to Jokhang Temple, to restaurants, and to the bazaars. Almost every morning as I strolled around, I was aware of a very elderly woman who would sit in the same spot in front of the Potala Palace; she seemed to notice me as well. She would acknowledged my presence with a smile and a small nod as she worked her prayer beads.

I would watch the movement of the wooden beads in her ancient fingers as she prayed. She looked to be old enough to have suffered through the terrible times of 1959 when so many Tibetans were forced to flee over the mountains to India, to safety and freedom. I wanted to talk to her, but didn't want to upset her and lose the nod that had become so sacred to me those mornings.

Finally, one Sunday morning, I asked my guide to help me speak to her. We sat next to her and my guide wished her tashi delek, meaning "blessings and good luck." She told us that she came to the palace to pray for her son and his family. Years before, she had sent her son with her brother and his wife to safety and had not seen them since. She wondered if during all the long years of separation her daughter-in-law had given birth to a boy or a girl. She said something that took me many years to understand: "I pray that they have learned to be happy."

Listening to the timeline of her story, I guessed that she must have been around ninety years old. Like many of the very old people up in the mountains, her face was deeply lined from the sun, the wind, and the pain of waiting, but she was quite agile still and moved with vigor.

After some time, I began to understand everything she was saying without my guide; she had such purity and devotion in her eyes that I still think of her all these years later. Her eyes glowed when she talked about happier times when her house was filled with guests, celebrations, and laughter. At that moment, I knew that I had come to Tibet not just to collect recipes and cooking lore, but to listen to and share peoples' life stories.

The woman spoke of how she'd often find herself adding more and more water to her kitchen pots to make broth for soups and meats to feed her steady stream of guests. A version of this broth, used as a base for many recipes, is found in every home.

Basic Broth

YIELDS 2 QUARTS

1 pound oxtail or other beef with bones, cut into pieces

1/4 teaspoon whole Szechuan peppercorns (see page 44)

5 or 6 cloves garlic

2-inch piece fresh ginger, crushed

3 quarts water

1/2 teaspoon salt

Combine all of the ingredients in a soup pot. Bring to a boil, lower the heat, and gently simmer uncovered, for at least 4 hours, until the meat is very soft.

Strain the broth and discard the solids.

Cool the broth and skim any fat from the surface. Store, covered, in the refrigerator for up to three days.

Tibetan Vegetable Noodle Soup [Tse Thenthuk]

Mount Kailash, in a remote far western region of Tibet, is a towering mountain profoundly sacred to many, including Buddhists, Hindus, and Jains. The area is the source of many major rivers and has deep mythological and spiritual importance. In the Hindu tradition, Lord Shiva the Destroyer of Evil and Sorrow lives atop it, while in Buddhism, it is believed to be the home of the Buddha of supreme bliss.

Though the journey to the region can be grueling, many make the pilgrimage to perform the kora, a pilgrimage in which one walks all the way around a sacred site. The circuit around Mount Kailash is about 32 miles long and is often completed by the devout in one day. For those who want to challenge themselves further or are more strictly devout, the circuit can be done with full-body prostrations, which involves kneeling, then lying flat on the ground with arms outstretched, showing complete devotion. They then make their way forward only as far as where their hands had touched; kneeling again, the process repeats again and again and can take several weeks to complete.

When we went on our Mount Kailash pilgrimage, one of the members of our group sadly fell victim to altitude sickness as we were making our way around the circuit. We turned back and came across another pilgrimage group; they were cooking this soup and offered to share it with us. The soup and their generosity really revived our spirits. It is common to see people stopping along the way like this, making soup for sustenance, as the journey is very demanding. Mount Kailash defeated us that trip, but I know I will go back to Tibet one day to complete my pilgrimage.

SERVES 4

3 tablespoons unsalted butter

2 cloves garlic, finely chopped

1-inch piece fresh ginger, peeled and minced

1 small red onion, diced

1 teaspoon Kopan Masala (page 113)

1 tomato, diced

1 tablespoon Tibetan Chile-Garlic Paste (page 374), plus more for serving

1 russet potato, peeled, boiled, and cut into 1-inch cubes

4 cups vegetable broth

4 ounces Japanese udon noodles or thick noodles of your choice

1 tablespoon soy sauce

Salt and freshly ground black pepper

Heat the butter in a saucepan over medium heat and cook the garlic, ginger, and onion until softened, 2 to 3 minutes. Add the masala and cook until fragrant, about 1 minute. Add the tomato and chile-garlic paste and cook, stirring until the tomato becomes soft, about 2 minutes.

Add the potato and broth and increase the heat to high to bring to a boil. Add the noodles and cook for 5 minutes or until the noodles are tender. Add the soy sauce and season with salt and pepper to taste. Serve hot with chile-garlic paste.

Ladakh Vegetable Stew with Handmade Pasta [Tschu Tagi]

SERVES 4 TO 6

1/2 cup whole-wheat flour

Salt

6 tablespoons warm water, plus more if necessary

2 tablespoons vegetable oil

1 small white onion, diced

2 cloves garlic, minced

1 small russet potato, peeled, boiled, and cut into 1/2-inch wedges

2 ripe tomatoes, seeded and coarsely chopped

1/2 cup chopped spinach

1/2 teaspoon ground turmeric

1/2 small head cauliflower, cut into small florets

1/2 cup fresh or frozen peas

5 cups vegetable broth

1/4 cup coarsely chopped fresh cilantro

The hostess at the Lobchang Guesthouse in Ladakh taught me this recipe during my stay there. Warm and hospitable, she had run the guesthouse for a long time. She told me she had been making this particular dish for fifty years and since she had no daughters of her own, she was happy to teach it to me. The first time she had ever helped make tschu tagi was her older sister's wedding. The dish was just one of an incredible number of dishes made for the party. She reminisced about the wedding as we worked together and sighed heavily that things were not done as they were back in the old days. Thankfully, this hearty, comforting stew with pasta lovingly made by hand is something that hadn't changed after all those years.

In a bowl, combine the flour and a pinch of salt. Add a tablespoon of water at a time, stirring until the flour and water come together to form a firm dough. Knead it with your hands for at least 10 minutes. Cover with plastic wrap and let rest for at least 30 minutes at room temperature.

Divide the dough into small balls, about 1 teaspoon each, and with your fingers, flatten the dough into a disk about 1 1/2 inches in diameter and 1/8-inch thick. Shape the dough around a handle of a round wooden spoon and pinch it together. Gently transfer each piece to a lightly floured plate and keep covered with a damp kitchen towel.

Heat the oil in pot over medium heat and cook the onion and garlic until softened, 2 to 3 minutes. Add the potato and salt to taste and cook, stirring, for 1 minute. Add the tomatoes, spinach, and turmeric and cook until the tomatoes begin to soften and the spinach is wilted, about 2 minutes.

Add the cauliflower, peas, and vegetable broth and increase the heat to high to bring to a boil. Add the pasta and cook, gently stirring, until the pasta is cooked through, 6 to 8 minutes. Stir in the cilantro just before serving.

Fermented Greens Soup

SERVES 4

1 cup Gundruk (page 213)

1 cup warm water

2 tablespoons vegetable oil

1 small white onion, finely chopped

1 dried red chile, coarsely broken

1 teaspoon cumin seeds

2 cloves garlic, minced

1-inch piece fresh ginger, peeled and minced

1 tomato, seeded and finely chopped

1/2 teaspoon ground turmeric

4 cups vegetable broth

Salt

Mustang is one of the most stunning places anywhere in the world. It was only opened to foreign visitors as recently as 1991 and I could not let the chance to visit this incredible place pass me by. After the bus ride, I took a plane from Pokhara to Jomsom in Mustang. This is not a flight for the squeamish, but if you're up to it, the thrilling flight path is along a gorgeous, narrow valley. The trick is to be sure to touch down in Jomsom by around 11:00 a.m. before the wind kicks up and landing is impossible for the rest of the day.

When I arrived, I of course went in search of something local to eat—just as my grandfather would have done upon finding himself in a new place. I was lucky to find this gundruk soup at the little lodge where I wound up staying.

Gundruk (page 213) is a staple food in Nepal made from greens (mustard, radish, or spinach). Fermented and dried, gundruk has a unique flavor. Karma, the cook at the lodge, was amused by my desire to learn this recipe. The very idea that there could be a recipe for a dish was totally alien to her. By the time we were done recreating it, I think this very shy cook was relieved not to have to answer any more of my questions.

My version here includes tomatoes, which are not normally found in gundruk. You can always leave the tomatoes out if you crave authenticity.

In a nonreactive (glass or stainless-steel) bowl, soak the gundruk in the water. Cover and let it hydrate for at least 10 minutes. Drain and finely chop.

In a Dutch oven, heat the oil over medium heat and fry the onion, chile, cumin, garlic, and ginger, stirring continuously until the onions begin to turn golden brown around the edges, 4 to 5 minutes. Add a few tablespoons of water to prevent burning if necessary.

Add the tomato and turmeric and cook, stirring until the tomato softens, 2 to 3 minutes. Mix in the gundruk and cook, stirring continuously until it is evenly coated. Add the broth and bring to a boil. Lower the heat to low, cover, and simmer until all the flavors are well blended and the broth is rich and thickened, 3 to 5 minutes. Season with salt to taste before serving hot.

Field of mustard plants in Tibet.

Bean Thread Noodles with Garlic Leaves

SERVES 4

1 teaspoon cornstarch

1 tablespoon low-sodium soy sauce

1 or 2 pinches cayenne pepper

1/2 pound pork loin, cut into 1/2-inch cubes

5 ounces bean thread noodles (available at Asian groceries)

3 tablespoons vegetable oil

1 red onion, thinly sliced

2 cloves garlic, minced

8 to 10 garlic leaves, coarsely chopped

1/2 teaspoon salt

Bean thread noodles, also known as cellophane noodles, are popular in Tibet and are seen on practically every Tibetan restaurant menu in the world. If you are in Tibet, you will find bean thread noodles in places ranging from simple food shops and people's homes to upscale restaurants. Generally, bean thread noodles are prepared simply with a small amount of meat, a few flavorings, and some fiery chutney or chile paste served on the side. If garlic leaves are out of season, substitute scallions.

Mix the cornstarch, soy sauce, and cayenne in a bowl. Add the pork and mix to evenly coat. Cover and refrigerate for at least 30 minutes or up to 2 hours.

Soak the noodles in 2 cups lukewarm water, for at least 20 minutes or up to half an hour, at room temperature. Drain.

Heat the oil in a wok or large skillet over medium-high heat and cook the onion and garlic until softened, about 3 minutes. Add the pork and fry for 2 minutes, stirring continuously until evenly browned, 3 to 4 minutes.

Add the noodles and garlic leaves and continue to stir until well combined and warm. Add 1 cup water and bring it to a boil. Lower the heat to low and simmer until the pork is cooked and the water has evaporated, about 5 minutes. Add the salt and serve hot.

Mung Bean Noodles [Laping]

SERVES 4

2 1/4 cups water, divided

1/2 cup mung bean starch (available at Asian groceries)

Vegetable oil

1 1/2 teaspoons soy sauce

Pinch of salt

1 tablespoon finely chopped scallions

Tibetan Chile-Garlic Paste (page 374), for serving

Laping is a popular street food in Lhasa and throughout Tibet. I enjoyed various versions of this dish and this was a simple, but satisfying, way to make it—with just a touch of soy sauce and served with hot sauce. The first time I made laping, I refrigerated it to cool it down quickly and the noodles became cloudy. Now I just leave the laping out on the kitchen counter to cool slowly for a beautiful, traditional translucent look. After it has fully cooled to room temperature, it should be refrigerated overnight so that it is fully set and firm before cutting.

In a pot, bring 2 cups of the water to a boil over medium-high heat.

Meanwhile, place the starch in a small bowl and slowly whisk in the remaining 1/4 cup water until the starch has dissolved. Slowly whisk the dissolved starch into the boiling water. Stirring continuously with a whisk, simmer until thickened and clear, 5 to 7 minutes.

Lightly oil a large, rimmed baking sheet. Pour and spread the mixture to about 1/2 inch thick. Let stand at room temperature until set and fully cooled, 3 to 4 hours. Refrigerate overnight to completely firm up.

Using a sharp knife, cut the mixture into 2 by 1/3-inch strips. Toss them with the soy sauce and salt. Top with the scallions and serve cool with chile-garlic paste.

Potato Noodles with Chile Paste [Shu-Ping]

SERVES 4 TO 6

2 1/4 cups water, divided

1/2 cup potato starch

Vegetable oil

1/2 teaspoon salt

1 1/2 teaspoons soy sauce

1 tablespoon finely chopped scallions

2 tablespoons Tibetan Chile-Garlic Paste (page 374), plus more for serving

I received a lesson in ingenious cooking tools when I watched these noodles being made. The man preparing them had taken the lid from an aluminum can and poked holes in it, fashioning himself an improvised noodle maker. He made a large block of potato starch dough and then dragged the lid across its surface, the noodles extruding from the holes as he went. Such lids are incredibly dangerous to work with, so even if you're tempted to make one in your kitchen, using a sharp knife to cut the noodles is a far safer way to go.

This dish is prepared similarly to laping (page 139), and the noodles share a translucent look, but noodles made of potato starch are much softer and more pliant than those made with mung bean starch.

In a pot, bring 2 cups of the water to a boil over high heat and then lower the heat to low.

Place the starch in a small bowl and slowly whisk in the remaining 1/4 cup water until the starch has dissolved. Slowly whisk the dissolved starch into the boiling water. Simmer until clear, 5 to 7 minutes.

Lightly oil a rimmed baking sheet with vegetable oil and pour the mixture onto it. The mixture should spread on its own, but be prepared to use a spatula to help it along. It should be no more than 1/3 inch thick. Let stand at room temperature until set, 3 to 4 hours. Refrigerate overnight for additional firming.

Using a sharp knife, cut into long thin noodles. Toss with the salt and soy sauce. Top with the scallions and chili-garlic paste and serve with more paste on the side.

Tibetan-Style Lo Mein [Thukpa Dangmo]

SERVES 4

1 tablespoon vegetable oil

8 ounces cooked lo mein noodles, preferably fresh

1 1/2 teaspoons cayenne pepper

2 tablespoons soy sauce

Salt

Pinch of sugar

3 scallions, finely chopped

This noodle dish provided me sustenance through my long journeys in Tibet and I love it. Lhasa was the central point of my travels, and each time I had a stopover there, I would get these noodles from the street carts outside Jokhang Temple. I would request stewed vegetables and meats be added to the noodles to make this a complete meal on the go.

While "thukpa" means noodles, "dangmo" means served at room temperature.

Heat the oil in a large skillet or wok over high heat. Carefully swirl to coat the bottom of the pan with the hot oil. Add the noodles, cayenne, soy sauce, salt to taste, and sugar and toss to combine and heat all the ingredients. Top with the scallions and serve cold or at room temperature.

Bhutanese Buckwheat Noodles with Chile and Scallions [Puta]

In the eastern part of Bhutan, people traditionally eat puta, or buckwheat noodles. The Bhutanese in this area have been making buckwheat cakes and these particular buckwheat noodles since time immemorial. When I stayed in Thimphu, I passed by a house everyday and was intrigued by a large ancient-looking wooden contraption in the yard. It turned out that it was a traditional pasta maker: a wooden handle is used to push the dough, and noodles are extruded and caught below. No one will ever be able to say with certainty who invented pasta, or when, but these machines seem to be one of the oldest pasta-making tools still in use.

As farmers gravitate towards growing more lucrative crops such as rice and potatoes, traditional foods, such as these Bhutanese buckwheat noodles, are in danger of vanishing. Puta is now often reserved for special occasions, though I have heard that some elders are trying to preserve this ancient food tradition.

This recipe calls for a contemporary pasta maker that can be either hand-cranked or electric.

SERVES 4

2 cups buckwheat flour

1/2 cup all-purpose flour

3 large eggs

2 tablespoons vegetable oil

1 red onion, thinly sliced

1 bunch scallions, coarsely chopped

1 fresh green chile (such as serrano), sliced

1 teaspoon soy sauce

Salt

Mix the flours, place on a work surface in a mound, and make a well in the center. Put the eggs and 1/2 teaspoon salt into the well and lightly beat to mix. Using a fork, gently incorporate the flour into the eggs a little at a time. Once the flour has been incorporated, use your fingers to blend the mixture well. Knead it with your hands to form a firm, smooth dough, 5 to 7 minutes.

Cover the dough with plastic wrap and let rest for 15 minutes.

Using a pasta maker, form the dough into thin noodles of your preference. If you're not cooking the noodles immediately, toss them with a little flour to keep them separated and store, tightly covered, in the refrigerator for up to 1 week.

To cook the noodles, bring 2 quarts water to a boil. Add the noodles and boil until firm and cooked, about 3 minutes. Drain. Heat the oil in a skillet over medium-high heat and fry the onion until golden, about 3 minutes. Add the noodles, scallions, chile, soy sauce, and salt to taste. Stir until well combined and warm, about 2 minutes.

Ritsha Village. Punakha. Bhutan.

GRAINS

From Asia to Afghanistan, rice is a deeply sacred element, inextricably embedded in many cultures. In the Himalayas, terraces are cut into mountainsides to create more land to cultivate rice, and there are more varieties of rice in the region than anywhere else in the world.

I am from Amritsar, a wheat-growing area, and while we enjoy rice very much in that part of India, it is not nearly as ubiquitous as it is up in the mountains. From the Himalayan foothills of Dehradun in India, where the most fragrant basmati rice is grown, to Bhutan with its famous red rice, everyone in the region plants rice. When I talk to people about the Himalayas, I often refer to the epiphany I experienced in Bhutan while I was staying in the city of Paro. Everywhere I went, people were closely connected to the land and to each other. A vital part of this connection is the cultivation of rice. Rice was literally planted everywhere it could possibly sprout and houses were flanked by rice paddies.

Whether for breakfast, lunch, dinner, a snack, drinks, wine, or sweets, rice is a component of many Himalayan dishes. This versatile grain is also used in religious offerings and is probably one of the most auspicious foods the people of the Himalayas consume. The planting and harvesting of rice are part of the religious landscape; the success of the family and the success of the harvest, interwoven with religious practice, are one and the same.

Thankfully, these days, you can easily find the world's best rice at gourmet food shops, health food stores, ethnic groceries, and even at many large chain stores. It is well worth your while to spend a little extra money to experience the wonderfully intense aroma and flavor of some of these newly available varieties of rice.

Pampore Saffron Rice Pilaf [Zafrani Pulao]

SERVES 6

2 cups long-grain basmati rice

3 tablespoons ghee (clarified butter) or vegetable oil, divided

1 red onion, thinly sliced

Salt

2-inch cinnamon stick

5 whole cloves

4 to 6 green cardamom pods, crushed open

Pinch of ground turmeric

4 cups water

1 teaspoon saffron threads, steeped in 2 tablespoons warm milk

1/4 cup walnuts, coarsely chopped

Pampore is a town in the heart of Kashmir and the center of saffron growing. From this region, known as the Saffron Valley, comes Kashmiri saffron, renowned for its deep maroon color and musky aroma. Many people consider this saffron, particularly what is grown in Pampore, to be the best in the world.

As you may know, saffron is the most expensive seasoning ingredient you can buy. At various times in history it was worth more than gold. It is so costly because it must be harvested very early in the day, just after the Crocus sativa, the saffron crocus, has opened its petals. The stigmas are pulled by hand—no machine can do this—and the harvesting season is very short, from the end of October to the beginning of November. It takes about 75,000 flowers to make one pound of saffron.

This rice dish, made wonderfully aromatic by the cinnamon, cloves, and cardamom, is the perfect way to showcase this special ingredient.

Thoroughly rinse the rice in a fine-mesh strainer under cold running water until the water runs clear. Soak the rice in a bowl, covered by 2 inches of cold water, for 15 minutes.

Heat 2 tablespoons of the ghee in a large heavy-bottomed pot over medium heat. Cook the onions with a pinch of salt, stirring and scraping the pan continuously, until golden brown, 8 to 10 minutes. Remove the onions from the pan and drain the excess fat on paper towels.

In the same pan, heat the remaining tablespoon of ghee with the cinnamon, cloves, cardamom, and turmeric, and cook over medium heat, stirring until the cinnamon unfurls, 1 to 2 minutes.

Drain the rice, add to the spices with 2 teaspoons salt, and continue to stir until the rice is well coated. Add 4 cups water and the saffron-milk mixture and bring to a boil. Lower the heat to low; cover and cook until the rice is tender and each grain is separate, about 15 minutes.

Fluff with a fork and serve hot, topped with the onions and walnuts.

Assamese Rice Cakes [Pitha]

MAKES 15 TO 20 PITHAS

1 cup rice flour

1 red onion, finely chopped

1/2 teaspoon salt

1/4 to 1/3 cup water

6 tablespoons mustard oil
(see page 45) or vegetable oil

Bihu, the great festival of Assam, celebrates the arrival of spring and what the Assamese consider the beginning of the new year. During the festival, Bihu dancers perform elaborate ritual dances and wear a gamosa wrapped around their heads to honor the holiday. The gamosa, a white and red woven cloth, is exceedingly important in Assamese culture and serves a variety of purposes, from ordinary to sacred. The direct translation of gamosa is "body wiping cloth," and though it is indeed used to dry off after baths, it is also offered to elders or honored guests as a sign of respect and is used in religious ceremonies and customs.

One of my most prized possessions is the gamosa that a Bihu dancer once gave me when he was happy with the pitha I had prepared for the dancers. Pitha, which are griddled cakes made of rice flour, are essential to Bihu festivities—it would be unthinkable to celebrate Bihu without eating them. Though they are so widely available at street stalls that most people don't bother making them at home anymore, I love making my own so I can come up with variations using lemon or orange zest, nuts, herbs, or other spices in the batter.

This recipe uses store-bought rice flour, but in Assam, pithas are typically prepared with rice that is first soaked in water and then ground.

In a bowl, combine the flour, onion, and salt and mix well with a wooden spoon. Make a well in the center and gradually add the water, gently mixing, until it reaches the consistency of pancake batter. Cover and let the batter rest for at least 10 minutes.

Line a baking sheet with paper towels. Heat a nonstick skillet or griddle with 1 tablespoon of the oil over medium heat. Swirl the pan to evenly coat with the oil. Pour small ladlefuls of batter (about 2 tablespoons) into the pan and spread round like pancakes. Cook until the edges brown and bubbles form on top, 2 to 3 minutes. Using a spatula or a flat spoon, turn the pancakes over and continue to cook until the second side is lightly browned, another minute. Drain the pancakes on the paper towels to remove excess oil.

Add another half-tablespoon of oil to the pan and continue to cook the pancakes, gently stirring the batter each time right before frying. Serve at room temperature or just slightly warm.

Clarified Butter Basmati Rice

SERVES 4 TO 6

2 teaspoons salt

2 quarts water

2 cups basmati rice

3 tablespoons ghee
(clarified butter), melted

Baisakhi is a spring harvest festival celebrated among Hindus at the beginning of the solar new year. It is one of the most important festivals among the Sikhs of Northern India. Celebrations can be found throughout India and much of the Himalayas. Baisakhi rituals include taking a bath in the waters of a pool at the Golden Temple, sacred to Sikhs, in Amritsar. Other sacred waters especially prized for this ritual include the Ganges and particular ponds and canals.

I once traveled up to Jammu and happened to be there during Baisakhi. There I decided to visit the Nagbani Temple, an old temple originally dedicated to Naag Devta, the Serpent God (many depictions of Lord Shiva show Naag Devta wrapped around his neck). Many years ago, the temple became an agricultural college, but nevertheless, people still come to make offerings of grains and cereals. On this occasion, I had felt overfed with the many sweet festival foods of Baisakhi and longed for something simple to eat, so I was grateful to have this simple, but delicious, rice dish at the temple.

The rice on its own is wonderful, but the clarified butter further enhances its superb bouquet of flavors. The rice is cooked in a large amount of water—normally, we would only use one quart of water to cook 2 cups of rice; here we use two quarts, so it need not be rinsed before cooking. When the cooked rice is drained, the water is reserved for feeding the cows as it is rich with nutrients.

In a large pot, combine the salt and water, and bring to a boil over high heat. Add the rice and return to a boil. Cook the rice until tender, about 15 minutes. Drain and transfer to a bowl. Evenly drizzle with the ghee. Gently mix and serve hot.

Pressed Rice with Yogurt and Nuts [Poha]

SERVES 6 TO 8 AS A SNACK

Vegetable oil, for frying

2 cups pressed rice, preferably the thick variety (see page 45)

1 teaspoon salt

1 cup plain low-fat yogurt, whisked smooth

1/4 cup sliced blanched almonds

Poha is one of the staple foods of Nepal. Also known as cheura in Indian grocery stores, it is made from parboiled rice that is rolled flat and dried. Traditionally, the rice was flattened in a wooden mortar before drying, whereas now it is pressed by a machine. Poha is available in both thick and thin varieties and can be eaten plain, toasted, or fried. The thick variety is often reconstituted with liquid, which makes it fluffy instead of crispy like the thin variety.

In Punjab, my grandmother used to make this dish as a snack. She would stir-fry the poha in hot oil until it puffed up and then added yogurt and other ingredients. To test if the oil is hot enough, fry one grain of pressed rice; if it expands and rises to the top right away, it's ready.

Line a baking sheet with paper towels. Heat about 3 inches of oil in a wok or Dutch oven over medium heat to 350°F. Fry the pressed rice a handful at a time and stir until evenly golden, 1 to 2 minutes. Remove with a fine-mesh strainer and drain on the paper towels to remove the excess oil.

Once cooled, season the poha with salt. Stir in the yogurt and top with the almonds. Serve immediately.

Bhutanese Red Rice with Nuts and Apricots

SERVES 4

1 cup Bhutanese red rice

Salt

4 cups water

2 tablespoons ghee (clarified butter) or vegetable oil

3 tablespoons shelled pistachios

12 shelled walnuts

5 or 6 dried apricots, coarsely chopped

I crossed into Phuntsholing, Bhutan, for the first time on a bus from Jaigaon, an Indian town in western Bengal. The two cities are not far from each other and yet they are worlds apart. Jaigaon is noisy and jangles the nerves with its frenetic commercial activity and constant influx of immigrants while Phuntsholing is serene and calm, a seemingly different world.

My guide met me at the bus station and brought me to his home for lunch where he served me this wonderful red rice dish. Professional guides such as he work to showcase the beauty of their country and often offer the hospitality of their homes as well. Everything in the kitchen had the look and feel of careful craftsmanship and the patina of long use. The entire cooking surface was made from clay and I was happily able to watch the cooking process from start to finish.

Bhutanese red rice has a rich, nutty aroma and is slightly chewy. The first time I saw it in Bhutan, I noticed it growing side by side with white rice and I couldn't understand what I was looking at. The color of the red rice made it seem as though it was growing in a shadow. Red rice is being used more and more in America and this dish is a great place to start.

Thoroughly rinse the rice in a fine-mesh strainer under cold running water until the water runs clear. Transfer to a bowl, cover with 2 inches of water, and soak for at least 30 minutes.

Drain the rice. In a heavy-bottomed saucepan, salt the 4 cups water and bring to a boil, add the rice, and return to a boil. Lower the heat to low and simmer until the rice is cooked, 20 to 25 minutes, depending on the age and quality of rice. Drain the rice well.

Melt the ghee in a nonstick skillet or saucepan over medium-low heat. Add the rice, pistachios, walnuts, and apricots and gently stir with a wooden spoon until well combined, 2 to 3 minutes. Serve hot.

Breakfast Fried Rice

SERVES 4

1 cup short grain rice

Salt

4 cups water

2 tablespoons ghee (clarified butter) or vegetable oil

1 large red onion, finely chopped

1 cup chopped cooked vegetables (optional)

1 teaspoon salt

1 medium egg, lightly whisked (you could use 2 eggs to make it heartier)

Red Chile Onion Chutney (page 369) or other spicy chutney, for serving

On my way up to the Tiger's Nest Monastery in Bhutan, I stopped at a broken prayer wheel that was covered with a corrugated tin roof. A monk told me that the wheel had served many generations, answering their prayers and giving them hope, and out of respect for the wishes and dreams of our ancestors, we must continue to protect and respect sacred objects. That morning I had this rice dish for breakfast and it has become a favorite comfort food of mine. It reminds me of the beauty of age-old customs and traditions.

The night before, I try to get the chutney, cooked rice, and vegetables prepared so that I can quickly toss everything together the next morning. This dish is also a great way to use up leftover rice and vegetables and is delicious any time of day.

Thoroughly rinse the rice in a fine-mesh strainer under cold running water until the water runs clear. Transfer the rice to a bowl, cover with 2 inches water, and soak for at least 30 minutes.

Drain the rice. In a heavy-bottomed saucepan, salt the water and bring to a boil, add the rice, and return to a boil. Lower the heat to low and simmer until the rice is cooked, 20 to 25 minutes, depending on the age and quality of rice. Drain the rice well and cool to room temperature.

Heat the ghee in a large skillet over medium heat. Add the onion and cook, stirring frequently, until soft, 3 to 4 minutes. Add the rice, vegetables (if using), and salt and cook, stirring until the rice is warmed through, about 4 minutes. Gradually add the egg and continue to stir until the egg is cooked and well combined with the rice, about 2 minutes. Serve hot with the chutney.

Bhutanese Crispy Rice [Zaw]

MAKES ABOUT 2 CUPS

1 cup white rice

Salt

4 cups water

2 tablespoons vegetable oil or
mustard oil (see page 45)

Zaw is a popular snack food in Bhutan much like potato chips or corn chips are in the United States. Traditionally, it is made for storing throughout the winter months when fuel for cooking becomes scarce. The rice is first boiled and then fried with a small amount of oil in a wok while continuously stirred. This simple cooking process dries the rice, preserving it so that it lasts for months; if not done correctly, it will not keep.

Most often, it is served plain and eaten by the handful, but it can also be made fancier with additional ingredients like Zaw Ma Gew (page 161), served to more esteemed guests. The first time I saw zaw in Bhutan, a little girl was eating it with a very big dollop of chile paste so I tried mine with chile paste too, but alas, it was way too spicy for me.

Thoroughly rinse the rice in a fine-mesh strainer under cold running water until the water runs clear. Transfer the rice to a bowl, cover with 2 inches water, and soak for at least 30 minutes. Drain.

In a heavy-bottomed saucepan, salt the water and bring to a boil, add the rice, and return to a boil. Lower the heat to low and simmer until the rice is cooked, 20 to 25 minutes, depending on the age and quality of rice. Drain well.

Line a baking sheet with several clean kitchen towels and spread the rice on it. Evenly cover with another layer of kitchen towels and press lightly to remove as much excess moisture as possible. Let it rest for 2 hours.

Line another baking sheet with several layers of paper towels. Heat the oil in a large wok or nonstick skillet over medium-low heat. Add the rice and gently stir with a wooden spoon, until darker in color and lightly crisp, 8 to 10 minutes.

Remove the rice from the oil with a fine-mesh strainer and spread it on the paper towels to remove excess oil. Let the rice cool completely before storing in a tightly covered, clean jar. Store in a cool, dark place for up to a month.

Growing rice in Ritsha Village.
Punakha, Bhutan.

Sweet Crispy Rice with Butter [Zaw Ma Gew]

MAKES ABOUT 2 CUPS

2 cups Zaw (page 158)

1/4 cup (1/2 stick) unsalted butter, softened

3 tablespoons sugar, preferably dark brown

2 teaspoons black sesame seeds, lightly toasted and coarsely ground

On one trip to Bhutan my guide took me to a government office to pick up a filming permit for my Holy Kitchens documentary series in which I explore the relationship between food, faith, and spirituality. Among the Bhutanese rules of public decorum is the requirement that one must wear the national dress for official outings, such as visiting a government office, going to work or school, or attending festivals, parties, and weddings. The people of Bhutan believe that wearing their national costume shows respect for tradition and there were many at the office wearing such attire.

While I was waiting, I was honored to be treated to zaw ma gew. To be offered the dish is a sign of great respect and means that you are a treasured guest. Traditionally, zaw ma gew is made by rubbing zaw (page 158) between your fingers with yak butter and then adding chopped nuts, dried fruit, and sometimes sugar. In Bhutan, there are different versions of this dish so feel free to improvise when you make your own. A savory version I like to make has dried chile flakes, salt, nuts, and dried mango powder, while another sweet version I do includes cinnamon, dried fruit, and sugar.

Zaw is generally eaten with bare hands, but hand out spoons to your guests if you'd like.

In a bowl, add the zaw and using your hands, gently rub the butter into the rice. Add the sugar and sesame seeds and mix until well combined. Serve in a bowl for everyone to share.

Tibetan Rice Porridge with Beef [Drethuk]

SERVES 6

1 cup short-grain rice
(such as sushi rice)

2 1/2 quarts water

1 teaspoon salt

1 pound boneless beef chuck,
trimmed of excess fat and finely
chopped by hand

Tibetan Chile-Garlic Paste
(page 374), for serving

Drethuk, a Tibetan comfort food, is typically not a highly seasoned dish, but before adding too many other seasonings, I recommend holding off so you can experience for yourself how simply most Tibetans eat. The recipe calls for beef chuck, but you could also use lamb or pork and add vegetables. Traditionally, a Tibetan would never use a blender to purée this dish, but would instead use a wooden butter churner to mash it to the preferred consistency.

In a large heavy-bottomed pot, combine the rice with the water and salt and bring to a boil, uncovered, over high heat. Lower heat to low and let simmer, stirring occasionally, until cooked to the consistency of mushy porridge, about an hour. (If you like a smoother consistency, let the porridge cool and carefully blend it to a smooth purée in batches. Return it to the pot and bring it to a boil again before lowering the heat to low.)

Add the beef and simmer, covered, for at least half an hour, whisking occasionally, until the mixture is thick and smooth.

Serve hot with chile-garlic paste.

Darjeeling Eggplant Biryani

SERVES 6

2 quarts water

2 cups basmati rice

3 tablespoons vegetable oil

1 teaspoon cumin seeds

1 pound Italian eggplant, cut into 1/2-inch chunks

2 red onions, sliced

1 1/2 teaspoons salt

Juice of 1 lemon

1/3 cup lightly packed, finely chopped fresh cilantro

One ritual that I really enjoyed while staying at Mrs. Sonam's Darjeeling inn was buying fresh seasonal produce from the vegetable vendor every morning at daybreak. While biryani is not native to the region, Mrs. Sonam always made this dish for me, knowing that I loved the simplicity and flavors of the tender eggplant combined with rice and the brightness of the lemon.

Bring the water to a boil over high heat in a large pot. Add the rice and return to a boil. Cook the rice until tender, about 15 minutes. Drain and keep warm.

In a large skillet with a tight-fitting lid, heat the oil over medium-high heat. Add the cumin, eggplant, and onion and stir to coat. Lower heat to low, season with the salt, cover, and cook, stirring frequently until the onions are caramelized and the eggplant is cooked through, 10 to 12 minutes. Stir in the lemon juice and cilantro. Gently mix the rice with the eggplant mixture and serve hot.

Siliguri Mung Dal with Rice [Khichdi]

SERVES 4

1 cup long-grain basmati rice

1 cup mung dal
(split mung beans)

2 tablespoons ghee (clarified
butter) or vegetable oil

1 red onion, finely chopped

6 cups water

1 teaspoon salt

Pinch of asafetida
(see page 40; optional)

Nepalese Lemon Pickle
(page 349), for serving

1 cup low-fat yogurt, for serving

You may find that sometimes rice recipes do not seem to come out perfectly. The rice is not cooked all the way or doesn't have the best, most aromatic flavor. This is a result of the age and quality of the rice, which can vary tremendously. As rice ages, it needs a little more water and longer cooking time. Ideally, you should buy your rice from a store that turns over its inventory quickly so your rice is always fresh. I recommend using your kitchen instincts to get the best possible results.

The fertile foothills of the Himalayas are renowned for their highly prized basmati rice, which is more aromatic than rice grown anywhere elsewhere in the world. This soul food dish of Siliguri, a city in the Darjeeling region, is another simple but comforting one-pot meal.

In Nepal, people make a similar dish with urad dal (split black lentils, page 169) instead of mung dal on the auspicious occasion of Maghe Sankranti, which is celebrated by taking a ritual dip in the holy rivers. It's a time during which the Nepalese people renew their faith in the heavenly powers.

Combine the rice and dal in a fine-mesh strainer and rinse under cold running water until the water runs clear. Transfer to a bowl, cover with 2 inches water, and soak for 30 minutes. Drain well.

In a Dutch oven or large heavy-bottomed pot, heat the ghee over medium-high heat. Add the onion and cook, stirring until soft, 4 to 5 minutes. Add the water, dal-rice mixture, salt, and asafetida, increase the heat to high, and bring it to a boil. Lower heat to medium and simmer, whisking occasionally until thick and smooth, about 30 minutes. Add more water, a half-cup at a time, if the mixture starts to dry out. Serve hot with lemon pickle and yogurt.

Srinagar. Kashmir. India.

Nepalese women with whom I shared dal bhaat.

Swayambhunath

On my way to the Swayambhunath Temple in Kathmandu (page 171), I was overwhelmed with the many layers of meaning built into this magnificent and sacred temple. The elaborate stupa's spire is decorated with thirteen gilded rings that symbolize the ladder that leads to enlightenment, Buddhahood, and Nirvana; the eyes painted on each face of the stupa are symbolic of wisdom and compassion.

I had climbed a flight of 365 steps to reach the stupa, the base of which is lined with prayer wheels. Holy mantras are written on the prayer wheels and it is said that one turn of the wheel bestows the same blessings as reading the mantra. After reaching the stupa, I met a woman and her mother who insisted on sharing their dal bhaat—the most popular dish in Nepal—and would not even consider my not accepting. The people of Nepal, like others throughout the Himalayas, are as generous and hospitable as any you are likely to meet anywhere in the world. As I looked at the eyes of the Buddha inside the temple and saw how little food the two women had in their bowls, I was reminded once again of the importance of such compassion and generosity.

The Nepalese National Dish of Lentils and Rice ⇒

The Nepalese National Dish of Lentils and Rice [Dal Bhaat]

SERVES 4 TO 6

1 cup urad dal (split black lentils), skin on

1/2 teaspoon ground turmeric

1/2 teaspoon salt

4 1/2 cups water, divided

3 tablespoons ghee (clarified butter), divided

1 cup basmati rice, rinsed and drained

1/2 teaspoon Szechuan peppercorns, finely ground (see page 44)

2 to 3 dried red chiles, halved and seeded

1/2 teaspoon jimbu (see page 42)

A generous pinch asafetida (see page 40)

1-inch piece fresh ginger, peeled and shredded

2 large cloves garlic, thinly sliced

This dish is so common that it is impossible to leave Nepal without having it at least once. In this recipe, the dal will thicken if it is not served at once, so if you intend to rewarm it later, you will need to thin it with 3 to 4 tablespoons water.

Combine the lentils, turmeric, salt, and 3 cups water in a large saucepan and bring to a boil over medium-high heat. Cook uncovered for about 20 minutes, stirring occasionally to make sure the lentils do not boil over or stick together. Lower the heat, cover, and simmer gently until the lentils are tender and have doubled in volume, about 50 minutes. If necessary, add more water to maintain a soupy consistency, and simmer 5 minutes more. Remove from the heat and set aside.

Melt 1 tablespoon of the ghee in a heavy-bottomed saucepan over high heat. Add the rice and cook, stirring frequently until the rice is translucent, 2-3 minutes. Add the remaining 1 1/2 cups water and stir gently until the water comes to a boil. Reduce the heat to its lowest setting, cover tightly and let simmer until done, about 17 minutes. Let the rice rest five minutes before fluffing with a fork.

In a small skillet, heat the remaining 2 tablespoons of the ghee over medium-high heat. Add the ground peppercorn, chiles, and jimbu and fry until light brown and fragrant, about 5 seconds. Add the asafetida, then immediately add the ginger and garlic and fry until lightly browned, about 10 seconds. Immediately pour the entire mixture into the lentils and stir well. Add the cooked rice and stir until well combined. Cover and allow the seasoning to develop for 5 minutes. Transfer to a serving dish and serve hot.

Swayambhunath Temple, Kathmandu, Nepal.

Tsampa

No one who is traveling in this part of the world would ever think of leaving home without a bag of tsampa. Imagine that before you leave your house every day, you stop by the kitchen, remove the little pouch that is always attached to your belt and gently work the strings loose. You open the pouch and a warm, wholesome aroma emanates from a tan colored powder. Is your supply a little low? Best not to take a chance, so you uncover your tsampa bowl, pour a little more of the grain into your pouch and tighten the strings before putting it back on your belt. Now you are ready to step out into the world with your bag of sustenance at your side.

Tsampa factory.

Now imagine that each and every person you meet during the day performs the very same ritual. When you sit down together, you all have a cup of hot butter tea and when you reach the last two sips, instead of finishing it, you add to it some of your store of tsampa, stirring the tea with the tips of your fingers until the tsampa forms a ball. Then you eat the ball, and you are satisfied. There are no vending machines with candy bars or potato chips nearby—just the bag of tsampa. As you go through your day, walking and working, when you find yourself needing something to eat, you pull pinches of tsampa from your pouch and let it dissolve on your tongue.

Tsampa is historically the most important staple food of Tibet. In Ladakh, it is known as ngamp. It is also used in Nepal where it can be made from any kind of toasted grain. In the Himalayan region of India, it is known as sattu and comes from barley or wheat. In Tibet, tsampa is flour made from toasted barley and is available in two varieties: Amdo tsampa, which is coarser, and regular tsampa, which has a finer texture.

In Tibet, tsampa finds its way into a huge number of dishes. In fact, tsampa is absolutely essential to any discussion of Tibetan foodways and hospitality. I can't think of another culture where there is one food that takes on so much importance. In the morning, tsampa is made into porridge—I like mine with butter and a little sugar. For lunch, it might be used to thicken a stew. Noodles for soups and stews are often made from tsampa. As a dough, it can be filled and turned into the dumpling known as momo (page 94) or it can be made into dense and filling bread. Whole barley grain is fermented into chang (beer) or changkue (wine). Mixed with butter and pasta, it becomes my favorite Tibetan dessert Bhatsa Marku (page 394).

Tsampa is also an important part of many festivals and ceremonies, from everyday rituals to sacred celebrations like the festival of Losar, which is celebrated during the first three days of the first lunar month of the year. Grains are exchanged as part of the wedding ritual, and pinches of tsampa are thrown in the air at religious ceremonies. In every way, tsampa is part of the Tibetan national identity and part of Tibetans' spiritual relationship to food.

Traditionally, tsampa is eaten in a wooden bowl, and I purchased several to take back to New York to use at the Rubin Museum Café. This was lucky for me because I learned something new about tsampa. I was surprised when the lady who sold me the bowls placed a small handful of whole barley grains into each one before packing it. I asked why, and she replied that this practice was auspicious and would ensure that the person who received the bowl would never go hungry. This sort of mindfulness about the blessing of food is everywhere in the Himalayas, but seems most intentional in Tibet.

TSAMPA AT HOME

To enjoy tsampa at home, you can either buy it (www.tibetantsampa.com/english.htm) or make it in your own kitchen. If you make it at home, you again have two choices. You can toast whole barley and then grind it in your spice grinder, which will give you the coarser Amdo tsampa. You can also buy already milled barley flour and toast it in a dry skillet over medium heat, which will result in a finer tsampa. In our taste tests at home, people overwhelmingly favored the tsampa made with the barley flour. Either way, you want to be sure to use a heavy-bottomed skillet and toast it over medium heat, stirring it continuously. I find that it is best to use a whisk for this and every minute or so I also give the pan a good shake. When the flour turns a nice tan color and smells toasty, it is done. It is best to toast only as much flour as you will need so that it will always have a warm and fresh toasty aroma.

Whatever you are cooking with the tsampa, it is traditional to take a pinch and let it melt in your mouth, which ensures that you will enjoy good fortune.

Tsampa Porridge [Pawa]

SERVES 4

2 cups water

1 teaspoon salt

1 cup tsampa (see page 46)

2 tablespoons unsalted butter

1 cup plain low-fat yogurt

1 dried red chile, coarsely ground, or 1/2 teaspoon chile flakes

Once, on my way from Kashmir to Jammu, the fog was too heavy to continue driving safely. We pulled over and heard the familiar sounds of a monastery—the chanting of Buddhist hymns, the knocking of wooden bowls, and the turning of prayer wheels—and decided that we must ask around for accommodations. We finally found a family that had recently relocated from Ladakh; they were kind enough to take us in.

In the morning we awoke to the sound of our hostess's clearly unhappy four-year-old daughter asking why there was no pawa for breakfast. We went to the kitchen to see what was amiss and there she was, on the verge of tears. And so our hostess made this pawa, which we then shared with the now much more content little girl.

As I happily dug into my bowl of tsampa porridge, I asked my hostess about the dish. She said that she had assumed we wouldn't like it so she hadn't prepared any that morning, thinking we would prefer eggs for breakfast. We did like it—very much as it turned out. It was simple, tasty food. The entire family sat around the dish talking to one another while scooping up porridge with their fingers and dipping it quickly in yogurt before popping it into their mouths. It was such a customary part of starting their morning that it simply couldn't be omitted as you can tell by the little girl's reaction.

In a saucepan, bring the water and salt to a boil over high heat. Lower the heat to low, and gradually add the tsampa, stirring continuously to avoid any lumps until the consistency is that of thick porridge. Stir in the butter, and serve hot with the yogurt topped with chile.

Phie-Mar

Butter Tea Tsampa Porridge [Phie-Mar]

SERVES 4

2 tablespoons unsalted butter

3 tablespoons sugar, preferably dark brown

2 cups Tibetan Butter Tea (page 420)

1 cup tsampa (see page 46)

The first time I returned to New York from Tibet, I came down with a bad case of tea fever. Everyone who visited my house received hot butter tea whether they wanted it or not. It took me some time to get out of this habit. I finally relented when my sister reminded me that it's not everyone's cup of tea. On the other hand, phie-mar is everyone's cup of tea. It is tsampa mixed with hot butter tea and sugar and eaten with fingers or with spoons any time of day.

Combine the butter and sugar in a wok or a skillet over medium heat and stir until the sugar is dissolved, 1 to 2 minutes. Add the tea and bring it to a boil. Lower the heat to low and gradually add the tsampa, stirring continuously to avoid lumps until the consistency is that of thick porridge. Serve immediately.

Tsampa and Milk Porridge [Chamdu]

SERVES 2

1 cup tsampa (see page 46)

2 1/2 cups hot milk

Salt

2 tablespoons unsalted butter, melted

My friend Tashi Chodron's brother, Lama Ugen Palden Rongdrol, is a monk who follows the palyul tradition of Tibetan Nyingma Buddhism. One of its intriguing features is lama dancing, a form of worship that is especially important around Losar, the Tibetan New Year. The particular dance for which Lama Ugen Palden Rongdrol is known is the Cham dance of awareness when confronting death, a wonderful expression of prayer in action, and deeply spiritual and beautiful. He teaches and performs around the world and is a great cook, too. On a retreat to the monastery in upstate New York where he resides, I enjoyed this breakfast dish each morning.

Whisk the tsampa into the hot milk and add salt to taste. Serve hot, drizzled with butter.

Tsampa Butter Tea

SERVES 4

2 cups Tibetan Butter Tea
(page 420)

1 cup tsampa (see page 46)

My fascination with tsampa began years ago when I miraculously picked up a wooden tsampa bowl from a thrift store in Brooklyn. I cannot imagine how it came to be there and obviously no one working there had any idea what it was. I felt that I was rescuing it. I used it for my cereal every morning, never failing to inhale the distinctive aroma of the wood—the smell of incense and fireplace smoke—that lets you know that the bowl had been used for a long time. My friend Tashi dropped in to visit one day and was shocked when she saw my bowl. She asked me to imagine the journey my bowl had made from some village in Nyingchi where the Moinba people live to New York. That is when I became obsessed with the craftsmanship of wooden tsampa bowls made by Moinba people. Once you have smelled one of them, you can never forget it.

The little I knew about the Moinba was that they were a relatively small indigenous group of artisans and farmers living in the Tibetan regions of Monyu and Nyingchi. I was in Lhasa, standing at the reception area of my hotel, when someone mentioned Moinba culture. I really wanted to dig deeper into it and before I knew it, I was seated in a small van with my driver friend, Jigme, following the Nyang River. I clearly remember the vast open valleys and Jigme playing loud (very loud) music, full of happiness since he would soon see his Moinba maternal grandparents.

We reached the town of Bayi where Jigme's family lived and drove up to their house. Most of his family greeted us in traditional dress and were wearing gaus, Tibetan Buddhist lockets made from sterling silver, turquoise, and red coral that signify blessings and good fortune. Even today when I see a similar ornament, I think of the bright colored gaus in Nyingchi.

A group of elders was praying by the base of a small hill and drinking butter tea. By that time I was addicted to this traditional tea and could easily have downed twenty cups in a day. After greeting the elders, Jigme introduced me and they insisted that we enjoy some hot butter tea and tsampa served in beautiful, ornamental wooden bowls. I still loved my bowl at home but upon seeing the elders' bowls, I was overcome with a terrible case of bowl envy.

Make the tea according to directions and serve the tsampa alongside. When you reach the last quarter-cup or so of tea, take some tsampa and stir it into the tea, mixing until it forms a ball. Pop the ball in your mouth.

Dal Lake, Srinagar.

VEGETABLES

On my trips through the Himalayas, I would often notice that during the times of day when the sun was most powerful, almost every house had some vegetable drying outside, whether it was eggplant, tomatoes, spinach, or even carrots. Sometimes small garlands of turnips or cauliflower could be found hanging outside the houses drying in the sun. All these vegetables were used in the winter to make hearty and nutritious comforting meals to combat the cold.

Buying fresh vegetables in the Himalayas can be an adventurous experience. In Kashmir, one of the greatest memories of my travels was the famed floating vegetable market on Srinagar's beautiful Dal Lake. Gently sailing amidst the lotus-filled waters are vendors selling all varieties of fresh vegetables in their bright and colorfully decorated shikaras (wooden boats). In Nepal, the street vegetable vendors are women who wear big bindis, bright saris, and vermillion in the parts of their hair. They sell many kinds of greens in the market square in the summer months.

These vegetable recipes are easy and rustic and represent the simple but resourceful lives of the Himalayan people.

Vaishno Devi Chickpeas Masala

SERVES 4 TO 6

2 cups dried chickpeas

1 teaspoon salt

1 teabag, preferably Darjeeling

3 tablespoons vegetable oil

2 red onions, finely chopped

2 cloves garlic, minced

1 tablespoon ground coriander

2 teaspoons ground cumin

1/2 teaspoon cayenne pepper

1 teaspoon ground turmeric

2 tomatoes, seeded and finely chopped

Juice of 1 lemon

2 fresh green chiles (such as serranos), coarsely chopped

I made the pilgrimage to the Vaishno Devi Temple in the Jammu region of the Himalayas with my grandfather when I was fourteen. Pilgrims bring these chickpeas to offer to others who are also on their way to seek the favor of the goddess. The chickpeas are a common form of puja, a kind of worship that can take different forms, all of which intend to show the sincerity and strength of one's dedication to Shri Mata Vaishno Devi Ji, the Shakti Goddess of the temple.

Spread the chickpeas on a light-colored plate or cooking surface to check for and remove small stones, debris, and damaged chickpeas. Rinse the chickpeas thoroughly under cool running water. Transfer to a pot and soak the chickpeas in 2 quarts water overnight, or for at least 6 to 8 hours. Drain the chickpeas.

Bring 6 cups fresh water to a boil in a pot over high heat and add the drained chickpeas with the salt and teabag. Lower the heat to a simmer, partially covering the pot. If any foam develops, skim it off during the simmering. Cook until the chickpeas are tender, but not totally cooked, about 1 hour, adding more water if needed. Drain the chickpeas and discard the teabag.

Heat the oil in a large skillet over medium-high heat. Add the onion and garlic and fry until the onion is soft and translucent, 3 to 4 minutes.

Add the coriander, cumin, cayenne, and turmeric and cook until fragrant, about 1 minute, stirring continuously. Add the tomatoes and chickpeas and stir until well blended. Add a cup of water and stir in the lemon juice and salt to taste, and cook until the chickpeas are tender all the way through, about 30 minutes more, again adding more water if needed. Remove 1 cup of the chickpeas and coarsely mash them. Transfer the mashed chickpeas back to the skillet and continue cooking until the dish thickens, about 10 minutes. Top with the chiles and serve hot.

Young Bhutanese monk carrying a bucket of ema datshi.

The Bhutanese National Dish of Cheese and Chiles [Ema Datshi]

SERVES 4

1 tablespoon vegetable oil

1 red onion, thinly sliced

1/2 cup coarsely chopped fresh green chiles (such as serrano)

3 cloves garlic, sliced

1 cup water

1 tomato, coarsely chopped

1 pound blue cheese, preferably Churu (page 268) or Maytag, crumbled

3 tablespoons coarsely chopped fresh cilantro

I was fortunate enough to meet Her Majesty, Ashi Dorji Wangmo Wangchuck, the Queen of Bhutan, a few of years ago, at the Rubin Museum of Art's annual gala. The queen was the guest of honor and was kind and gracious.

For the gala, I created a special version of ema datshi, the national dish of Bhutan, which included seasonal vegetables, traditional Bhutanese cheese, and chiles. There are numerous versions of ema datshi and in Bhutan, it's served in both homes and restaurants. This recipe calls for traditionally used vegetables, but feel free to vary it by adding other cooked seasonal vegetables. Typically, ema datshi is very spicy, so you may want to adjust the level of heat to your taste.

In a heavy-bottomed skillet, heat the oil over medium heat. Add the onion, chiles, and garlic, and cook, stirring until the onions soften, about 1 minute. Add the water and tomato and bring to a boil. Lower the heat to low and add the blue cheese and cilantro, stirring continuously until well combined, 3 to 4 minutes. Serve warm or at room temperature.

Dechen Phodrang Monastery. Thimphu, Bhutan.

Cabbage and Pea Stir-Fry

SERVES 4

1 tablespoon vegetable oil

2 dried red chiles

1 teaspoon Kashmiri or Hungarian paprika (see page 43)

2 cloves garlic, thinly sliced

1/2 teaspoon jimbu (see page 42)

1 teaspoon ground turmeric

1 tomato, seeded and coarsely chopped

Salt

1/2 head green cabbage, thinly sliced

1 cup thawed frozen peas or 1 cup fresh peas, blanched in boiling water for 3 minutes

1/4 cup fresh cilantro leaves

This cabbage dish makes a great accompaniment to any meat dish. It was served to me in Mustang, Nepal. I had variations of it in Tibet as well, but only in Mustang do they make it with jimbu. It is hearty, satisfying, and bound to be a hit with vegetarian guests.

In a skillet with a tight-fitting lid, heat the oil over medium-high heat and fry the chiles until darker in color, about 1 minute. Add the paprika, garlic, jimbu, turmeric, tomato, and salt to taste and cook, stirring continuously, for 30 seconds. Top the mixture with the cabbage and lower the heat to low. Cover and let cook for 5 minutes.

Stir the cabbage into the tomato mixture until well coated. Cover and cook, stirring occasionally until the cabbage is soft and almost completely cooked, about 10 minutes. Stir in the peas and cook for another 2 minutes.

Top with cilantro and serve hot.

Sun-Dried Eggplant with Garlic Butter

SERVES 4

1 pound Japanese or Chinese eggplants

3 tablespoons unsalted butter

4 cloves garlic, thinly sliced

1/4 cup water

Salt

I got lucky and happened to be in Trongsa, Bhutan during the peak of eggplant season, and I was able to convince a local woman to show me how to prepare this dried eggplant dish. She didn't understand why I wanted to learn how to make dried eggplant during the summer when the fresh variety was readily available, but having always used fresh eggplants, I was keen to give the sun-dried version a try. Sun-dried eggplant has a more intense flavor and firmer texture than fresh eggplant and this is a great way to enjoy it. In this version for the home cook, we use the oven for convenience.

Preheat oven to 150°F or the lowest setting possible.

Trim and discard the stem ends of the eggplants and slice them lengthwise into 1/3-inch slices. Arrange the eggplant slices side by side on wire racks. Set on the oven racks and bake until the eggplants are shriveled and dry, flipping them every half hour for about 12 to 14 hours total.

Once dried, remove the eggplant from the oven and allow them to thoroughly cool on the wire racks before storing them in clean airtight containers.

Melt the butter in a skillet over medium heat and cook the garlic, stirring continuously, until golden, about 3 minutes. Add the water, dried eggplant, and salt to taste and stir well to evenly coat the eggplants. Cook until all the water has been absorbed. Served hot or at room temperature.

Sikkimese Turmeric and Ginger Potatoes

SERVES 6

4 russet potatoes
(about 1 1/2 pounds)

Salt

2 tablespoons mustard oil (see
page 45) or vegetable oil

2 cloves garlic, finely chopped

2-inch piece fresh ginger, peeled
and finely chopped

1 tablespoon cumin seeds

1/2 teaspoon ground turmeric

2 teaspoons ground coriander

2 tablespoons coarsely chopped
fresh cilantro

I was working on this book at the Hill View Lodge in Gangtok, the capital of Sikkim, when I fell ill for several days. Being so far from home, I was really quite miserable. Luckily for me, the cooks at the lodge liked me because I kept sticking my head into the kitchen trying to learn their recipes. They peppered me with questions about hotel and restaurant operations in my hometown of Amritsar and in New York, which they especially could not hear enough about. They were amazed that an American cook could rise to the level of writing a book, and the idea of a cookbook itself—an actual volume containing recipes—totally mystified them.

In a beautiful gesture of friendship towards a fellow cook, the head chef at the hotel prepared these potatoes for me, insisting that they alone would bring my health back. Indeed, after I ate a dish of them, I felt instant relief. This recipe contains ginger and turmeric, which in the Ayurvedic tradition, convey powerful health benefits. Now whenever a friend or family member gets sick I cook this comforting, simple-to-make dish. Afterwards, even once they're healthy, they ask that I make them more.

Wash the potatoes well and cut them into 1/2-inch cubes. Fill a pot with salted water and add the potatoes. Bring to a boil and cook until tender over medium-high heat. Drain and keep warm.

Heat the oil in a heavy-bottomed skillet over high heat until the oil is smoking. Lower the heat to medium and add the garlic, ginger, cumin, and turmeric and fry, stirring continuously until fragrant, about 2 minutes.

Add the potatoes and ground coriander and gently stir until the potatoes are well coated with the mixture. Season with salt and stir in the cilantro.

Kashmiri Garam Masala Mustard Greens

SERVES 4 TO 6

2 pounds mustard greens

3 tablespoons mustard oil (see page 45) or vegetable oil

1/4 teaspoon asafetida (see page 40)

1 teaspoon cumin seeds

3 cloves garlic, thinly sliced

1 dried red chile

2 scallions, finely chopped

2 tomatoes, finely chopped

1 teaspoon ground turmeric

Salt

1 cup water

1 teaspoon Kashmiri Garam Masala (page 39)

My good friend Deepak Kaul is from Kashmir and he claims that his mother is the best cook in his hometown of Pampore. Deepak has cooked this dish for me— his mother prepares it during Kashmir's short growing season when mustard greens are available—and it truly is a wonderful treatment of these leafy greens. It's such a delicious dish that it's hard not to believe Deepak's stories of his mother's legendary cooking abilities.

I have eaten variations of this dish where cooks do not season it with garam masala, but Deepak's mother's addition is a good one. This recipe can be made with other greens, such as spinach or kale, which are equally delicious.

Remove and discard the tough stalks from the mustard greens and chop the leaves coarsely.

Heat the mustard oil in a heavy-bottomed skillet over medium heat and fry the asafetida and cumin until darker in color and fragrant, about 1 minute. Add the garlic, chile, and scallions and cook, stirring, for 1 minute. Add the tomatoes and turmeric and cook, stirring, until very soft and the liquid has evaporated, 5 to 6 minutes. Add the greens and salt to taste, and cook, stirring continuously, until well combined. Add the water and cook until the greens are tender and the flavors are well combined, 8 to 10 minutes.

Season with the garam masala and serve hot.

Dharamshala Peas and Carrots [Gajar Matar]

SERVES 4 TO 6

2 tablespoons vegetable oil or peanut oil

1-inch piece fresh ginger, peeled and minced

3 carrots, peeled and coarsely chopped (about 1 pound)

1 tablespoon cumin seeds

1/2 teaspoon ground turmeric

1/2 teaspoon cayenne pepper

Salt

1 cup freshly shelled peas or thawed frozen peas

4 fresh green chiles (such as serranos), split lengthwise

Dharamshala, India is His Holiness the Dalai Lama's home in exile and the seat of the exiled Tibetan government. In 1959, the 14th Dalai Lama fled Tibet for Dharamshala and today the majority of the Tibetan diaspora lives in India. Living in exile obliges people to take the dishes from home and learn to make them in new ways.

An elderly woman in Dharamshala named Tenzing introduced me to this peas and carrots dish. I thought it was a traditional Tibetan dish until I got back to New York and made it for my Tibetan friend Tashi. I was so proud that I was able to prepare a dish for her from her native country. But when she saw what I had cooked and that I called it Tibetan, she laughed and shook her head. It turned out that this dish is a relatively new recipe that has emerged as a result of the Tibetan diaspora. Whatever its origins, it reminds me that I am grateful for the presence of Tibetans in India. They have enriched our spiritual lives immeasurably with their constant mindfulness of life's many blessings.

Heat the oil in a heavy-bottomed skillet with a tight-fitting lid over medium heat and fry the ginger until darker in color and fragrant, about 1 minute. Add the carrots, cumin, turmeric, cayenne, and salt to taste. Cook, stirring continuously, until well coated. Lower the heat to low and cover. Stir occasionally until the carrots are cooked, 10 to 12 minutes. Add a few tablespoons of water if the pan gets too dry. Stir in the peas and cook for another 2 minutes. Top with the chiles and serve hot.

Spiced Black Chickpeas [Kala Channa Masala]

SERVES 4 TO 6

1 cup black chickpeas, picked over and rinsed

7 1/2 cups water, divided

Salt

Pinch of baking soda

3 tablespoons vegetable oil or mustard oil (see page 45)

2 red onions, sliced

2 cloves garlic, minced

1 teaspoon ground turmeric

Pinch of asafetida (see page 40; optional)

2 whole green cardamom pods

1 teaspoon cumin seeds

1 teaspoon cayenne pepper

The common chickpea is popular all over the world. It is highly nutritious, easy to grow, and keeps very well when dried. Staple foods like the chickpea store well and are an essential part of the diet of people throughout the Himalayas where the winters are long and harsh and the growing season is short.

Kala channa, or black chickpeas, are much smaller and usually take longer to cook than the more common light-colored chickpea. To my mind, kala channa are far more flavorful.

Place the chickpeas in a large bowl, cover with cold water, and soak overnight or at least 6 hours.

Drain the chickpeas and place them in a Dutch oven with 6 cups salted water. Bring to a boil over medium-high heat. Add the baking soda, lower the heat to medium-low, cover, and simmer gently, stirring occasionally until the chickpeas are tender, 45 minutes to 1 hour. Drain and cover to keep warm.

Heat the oil in a heavy saucepan over medium heat. Add the onions and garlic and fry until golden brown, 4 to 5 minutes. Add the turmeric, asafetida (if using), cardamom, and cumin and cook, stirring, until very fragrant and darker in color, about 1 minute. Immediately add 2 tablespoons water to avoid burning the spices.

Stir in the chickpeas, cayenne, and 1 1/2 cups water and bring to a boil. Lower the heat to low and cook, stirring occasionally, until the water has evaporated. Season with salt to taste and serve hot.

Wild Fiddlehead Ferns with Garlic Butter [Nakey]

SERVES 4

Salt

1 pound fiddlehead ferns

2 tablespoons unsalted butter

4 cloves garlic, minced

1 red onion, sliced

1 tomato, seeded and coarsely chopped

1/2 teaspoon freshly ground black pepper

1 teaspoon fresh lemon juice

My friend Evan has a weekend place in the Catskills, a rural area north of New York City, where he spends time foraging in the forest for hard-to-find wild foods. Foraging is a way of life for people in the Himalayas and I was delighted when Evan told me that he enjoyed doing it as well.

You probably cannot imagine my surprise when Evan invited me to share a wonderful spring treat that turned out to be fiddlehead ferns. I had enjoyed this fiddlehead fern dish years before in Bhutan at The Organic Restaurant on Chang Lam in Thimphu, but never thought I would find these ferns on an American table.

Of course, foraging is now increasingly popular among dedicated foodies. Through Evan and other American foragers, I have learned about a number of sought-after wild foods, including rhubarb, lamb's quarters, wild mushrooms, dandelions, wild blueberries, strawberries, and ramps, among others.

Bring a large pot of salted water to a boil.

Remove the papery particles from the fiddleheads, slit the ferns in half, and thoroughly wash them under cold running water. Transfer them to the boiling water and cook for 2 to 3 minutes until cooked, but still firm. Drain.

Melt the butter in a large skillet over medium heat. Add the garlic and fry, stirring until golden brown on the edges, about 2 minutes. Add the onion and cook until golden brown, 3 to 4 minutes. Add a few tablespoons of water if the onions are in danger of burning.

Add the tomato and cook until the mixture begins to dry, 3 to 4 minutes. Add the fiddleheads and 1/2 teaspoon salt and cook 1 to 2 minutes more, until warm and well coated. Season with the pepper and lemon juice and serve.

Mushroom with Cheese and Chiles

SERVES 4

1 tablespoon vegetable oil

1 pound chanterelle mushrooms, cleaned and coarsely chopped

1/2 cup coarsely chopped fresh green chiles (such as serranos)

3 cloves garlic, minced

1 cup water

1 pound blue cheese, preferably Churu (page 268) or Maytag, crumbled

1/2 teaspoon salt

In Bhutan, mushrooms are considered an important health food and eating them is like taking a dose of preventive medicine. The chef who taught me this dish was puzzled at my surprised expression when he threw a very large quantity of chanterelle mushrooms into the pan to make this recipe. In the West, chanterelles are an expensive delicacy, but in Bhutan, they grow abundantly in the wild. Bhutanese people forage for them, selling them by the side of the road for relatively little money.

In a heavy-bottomed skillet, heat the oil over medium heat. Add the mushrooms, chiles, and garlic and stirring, cook until lightly browned, about 2 minutes. Add the water and bring it to a boil. Lower the heat to low and add the blue cheese and salt, stirring continuously until well combined, 2 to 3 minutes.

Serve warm or at room temperature.

Chanterelles in Bhutan, picked by women every morning.

Thikse Monastery Squash and Potatoes

SERVES 4 TO 6

2 tablespoons vegetable oil

2 boiled russet potatoes, peeled and cut into 1-inch cubes

1 teaspoon ground turmeric

2 or 3 summer squashes (about 2 pounds), trimmed and cut into 1-inch cubes

Pinch of asafetida (see page 40)

1 teaspoon ground coriander

1 tablespoon ground cumin

Salt

1 cup water

On a trip to the Thikse Monastery in Ladakh a number of years ago, I was nodding off in the car when I was pleasantly woken by chanting from the temple. We had arrived, and soon an enthusiastic young monk named Dharma guided me around the monastery. He brought me to its kitchen that had been built for the exclusive use of His Holiness the Dalai Lama. Dharma asked if I were hungry and when I admitted I was, he checked the time and placed a comforting hand on my arm. He told me that lunch was not until one o'clock but that he would keep me company until then so that I would not feel alone. This recipe is for the dish we had for lunch later that day.

Heat the oil in a large saucepan over medium heat, add the potatoes and turmeric, and cook, stirring, until well coated, about 2 minutes. Add the squash, asafetida, coriander, cumin, and salt to taste and continue to cook, stirring continuously, until well combined. Add the water and bring to a boil. Lower the heat to low and simmer until the potatoes have absorbed most of the liquid and the mixture is dry, 4 to 5 minutes. Add a few tablespoons of water if the liquid evaporates too quickly. Serve hot.

Thikse Monastery, Ladakh, India.

Pahalgam Squash Yogurt Curry [Yakhni]

SERVES 4 TO 6

1 tablespoon fennel seeds

1-inch cinnamon stick

3 whole cloves

3 whole green cardamom pods

1-inch piece fresh ginger, peeled and chopped, or 1 teaspoon ground ginger

1/2 teaspoon Kashmiri Garam Masala (page 39)

1/2 teaspoon ground turmeric

1 teaspoon Kashmiri or Hungarian paprika (see page 43)

2 tablespoons vegetable oil

2 pounds zucchini or summer squash, cut into 2-inch cubes

1 teaspoon salt

1 teaspoon sugar

1 cup plain low-fat yogurt, whisked smooth

Cooked basmati rice, for serving

Pahalgam is a beautiful place in Kashmir through which the Lidder River flows. Surrounded by tall pine tree forests, Pahalgam is a popular destination for tourists and sports fishermen alike. It's a perfect little pocket of paradise only a two-and-a-half-hour bus ride from Srinagar, the capital of Kashmir. After I graduated from cooking school in 1994, I spent several weeks wandering around this region and fell in love with its unique beauty. I had eaten this squash curry dish from a roadside stall, served in a beautiful brass pot.

This traditional yogurt sauce is thin, creamy, and fragrant with aromatic spices such as fennel seeds, cinnamon, cardamom, cloves, and vibrant and sweet red Kashmiri paprika. Tempering the mixture with water before adding the yogurt helps prevent curdling.

Lightly roast the fennel seeds, cinnamon, cloves, and cardamom pods in a cast-iron or heavy-bottomed skillet over medium heat, stirring continuously until fragrant, 1 to 2 minutes. Remove from the skillet and cool. Transfer to a spice grinder and grind to a fine powder.

Mix together the ground spices, ginger, garam masala, turmeric, and paprika and to it, add the oil and 4 to 5 tablespoons water to make a fine paste.

In a large saucepan, preferably nonstick, cook the spice mixture over medium heat, stirring continuously, until the mixture become dry and the oil separates out, 2 to 3 minutes. Add the squash, salt, and sugar and continue to stir until well coated, about 2 minutes. Add 1/4 cup water and bring to a boil. Lower the heat to low and simmer for another 2 minutes. Add 2 to 3 tablespoons cold water and gradually add the yogurt, stirring continuously until all of the yogurt is incorporated. Continue to cook until squash is cooked through and the mixture is thick. Serve hot with basmati rice.

Mustard plants in Tibet.

Gundruk

The preparation of gundruk, a Nepalese dish of fermented dried greens, varies from family to family. Since the season for growing these greens is short, families store them to use during the cold winter months. The process of making gundruk occurs during the harvest, in October and November, when greens are abundant. First, they are seasoned and salted to drain off any moisture. There are different ways to do this, but the one used in this recipe is the traditional method that my friend Deepak taught me. Once the greens are very soft and wet, they are placed in baskets lined with banana leaves to dry in the sun. Traditionally, small children stand on the baskets and use the bottoms of their feet to press out the excess water. The water is discarded and using a wooden spoon, the leaves are packed into broad-necked earthenware pots. (I learned the hard way never to use aluminum utensils because the metal will leave behind an unpleasant taste.) The pots are then placed in the sun to ferment for at least a week. The longer the greens sit, the more fragrant they become. Finally, the fermented greens are removed from the pots and spread on bamboo or straw mats to dry completely before being stored for future use.

Most Nepalese will not share their gundruk with anyone other than their favorite relatives and closest friends, so if you are ever offered some in a Nepalese home, you will know just how valued you are.

Fermented Dried Greens ⟹

Fermented Dried Greens [Gundruk]

MAKES ABOUT 1 CUP

1 pound fresh mustard greens, radish greens, or spinach

1/4 cup salt

Remove any thick or tough stems and yellowed leaves. Gently rinse and dry using a salad spinner. Tear the large leaves in half, salt them liberally, and spread them on a large baking sheet lined with paper towels. Place in the sun, turning the leaves frequently until the moisture is completely removed and the greens are wilted, 2 to 3 hours. If using an oven, place the leaves on a wire rack over a baking sheet and bake at 150°F for 4 to 6 hours, until soft and leathery in texture. Gently press the leaves in a colander to remove any excess water and drain.

Wash the leaves once again and gently crush the wet leaves into a clean earthenware container, glass jar, or clay pot, pushing firmly with a wooden spoon and making sure there are no air bubbles. Cover the container with a clean cloth and let rest in a warm place for a day, preferably in the sun.

Beginning on the second day, uncover the jar and press the greens every morning with a clean wooden spoon to further compress them. The leaves are generally fermented within 6 to 7 days, depending on the ambient temperature.

Once the leaves taste sour enough and are completely fermented, drain the excess liquid, spread the greens on a clean kitchen towel, cover with cheesecloth, and let rest in the sun until completely dry. The greens can also be placed on a wire mesh rack and oven-dried at the lowest possible temperature, not above 150°F. If using a convection oven, evenly spread the leaves on a wire rack over a baking sheet and bake them overnight, 8 to 12 hours at 150°F, to dry all the moisture. In a conventional oven, the drying time may be up to 18 hours. Let cool completely on the rack before storing in a clean jar.

TVP Masala

SERVES 4

2 cups large textured vegetable
protein (TVP) nuggets

2 teaspoons cumin seeds

2 tablespoons coriander seeds

2 whole green cardamom pods

3 tablespoons vegetable oil or
mustard oil (see page 45)

1 red onion, sliced

2 cloves garlic, minced

1 tomato, coarsely chopped

1 teaspoon ground turmeric

Pinch of asafetida (see page 40;
optional)

1 teaspoon salt or more to taste

1 1/2 cups water

3 tablespoons coarsely chopped
fresh cilantro

Flatbread for serving

When I was training in Hotel Soaltee Oberoi (now known as Crowne Plaza) in 1993, after my shift, all of us cooks would get together outside the gates of the hotel for a snack of nutri nuggets and rice sold by a roadside vendor. I still remember how the earthiness of the spices combined with the spongy nuggets hit the spot after a long day's work.

In India, nutri nuggets, made from soy beans, are a popular source of protein. Here in the United States, they are known as TVP, or textured vegetable protein, and are available at South Asian groceries or health food stores. If you purchase it from a health food store, just be sure you buy the variety that comes in large pieces. Many vegetarian friends of mine say that this dish satisfies all of their meat cravings.

Soak the TVP nuggets in warm water for at least an hour. Drain and set aside.

Combine the cumin, coriander, and cardamom in a spice grinder and grind to a fine powder.

In a skillet, heat the oil over medium heat and cook the onion and garlic, stirring frequently, until the onion becomes soft, 3 to 4 minutes. Add the tomato, turmeric, asafetida, and ground spices and cook, stirring continuously until the tomato softens, 2 to 3 minutes.

Add the TVP nuggets and salt and toss gently to mix well. Add 1 1/2 cups water and bring to a boil. Lower the heat to low, add the cilantro, and simmer until the nuggets are tender and have absorbed the flavors of the sauce, which should be slightly thickened, 10 to 12 minutes. Serve hot with flatbread.

Monks' Seitan with Bok Choy

SERVES 4

1 pound baby bok choy

2 tablespoons vegetable oil or peanut oil

2 cloves garlic, sliced

1-inch piece fresh ginger, peeled and minced

1 cup seitan, cut into 1-inch cubes

3 tablespoons water

Salt

Seitan, made from vital wheat gluten, has a nice, meaty chew to it and is very satisfying. When I was in Tibet, I noticed that seitan was becoming more popular as it was carried in many stores and appeared on restaurant menus. The best way to prepare it at home is to use Arrowhead Mills Vital Wheat Gluten. Seitan can also be found already prepared in some supermarkets, Asian groceries, and health food stores. Unless you have ordered a dish made with tofu, seitan is what you usually are getting in an Asian restaurant when you order mock duck or other dishes designed to mimic the texture of meat.

Discard the outer leaves of the bok choy if they appear dirty or old and cut off the hard ends of the stems. Gently pull apart the leaves, clean under cold running water, and dry.

Heat the oil in a wok or a skillet over medium-high heat and fry the garlic and ginger until fragrant, about 1 minute. Add the seitan and bok choy and cook, stirring continuously, until well coated. Add the water and salt to taste and cover for 1 minute. Uncover and cook until all the water has been absorbed. Serve hot.

Dried fish in Assam.

FISH

As the beautiful rivers of the Himalayas flow by, they not only reflect the world's highest peaks, but carry with them many varieties of coldwater fish. They are the lifeline for the communities that develop around the banks.

One such community has settled around the Kosi River basin. The Kosi is the largest river of Nepal and one of the tributaries of the River Ganges. The fishermen go out in wooden canoes early in the morning to catch fish, mostly in groups. Fish vendors then sit by the banks of the river and sell the fresh fish caught that very morning. The fishing community is very closely knit—they do everything together, not just fishing, but social activities, marriages, and celebrations.

Fish also has a spiritual context in the Himalayan region. In Kashmir, fish is a very important delicacy cooked on festivals such as Gada Bhatta in December, the name of which literally translates to fish and rice. A plateful of rice and fish is placed on the top floor for the "Ghar Devta," the deity who is the protector of the house, to invoke his blessings for prosperity and good fortune and to keep the evil eye away. In Bhutan, one of the eight auspicious symbols is the Sernya, a pair of golden fish that represents good fortune and abundance. During the Saga Dawa festival celebrating the life of Buddha—from birth to Nirvana—Buddhists buy live fish in large quantities and free them in the streams to earn good karma and blessings from Buddha.

Tibetans traditionally do not eat fish, though in present times, eating fish has become popular. Fish was considered an embodiment of the dragon and eating it was taboo.

Saffron-Yogurt Fish Curry

SERVES 4

1 pound red snapper fillets or any firm-fleshed fish, cut into 2-inch pieces

1 teaspoon salt

1/2 teaspoon ground turmeric

3 tablespoons ghee (clarified butter) or vegetable oil

1 teaspoon cumin seeds

Pinch of asafetida (see page 40)

1 teaspoon saffron threads

2-inch piece fresh ginger, peeled and minced

1 whole clove

2 cups low-fat Greek-style yogurt

2 teaspoons ground coriander

2 fresh green chiles (such as serranos), split lengthwise and seeded

1 teaspoon Kashmiri Garam Masala (page 39)

1 cup water

Cooked rice, for serving

When adding yogurt to this or any other hot dish, you want to carefully control the heat under the pot. Be careful not to let the sauce boil after you've added the yogurt or the sauce may curdle. I recommend Greek-style yogurt, now widely available, because it is extra thick and adds a beautiful tartness to the finished curry.

Kashmiris mostly use river fish such as carp or trout, but catfish, monkfish, or mahi mahi would work well. Just make sure you choose a firm-fleshed fish so that it holds together while simmering in the sauce.

Gently rub the fish with 1/2 teaspoon of the salt and turmeric and let rest, covered, in the refrigerator for 15 minutes or up to 1 hour.

Heat the ghee in a heavy-bottomed skillet over medium heat. Place the fish in the pan in one layer and let it cook until the outside is golden and opaque, about 2 minutes. Carefully turn the fish on to the other side and cook until golden, about 2 minutes more. Remove fish with a slotted spatula and place on paper towels to drain the excess fat.

Return the pan to medium heat, add the cumin seeds, asafetida, saffron, ginger, and clove and fry until fragrant, about 1 minute. Lower the heat to low and add the yogurt, stirring continuously until it becomes reddish. Add the coriander, chiles, and garam masala and mix well.

Add the fish, the remaining 1/2 teaspoon salt, and the water. Stir gently and bring to a simmer. Be careful not to let the sauce boil as that will cause the yogurt to curdle. Cover and simmer over low heat for about 10 minutes until the fish is cooked and the sauce has thickened. Serve warm with rice.

Leh Sour Fish Stew

Traveling in places like Ladakh, which is so steeped in the spirituality of the Himalayas, you sometimes get caught up in the transcendent quality of the air, the sky, and the landscape. There really is this sense in Ladakh of being close to the sky and even closer to the gods. I was looking over my diary from my trip fifteen years ago to Leh, the capital of Ladakh, and realized that sometimes in my hurry to document the recipes and foodways of the local culture, I'd forget to appreciate the splendor of this awe-inspiring place.

While roaming the streets of Leh during that trip, I came upon the Himalaya Café located near the main bazaar. The café, run by a mother and her son, prepared foods from Tibet, Kashmir, and Ladakh. Not only was the food very good, the mother-son pair were extremely hospitable.

This stew is one that I enjoyed at their café. It reminded me of another fish dish I had tried in Myanmar, and when I asked for the recipe, and later prepared it, I found that the two stews were nearly identical. When I find a recipe that crosses borders such as this one, it reminds me of the birds that freely take wing and go where they will.

Sindh River from Sindhu Ghat.

SERVES 4 TO 6

2 scallions (green onions), chopped

1 tablespoon fish sauce (available at Asian groceries)

1/2 teaspoon ground turmeric

Freshly ground black pepper

1/2 teaspoon salt

One whole red snapper, scaled, cleaned, and cut into large pieces

6 tablespoons vegetable oil

1 red onion, finely chopped

3 cloves garlic, minced

3 tomatoes, peeled, seeded, and coarsely chopped

1/2 teaspoon Kashmiri or Hungarian paprika (see page 43)

4 cups water

3 tablespoons chopped fresh cilantro

2 scallions, chopped

Juice of 1 lemon

Mix the scallions, fish sauce, turmeric, pepper, and salt in a nonreactive (glass or stainless-steel) bowl. Gently coat the fish with the marinade, cover, and let rest in the refrigerator for 30 minutes or up to 2 hours.

In a blender, combine 2 tablespoons of the oil, the onion, and garlic and purée to a coarse paste. Add a few tablespoons of water if necessary.

In a pot, heat the remaining oil over medium heat, add the onion paste, and cook, stirring continuously, until the paste begins to caramelize, 6 to 8 minutes. Add a tablespoon or two of water if the mixture begins to stick to the bottom of the pan. Add the tomatoes and paprika and cook, stirring occasionally, until the tomatoes begin to dry, 3 to 4 minutes. Add the water and the marinated fish and bring to a boil over high heat. Lower the heat to low and simmer until the fish is cooked, 4 to 5 minutes, depending on the thickness of the fish. Serve hot in bowls, topped with the cilantro, scallions, and lemon juice.

Gulmarg woman selling fish.

Leh, Ladakh.

Assamese Sour Fish

SERVES 4

1 pound monkfish fillet, cut into
1-inch cubes

1 teaspoon salt

2 teaspoons ground turmeric,
divided

3 tablespoons mustard oil (see
page 45) or vegetable oil

2 dried red chiles

1 teaspoon yellow mustard seeds

1 can tomato purée (14 ounces)

1 cup water

Juice of 1 lemon

Pinch of sugar

Cooked rice, for serving

When I began my studies at the Welcomgroup School of Hotel Management, my roommate, Pallav, was from the northeastern Indian state of Assam. During our first month at the school, he made this dish for us and I loved its straightforward nature and surprising tartness. Whenever I have this dish, it reminds me of my carefree days as a student and the friendships I made then that endure to this day.

Pat the fish dry with paper towels. Gently rub the fish with the salt and 1 teaspoon of the turmeric. Transfer to a bowl, cover with plastic wrap and let rest for at least 10 minutes or up to half an hour.

Line a plate with paper towels. Heat the oil in a nonstick skillet over medium-high heat and gently place the fish in one layer without crowding. Cook until browned and crisp on both sides, 3 to 4 minutes. Using a slotted spatula, transfer the fish to the plate and keep warm.

Lower the heat to medium and to the same oil add the chiles and mustard seeds. Cook until the seeds begin to pop and become very fragrant, about 1 minute. Add the tomato purée, water, and the remaining 1 teaspoon turmeric and bring to a boil. Lower the heat to low, return the fish to the tomato sauce, and simmer until sauce is slightly thickened, about 5 minutes. Stir in the lemon juice and sugar and serve hot with rice.

Manali Fenugreek Fish Curry

SERVES 6

2 (1-ounce) bunches fresh fenugreek leaves, or 1/2 cup dried methi leaves (see page 42)

1 1/2 pounds tilapia fillets, cut into 2-inch pieces

Juice of 1 lemon

2 teaspoons salt, divided

2 tablespoons vegetable oil

2 red onions, finely chopped

1-inch piece fresh ginger, peeled and minced

3 cloves garlic, minced

2 tomatoes, seeded and finely chopped

1 tablespoon ground cumin

2 fresh green chiles (such as serranos), seeded and chopped

1 teaspoon cayenne pepper

1 1/2 cups water

Cooked rice, for serving

While making my way to Leh, Ladakh through Manali, a scenic Himalayan hill station and jumping-off point for traveling to Ladakh, my driver took me to his family home for a hearty meal before we made the much-anticipated drive. His wife showed me how to make this wonderful fish curry that incorporated fenugreek from her kitchen garden. She had prepared it with trout, but pretty much any fish can work in this preparation. Here, I've chosen tilapia, which has a nice firm texture and is relatively inexpensive.

If using fresh fenugreek leaves, remove the leaves and discard the stems. Wash the leaves under cold running water and pat dry with paper towels. If using dried leaves, remove the stems and crush the leaves with your hands.

Gently rub the tilapia with the lemon juice and 1 teaspoon salt. Cover with plastic wrap and let rest in the refrigerator for at least an hour, up to 2 hours.

Heat the oil in a heavy-bottomed skillet over medium-high heat. Add the onions, ginger, and garlic and cook, stirring continuously, until golden brown, 5 to 7 minutes. Add the tomatoes, cumin, chiles, cayenne, 1 teaspoon salt, and the fenugreek and cook, stirring occasionally, until the mixture seems dry. Add the fish and water and bring to a boil. Lower the heat to low and simmer until the sauce thickens and the fish is cooked through, 5 to 7 minutes. Serve hot with rice.

Bengali Mustard Fish Curry

SERVES 4

3 cloves garlic, coarsely chopped

1-inch piece fresh ginger, peeled and coarsely chopped

2 fresh green chiles (such as serranos), coarsely chopped

2 tablespoons mustard oil (see page 45) or vegetable oil

2 dried red chiles, broken in half

2 tablespoons yellow mustard seeds, ground to powder in a spice grinder

1 red onion, finely chopped

1 teaspoon ground turmeric

1 teaspoon cayenne pepper

1 teaspoon Kashmiri or Hungarian paprika (see page 43)

1 pound carp, cut into 1 1/2-inch cubes

1 1/2 cups vegetable broth or water

1 teaspoon salt

While living in Kolkata, I understood that a river never ends—it flows into the sea, evaporates into clouds, and comes back to nourish the earth as rain. The rivers, originating in the Himalayas, are a plentiful source of fish and this curry showcases a local favorite.

Kasundi, a traditional Bengali sauce, is used as the curry's base. Kasundi is made of mustard seeds ground into a paste with salt, garlic, and ginger and sometimes green mango. You can make this dish by substituting a tablespoon of Dijon mustard for the mustard seeds. In Bengal, the freshwater fish rohu is generally used, but carp has a similar taste and is a good alternative.

In a food processor, combine the garlic, ginger, and green chiles and process to a smooth paste, adding a little water if necessary.

Heat the oil in a skillet over medium heat and fry the red chiles, stirring continuously, until darker in color, about 1 minute. Add the ginger-garlic paste and ground mustard and cook until fragrant, about 2 minutes. Add the onion, turmeric, cayenne, and paprika and fry until softened, 4 to 5 minutes. Add the fish, vegetable broth, and salt, and bring it to a boil. Lower the heat to low and simmer until the fish is cooked through, about 3 minutes. Serve hot.

Bhutanese Five-Chile Sea Bass

SERVES 4

3 tablespoons vegetable oil

2 white onions, thinly sliced

3 cloves garlic, coarsely sliced

5 whole dried red chiles

1/2 teaspoon ground Szechuan peppercorns (see page 44)

1 pound sea bass, cut into 2-inch cubes

2 cups vegetable broth or water

1 teaspoon salt

During a class I was teaching to children in the Balakha Village outside of Paro, Bhutan, we talked about cooking in the United States. The next day, one of the little girls in my class brought me a dish of some fish from home that she had helped her mother prepare. Her face was proud and expectant as I tasted it. The fish was so hot, sweat started pouring down my face. Even so, I managed to joke with her that the fish wasn't too spicy at all. She quipped that indeed it really wasn't very spicy since they only had five chiles at hand. Normally, the little girl said, her mother would have added at least ten!

Some people in Bhutan refer to this dish as Fish with Vegetables because chiles are thought of as a vegetable and not just a spicy seasoning ingredient. If five chiles are too hot for your taste, you can always reduce their number.

Heat the oil in a skillet over medium heat and cook the onions, garlic, chiles, and Szechuan pepper, stirring continuously until the onions soften, 3 to 4 minutes. Add the fish, broth, and salt and bring to a boil. Lower the heat to low, cover, and simmer until the fish is cooked through, 6 to 8 minutes.

Leh. Ladakh.

Gorkhali Chile Shrimp

SERVES 4

MARINADE

1 tablespoon ground cumin

1 teaspoon ground turmeric

1/4 teaspoon freshly grated nutmeg

1/2 teaspoon Szechuan peppercorns (see page 44) or timur, roasted and ground

2 tablespoons fresh lemon juice

1 tablespoon chile paste, such as Sriracha

1 clove garlic, minced

1 tablespoon minced peeled fresh ginger

1 tablespoon honey

1 teaspoon salt

1/2 teaspoon freshly ground black pepper

Gorkhas are the soldiers of Nepal who began serving in the British Army more than 200 years ago. They are known throughout history for their loyalty, strength, and valor. This dish, one of the more popular recipes from Nepal, is a tribute to their legacy.

Every time I travel to Nepal, I make sure to get a small container of timur, which is also known as Nepali pepper and belongs to the family of Szechuan peppercorns. This recipe uses Szechuan peppercorns, which can be easier to find. Both leave a distinct tingly sensation in the mouth and have notes of citrus flavor. If you can find it, timur has a much stronger flavor and a deeper color.

To make the marinade, in a small nonreactive (glass or stainless-steel) bowl, whisk all of the ingredients into a smooth paste.

Pour the marinade over the shrimp in a large bowl. Mix well, cover, and let marinate in the refrigerator for at least 1 hour, but not more than 4 hours.

SHRIMP

1 pound shrimp (26–30 count), peeled and deveined

2 to 4 tablespoons vegetable oil

1 clove garlic, minced

1-inch piece fresh ginger, peeled and finely chopped

1 tablespoon minced fresh green chile (such as serrano)

1 teaspoon ground cumin

1 cup finely chopped onion

1 cup chopped tomato

2 tablespoons honey

1/2 teaspoon salt

1/2 teaspoon freshly ground black pepper

5 dried red chiles

1 cup diced red bell pepper, in 1-inch squares

1 cup sliced scallions, cut in 1-inch lengths

2 tablespoons chopped fresh cilantro, for garnish

Cooked rice and flatbreads, for serving

If cooking outdoors, heat a charcoal or gas grill to high heat. Grill the shrimp, turning occasionally, until cooked through, about 5 minutes. If indoors, heat 2 tablespoons oil in a wok or a heavy-bottomed skillet over high heat and sauté the shrimp for about 5 minutes. Keep the shrimp warm while preparing the rest of the dish.

In a blender or food processor, process the garlic, ginger, green chile, cumin, onion, tomato, honey, salt, and pepper into a smooth paste.

In a heavy-bottomed saucepan, heat 2 tablespoons oil over medium heat. Fry the red chiles until darkened slightly, 1 minute. Add the paste and fry until the oil starts to separate out from the spices, 5 to 8 minutes. Add the bell pepper and scallions and stir thoroughly to coat them. Lower heat to low, cover and let cook until vegetables are softened, about 10 minutes.

Add the shrimp and cook until the shrimp are just cooked through, 2 minutes. Be careful not to overcook the shrimp. Season with additional salt and pepper to taste, if needed. Top with chopped cilantro and serve with rice and flatbreads.

Lhasa Fried Red Snapper

SERVES 4

MARINADE

1 tablespoon soy sauce

1 tablespoon sugar

1 teaspoon rice vinegar

2 teaspoons cornstarch

1-inch piece fresh ginger, peeled and minced

FISH

2 whole red snappers, each 1 to 1 1/2 pounds, scaled and gutted

1/4 cup vegetable oil

Tibetan Chile-Garlic Paste (page 374), for serving

According to local myth, migratory birds wading in waters at much lower elevations carry fish eggs that have stuck to their legs through the mountains, leaving the eggs behind to hatch in the Himalayas' pristine waters. Fish is available throughout the Himalayas, but is usually eaten simply fried with some hot chiles or chile paste as in this recipe.

In a bowl, combine all the ingredients for the marinade.

Wash the fish and pat dry with paper towels. Cut the fish into 1 1/2-inch-thick steaks with a heavy, sharp knife. Add the fish to the marinade, cover with plastic wrap, and let it rest in the refrigerator for 1 to 2 hours.

Remove the fish from the marinade and pat dry with paper towels. Make sure the fish is dry to prevent the oil from spattering.

Line a platter with paper towels. Heat the oil in a large heavy-bottomed skillet over medium-high heat until hot, but not smoking. In batches, gently fry the fish in a single layer without crowding until well browned and cooked through, about 3 minutes on each side. Drain on the paper towels to remove excess oil before serving.

Serve with chile-garlic paste.

Ginger-Garlic Fried Fish

SERVES 4

1 tablespoon ground turmeric

1-inch piece fresh ginger, peeled and minced

3 cloves garlic, minced

1 tablespoon ground cumin

1 teaspoon cayenne pepper

1 teaspoon salt

1/4 cup vegetable oil, divided

1 onion, thinly sliced

1 pound sea bass fillets, cut into 3-inch pieces

1 lemon, cut into wedges

In Jammu, I first tasted this dish during Ramadan as part of a large celebratory meal to break the daily fast. Many people think of Ramadan as a time of great austerity and it is—in part. But it is also Islam's greatest period of celebration, when Muslims enjoy all of their favorite feast foods once the day's fast is over.

During dinner, my companions weren't eating any of the fried fish that had been placed on the table. I, on the other hand, kept taking more because I hadn't eaten fish in weeks and the one on the plate before me was perfectly moist and flavorful. Its simplicity stood out in contrast to some of the more elaborate dishes typical of a Ramadan feast.

In the Himalayas, the ginger-garlic paste used to coat the fish is usually pounded smooth in a mortar and pestle. In this recipe, I've left the ginger and garlic chopped fine because I prefer the coarser texture. You're welcome to use a mortar and pestle or a food processor to try the smoother version. Though this recipe is made with sea bass, try it with other varieties of fish, or even chicken.

In a bowl, combine the turmeric, ginger, garlic, cumin, cayenne, salt, and 1 tablespoon of the oil and mix to a thick, coarse paste. (The paste keeps well in the refrigerator for up to a month.)

Add the onion and fish to the paste and gently rub to evenly coat the fish with the paste. Cover with plastic wrap and let rest in the refrigerator for at least 1 hour, up to 4 hours.

Line a baking sheet with paper towels. Heat the remaining 3 tablespoons oil in a nonstick skillet over medium-high heat. Add the seasoned fish and onion, and fry, turning carefully with a spatula until the fish is cooked through, about 3 minutes each side. Transfer to paper towels and drain the excess oil. Serve hot with the lemon wedges.

Srinagar. Muslim men washing hands and
feet before prayers at Jama Masjid.

Friday prayers. Jama Masjid.

Traditional Bhutanese farmhouse.

POULTRY, EGGS, & CHEESE

Up in the Himalayas, chicken is typically stewed. They only wind up in the pot after they can no longer produce eggs, and because the chickens are so old, they need to cook for a long time in order to tenderize them.

Chicken in the Himalayas is also traditionally cooked on the bone and cooks leave the skin on since consuming fat is important for surviving the area's harsh winters. For convenience, almost all of the recipes in this section call for boneless chicken breast. But if you'd like to use a whole stewing bird for authenticity and a richer taste, choose one that weighs about five pounds, chop it into pieces with a strong cleaver, and then cook them on the bone.

Jwanu Chicken Stew [Tarkari]

After finishing cooking school in 1994, I took a bus from Kathmandu, the capital of Nepal, to Pokhara, the country's second largest city. An elderly woman approached the bus window and asked me to deliver a fragrant box of food and some sweaters she had made to her grandson in Pokhara. Did I mention that the food smelled delicious? It did! I accepted the packages and asked her how I would recognize her grandson. She gave me a description that would have fit roughly three-quarters of the young men in Nepal, but she expressed absolutely no doubt that I would find her grandson. I was less sure. Nevertheless, the look in her eyes redoubled my determination to deliver the package to its rightful owner.

All the way to Pokhara, the smell of the food in the box tempted me greatly. I was almost hoping that I would not find the grandson when I got to Pokhara and that I'd be able to enjoy for myself whatever was in the box. It turned out, however, that the elderly woman's optimism proved to be well founded. I located the grandson at the bus depot and he was relieved and very happy to receive the sweaters and the food. He was so grateful in fact that he embraced me like a brother. He told me that nothing less than an invitation to his home would do, and that I must share the food I had brought for him. I tried to resist since I could tell he didn't have much, but he insisted that he would bring shame upon his grandmother if I didn't share her food with him. Perhaps the love and the blessings of our elders add to the flavors of the food they cook, for their meals always satisfy us more than any other food.

In recreating the woman's recipe, I use jwanu seeds which are also known as lovage seeds, but celery seeds will work well, too.

SERVES 4 TO 6

2 pounds boneless, skinless chicken breast, cut into 1-inch cubes

1 teaspoon ground turmeric

1 teaspoon salt

Juice of 1 lemon

2 tablespoons vegetable oil

2 dried red chiles

1 tablespoon jwanu (lovage seeds) or celery seeds

1 tablespoon carom seeds (see page 41)

1 teaspoon cumin seeds

1 white onion, finely chopped

1-inch piece fresh ginger, peeled and minced

2 cloves garlic, minced

1 tomato, seeded and coarsely chopped

1 teaspoon cayenne pepper

2 1/2 cups water (you could use chicken broth here with excellent results)

1/2 pound chopped fresh spinach

2 tablespoons chopped fresh cilantro

Cooked rice, for serving

In a large bowl, combine the chicken with the turmeric, salt, and lemon juice and let rest for 20 minutes.

Heat the oil in a heavy-bottomed pan over medium-high heat. Add the chiles, jwanu seeds, carom seeds, and cumin and fry until fragrant and slightly darker in color, about 1 minute. Add the onion, ginger, and garlic and cook until golden, 3 to 4 minutes. Add the tomato and cayenne, and cook, stirring, until soft.

Transfer the chicken pieces to the pan and cook, stirring occasionally, until well combined, 5 minutes. Add the water and bring to a boil. Lower the heat to low and simmer, covered, until the chicken is cooked, 10 to 15 minutes. Stir in the spinach and cook uncovered until the sauce is reduced and thickened. Taste and add more salt, if necessary. Top with cilantro and serve hot with rice.

Tibetan Spicy Chicken Meatballs

My guide in Tibet in 2009 threw a party on the occasion of his daughter's departure to study in Shanghai. The party was held, to my delight, at my favorite little restaurant where I had enjoyed spicy chicken meatballs nearly every day I had been in Lhasa. It turned out that my guide's wife was related to the meatball maker and he had offered the use of his restaurant for the farewell party.

When I arrived, I peeked in the back and found the restaurant's cooks busy at work and laughing as they shared jokes while preparing different dishes. They accepted my offer of help. I was parked, happily, right next to the master meatball maker. Working with amazing speed and efficiency, he shaped the balls with a tablespoon, squeezing the mixture with his other hand, and flipped them into the fryer. I kept the fire going while stirring the meatballs and fished them out of the hot oil as they were done.

The party guests loved the dish and the meatball maker graciously agreed to share his secret recipe with me. These meatballs are perfect as bite-size hors d'oeuvres and can be made ahead of time and frozen.

SERVES 4 AS A MAIN COURSE

1 pound finely minced chicken breast

1 teaspoon salt

1/2 teaspoon freshly ground black pepper

4 cloves garlic, minced

1/2 teaspoon cayenne pepper

2 tablespoons fresh breadcrumbs

Vegetable oil for frying, plus 2 tablespoons for finishing the dish

5 tablespoons Tibetan Chile-Garlic Paste (page 374)

In a bowl, combine the chicken, salt, black pepper, garlic, cayenne, and breadcrumbs and mix well with a wooden spoon or your hands. Cover with plastic wrap and refrigerate for at least an hour to chill thoroughly.

Line a baking sheet with paper towels. Heat at least 3 inches of oil in a deep-fryer or wok over medium heat to 350°F. Gently spoon out rounded tablespoons of seasoned chicken into the oil and fry until cooked through and lightly crisp, about 5 minutes. Remove with a slotted spoon and drain the excess oil on the paper towels and keep warm. Repeat with the remaining chicken mixture, frying the meatballs without overcrowding.

When all the meatballs are cooked, heat 2 tablespoons oil in a large skillet over medium heat and add the chile-garlic paste, stirring until hot, about 2 minutes. Add the meatballs and stir until well coated with the chile sauce and heated through. Serve hot.

Spiced Hard-Boiled Eggs [Masala Anday]

SERVES 3 TO 4

1 tablespoon vegetable oil

1 teaspoon black mustard seeds

1 teaspoon ground turmeric

Pinch of cayenne pepper

6 to 8 curry leaves (see page 42), coarsely chopped

Salt

6 medium eggs, hard-boiled and shelled

This recipe was the specialty of a woman in Dalhousie, a hill station in the lower Himalayas. My mother and I traveled to Dalhousie quite often when we were opening a small motel there in 1997. When we had some free time, she would take me hiking. On most of these occasions we had these spiced eggs to sustain us during the hike. Traveling in the high peaks takes a great deal of stamina and these eggs, highly seasoned and packed with protein, are just what you want to be carrying with you.

One day, we hiked in Subhash Chowk, an overlook with a perfect view of the valley below and a favorite spot of my mother's. My mother also liked this area because of the bands of mischievous monkeys who congregate there and make a game of entertaining the tourists in return for food. At one point during our walk, we stopped to watch the monkeys play. One of them came up to my mother and tried to pull off her sari. She let go of the bag of eggs momentarily to try to keep her sari from being ripped off. All of a sudden, the monkey ran off, seemingly laughing at her. Unseen by either of us, one of his confederates had snuck alongside her and made off with the eggs. She grumbled that this was what she got for wearing a sari. (She hardly ever wore traditional saris, but had worn one on this occasion for a business meeting.) Still, she harbored no lasting resentment toward the monkeys since they were just trying to get their daily bread, or, in this case, her daily eggs.

I have tasted many variations of these hard-boiled eggs with different spice combinations so please feel free to experiment.

In a skillet, heat the oil over medium heat. Fry the mustard seeds, stirring continuously, until they begin to sizzle, about 1 minute. Add the turmeric, cayenne, curry leaves, and salt to taste and cook until well combined, about 1 minute.

Add the eggs and continue to stir gently until the eggs are well coated and warm, about 2 minutes. Store, covered, in the refrigerator, but let them come to room temperature before eating.

Bhutanese Chicken with Chiles and Garlic

SERVES 4

3 tablespoons vegetable oil

1 white onion, thinly sliced

3 cloves garlic, thinly sliced

2 russet potatoes, cut into 1-inch cubes

1 whole chicken (about 3 pounds), skinned and cut into 8 pieces

1 teaspoon salt

3 cups vegetable broth or water

1 fresh green Thai chile or jalapeño, coarsely sliced

2 tablespoons crumbled blue cheese, preferably Churu (page 268) or Maytag

I received a call one day from my friend Lindsay Chapman who excitedly told me that she had just met a special person. Lindsay, who was running the Café at the Rubin Museum, had spoken with a couple dining there only to discover that the man was a well-known chef in Bhutan. I immediately ran over to the café to meet him. How could I pass up this opportunity to learn about Bhutanese cooking? Both the chef and his wife very kindly agreed to come to my home where I peppered them with questions about their country and its cuisine for several hours. At that time, I was working on the menu for a gala at the Rubin Museum at which the Queen of Bhutan was to be the guest of honor, so I was lucky that the Bhutanese chef was able to teach me both ema datshi (page 187) and this chicken dish. Both dishes have a simplicity and straightforwardness that aptly reflects the values of the people of Bhutan.

In a Dutch oven or a large heavy-bottomed saucepan, heat the oil over medium heat. Add the onion, garlic, and potatoes, and cook until the onion is soft, 3 to 5 minutes. Add the chicken and salt, and stir until the chicken is well coated. Add the broth, chile, and cheese and bring to a boil. Lower the heat to low, cover, and simmer until the chicken and potatoes are cooked, 30 to 40 minutes. Serve hot.

Chicken with Rice Noodles and Szechuan Pepper

SERVES 4

4 cups water

1 pound boneless, skinless chicken breast, cut into 1-inch cubes

2 cloves garlic, minced

1 teaspoon salt

1 small carrot, peeled and sliced on the diagonal

2 fresh green jalapeño chiles, thickly sliced

8 ounces fresh Chinese flat rice noodles

1/2 teaspoon Szechuan peppercorns, coarsely crushed with a mortar and pestle (see page 44)

This delicious dish is commonly made with Szechuan peppercorn, known as emma, in Tibet. Adding the pepper right before serving preserves its fresh, intense flavor. I was lucky enough to pass through the city of Paro in Bhutan during the emma harvest, and the aroma in the air was intoxicating. Even today, the fragrance takes me back in time to that day in Paro.

In a pot, bring the water to a boil. Add the chicken, garlic, salt, carrot, and chiles, and bring to a boil again. Lower the heat to a simmer and cook until the chicken is almost done, about 20 minutes. Add the noodles and stir frequently until cooked and most of the liquid is absorbed, about 5 minutes. Add the peppercorns just before serving.

Chicken-Wrapped Chiles

The man who prepared this dish for a Tibetan wedding I attended had a weather-beaten face etched with lines that reflected his happy and friendly personality. Everyone who approached him did so with a smile and his face in turn lit up. Although he was 84 years old, with his agile body and sharp mind, he could have easily passed for someone in his late fifties.

After I arrived, he offered me, with a twinkle in his eye, a piece of this chicken. I knew it was going to be very spicy, but I also knew I couldn't decline his offer. As it turned out, the chicken was even hotter than I had expected. It is not true, as many Westerners believe, that all Indians enjoy very hot, spicy food. In Punjab, where I'm from, we do not eat food this spicy. I managed to down the chicken, which was delicious even though my mouth was on fire. I asked him how the people in the area could possibly consume food so hot and he said, "Up here in the mountains, we would never marry a woman who couldn't eat a hot chile." Everyone in the room burst out laughing at what was apparently a well-worn joke that's told at every wedding. I was quite happy to play his set-up man.

Here is his recipe for daring types who aren't afraid of a dose of heat. The pickled green Indian chiles can be found in Indian grocery stores, but feel free to substitute serrano or bird's eye chiles.

SERVES 4

1 pound boneless, skinless
chicken breast

Salt

20 to 30 pickled green Indian
chiles, or serrano or bird's eye
chiles

Vegetable oil for frying, plus 2
tablespoons for finishing the dish

3 cloves garlic, minced

2 dried red chiles, coarsely
crushed

5 tablespoons hot sauce
(such as Sriracha)

1 teaspoon sugar

4 to 6 lettuce leaves

1/4 cup sesame seeds,
lightly toasted

With a sharp knife, slice the chicken into thin strips. (You will need the same number of strips as you have chiles.) Season with salt and let rest for at least 10 minutes.

Gently wrap a chicken strip around each chile and secure with a toothpick.

Line a baking sheet with paper towels. Heat 3 inches of oil in a deep-fryer or a wok to 350°F over medium heat. Working in batches, carefully transfer the chicken to the fryer and fry until cooked through, gently stirring for even cooking, about 5 minutes. Remove with a slotted spoon and drain on paper towels. Once the chicken has cooled and is easy to handle, remove the toothpicks.

Heat 2 tablespoons oil in a large skillet over medium heat and fry the garlic until golden, about 2 minutes. Add the dried chiles and hot sauce and stir for 1 minute. Add the chicken and gently stir until evenly coated and warm.

To serve, line a platter with lettuce leaves, spoon on the hot chicken and sauce, and garnish with the sesame seeds.

Mrs. Sonam's Spicy Omelet

SERVES 4

6 large eggs

2 tomatoes, finely chopped

2 scallions, finely chopped

2 tablespoons chopped fresh
cilantro

1/2 teaspoon salt

1/4 teaspoon freshly ground
black pepper

2 tablespoons vegetable oil

2 dried red chiles, coarsely
crushed

While I was a student in cooking school, I traveled to one of the world's great tea growing regions, Darjeeling. I wound up staying at a small guesthouse run by a Mrs. Sonam. The first thing I did after I settled in was purchase a hot plate so I could brew tea. My aim was to learn all I could about the teas of Darjeeling. Tea was at that point my obsession and I quickly fell in with a group of similarly passionate fellow travelers.

Mrs. Sonam herself was an expert on teas, and would sometimes join us in our sessions. Some mornings, when I was rushing to work, Mrs. Sonam would make this omelet especially for me along with a cup of steaming hot tea so that I did not leave the guesthouse hungry.

Break the eggs into a bowl, add the tomato, scallions, cilantro, salt, and pepper and whisk until very foamy.

Heat the oil in a nonstick skillet over medium heat and swirl to evenly coat the pan. Add the chiles and fry until slightly darker in color and fragrant, about 30 seconds. Evenly pour the egg mixture into the hot oil and gently swirl the pan again. Let it set for 20 to 30 seconds. Repeat swirling the pan to evenly spread the egg mixture. Continue to cook for 45 seconds to 1 minute, then using a spatula, carefully turn the omelet over. Cook for another minute until the eggs are cooked. Slide it onto a serving plate and serve hot.

Viku-Niku Chicken

Woman in Kashmir.

This is a Kashmiri-style chicken recipe that I created with a cook whose nickname was Niku. Niku worked for Lawrence Gardens, a catering company in my hometown of Amritsar that I started when I was seventeen. Niku was from Kashmir and loved the flavors of his native cuisine. He wanted to prepare everything we served Kashmiri-style. It was only with great reluctance that he would put aside his favorite flavorings as he cooked pots of curry for weddings and family gatherings. As the wedding season approached, I agreed to put a Kashmiri dish on the menu, thinking that it would make him happy. Indeed, he was initially thrilled—but then grumbled when I required him to change the dish so it would be sure to appeal to our local customers. He said he understood, but when I offered to call it Niku's Kashmiri Chicken, he asked me not to because I had changed the recipe too much. Instead, he suggested that we name the dish after our two nicknames, and the name stuck. Viku-Niku Chicken became a mainstay on our Lawrence Gardens Catering Company menu.

There is no extra liquid added to this dish during cooking, a method which is not uncommon in Nepal and Kashmir. Keep a careful eye on the heat and make sure you use a heavy-bottomed pot to cook it in so the chicken doesn't burn.

SERVES 4

2 tablespoons cornstarch

Juice of 1 lemon

1 teaspoon salt

1 teaspoon Kashmiri or
Hungarian paprika (see page 43)

3 cloves garlic, minced

1-inch piece fresh ginger, peeled
and minced

3 tablespoons vegetable oil,
divided

1 pound boneless, skinless
chicken breast, cut into 1-inch
cubes

2 Spanish onions, thinly sliced

10 whole raw cashews, coarsely
ground

1 teaspoon saffron threads,
steeped in 1/4 cup warm water

1/4 cup plain low-fat yogurt,
whisked smooth

In a bowl, combine the cornstarch, lemon juice, salt, paprika, garlic, ginger, and 1 tablespoon of the oil and mix well to a smooth, thick paste. Add the chicken and gently rub it with the marinade to evenly coat it. Cover with plastic wrap and let it rest for at least 2 hours in refrigerator.

Heat the remaining 2 tablespoons oil in a heavy-bottomed skillet over medium-high heat. Add the marinated chicken and cook, stirring occasionally, until it begins to turn golden brown at the edges, 5 to 7 minutes. Add the onions and continue cooking until the onion softens, another 5 to 7 minutes. Stir in the cashews, saffron, and yogurt and mix well, until evenly blended. Lower the heat to low, cover with a tight-fitting lid, and let simmer in its own juices for 10 to 12 minutes. Stir occasionally to prevent scorching. Salt to taste and serve hot.

Peshwari Chicken Skewers

Saroj was my auntie next door in Amritsar when I was growing up, and she was a very important person in my life. She was not a blood relative but rather my mother's very close friend who was almost like a member of our family. I loved going next door to see Saroj Auntie because she always had treats for me.

In her backyard was a curry tree I would raid so I could use the leaves to make dishes for dinner. Of course, she'd always spot me filching leaves and would good-naturedly yell at me through the window to put them back on the tree. In return for stealing her curry leaves, I always brought her a little of the dish and we would talk about how I made it.

Saroj Auntie had a different cooking style from my Biji, and I learned quite a lot from her. She was from the Peshawar region in Pakistan, where the food is often richer and more heavily laden with spices and clarified butter. She also used rendered fat from the meat in her cooking, not normally used in our home. When I opened my catering company, she was my very first customer and helped to spread the word to key potential customers. Auntie enriched my cooking repertoire a great deal. She was a very dear and affectionate woman and I miss her terribly. This is one of her signature dishes.

SERVES 4

2 pounds boneless, skinless chicken breasts, cut into 1-inch cubes

1 teaspoon salt

Juice of 1 lemon

1 teaspoon cumin seeds

1 teaspoon coriander seeds

3 whole green cardamom pods

1 teaspoon Pakistani Garam Masala (page 39)

2-inch piece fresh ginger, peeled and minced

2 fresh green chiles (such as serranos), finely chopped

3 cloves garlic, minced

1/2 cup plain Greek-style yogurt

1 teaspoon Kashmiri or Hungarian paprika (see page 43)

1/4 cup ghee (clarified butter) or vegetable oil, divided

2 teaspoons Chaat Masala (page 39)

Chutney of your choice, for serving

In a nonreactive (glass or stainless-steel) bowl, season the chicken with salt and lemon juice. Cover with plastic wrap and let rest in the refrigerator for 15 minutes or up to 2 hours.

In a spice grinder, combine the cumin, coriander, and cardamom and grind to a fine powder. In a bowl, combine the spice mixture, garam masala, ginger, chiles, garlic, yogurt, paprika, and 2 tablespoons of the ghee and whisk well until smooth. Pour the marinade over the chicken and mix until well coated. Cover and let it rest for another 15 to 20 minutes.

Heat a grill to high and cook the chicken pieces, basting occasionally with the remaining ghee, until cooked through, 4 to 5 minutes each side. (If you don't have outdoor cooking facilities, you can cook the chicken using your oven broiler, adding 2 to 3 minutes cooking time to assure doneness.)

Sprinkle with the chaat masala and serve hot with chutney.

Himalayan cheese

Cheese is an intrinsic part of Himalayan cuisine, an excellent source of nutrition, given the extreme climate conditions. It is very rich in protein as the female yak, the dri, produces milk with twice the proteins and minerals of cow's milk. Yak milk is widely used in recipes ranging from the national dish of Bhutan, ema datshi (page 187), to day-to-day home fare. It adds a wonderful dimension of flavor to many dishes, especially ones that are vegetable-based.

Himalayan cheeses have only recently become available in the U.S. at certain gourmet grocery stores. Since yak milk is not readily available, I have tried to give ingredient substitutions based on the cheese's texture, taste, and process by which it is made to give you the closest approximation to the real thing.

Selling churkham in Lhasa. Tibet.

Tibetan Fresh Yogurt Cheese [Chuship]

MAKES ABOUT 12 OUNCES

2 quarts plain whole milk yogurt

1 teaspoon salt

Pinch of sugar

Usually made with yak's milk, this fresh, creamy cheese is commonly stirred into Tibetan soups and stews. To impart the closest flavor to chuship without yak's milk, I use yogurt. Be sure to use whole milk yogurt, not reduced fat, as it creates a much richer, tastier cheese.

Place four layers of cheesecloth in a colander set over a bowl. Add the yogurt and let it drain overnight in the refrigerator.

Mix the drained yogurt with the salt and sugar in a heavy-bottomed saucepan and bring to a boil over medium-high heat. Gently and continuously stir until the curds separate from the whey, about 5 minutes.

Repeat the layering of cheesecloth in a colander and drain the curds again until cooled to room temperature, about two hours.

Gently press the curds with the back of a spoon to remove excess whey. Transfer the curds to a storage container and discard the whey. The texture and consistency is very much like cottage cheese but with a little bit of that tart yogurt flavor. Refrigerate for up to 1 week, tightly covered.

Bhutanese Ripened Cheese [Churu]

MAKES ABOUT 12 OUNCES

2 quarts plain whole milk yogurt

2 teaspoons salt

Pinch of sugar

2 tablespoons ghee (clarified butter) or vegetable oil

This very strongly flavored cheese is intensely aromatic and flavorful. People snack on it and use it in dishes such as the popular Bhutanese ema datshi (page 187) and in momo fillings. In recipes, gorgonzola or other blue cheeses, which are similar in taste, can be used in its place. At the Sunday market in Paro, I would often see women coming bright and early to fill their bags with churu.

Place four layers of cheesecloth in a colander set over a bowl. Add the yogurt and let it drain overnight in the refrigerator.

Mix the drained yogurt with the salt and sugar in a heavy-bottomed saucepan and bring to a boil over medium-high heat. Gently and continuously stir until the curds separate from the whey, about 5 minutes.

Repeat the layering of cheesecloth in a colander and drain the curds again until cooled to room temperature, about two hours.

Gently press the curds with the back of a spoon to remove excess whey. Discard the whey.

In a heavy-bottomed skillet, heat the butter over medium-low heat. Add the curds and cook, stirring continuously, until they turn yellowish, 5 to 6 minutes. Once the fat begins to separate out at the sides, remove the solids and let cool at room temperature.

Transfer to a clean, airtight, nonreactive container and let ferment in a cool dark place until it smells like strong blue cheese, 2 to 3 weeks. Transfer to the refrigerator and keep for up to a month.

Tibetan woman selling yogurt in Leh.

Tibetan Dried Cheese [Churkham]

As I was walked towards Potala Palace for the first time, I was awestruck by its beauty and grandeur. Having weathered many years, it stands powerful, untouched by the tests of time.

As I performed parikrama, the act of moving around a sacred object or place, clockwise around the palace, I came across carts selling small, hard, candy-like pieces strung together by a thread. Not understanding the language, it took me a while to realize that they were selling churkham, dried yak cheese.

I had never seen cheese being sold on the streets in this way and bought myself a garland of it. The cheese was hard, but I was determined to finish the one little piece I had been chewing for almost 20 minutes. The trick is not to bite right into it, but to let it slowly crumble and melt in your mouth while savoring the milky, earthy flavor that intensifies as you chew.

I learned that it is common for travelers to bring this cheese with them as a snack, along with the ubiquitous tsampa, for a quick bit of sustenance. Children enjoy nibbling on it, too. In Bhutan, they have a similar dried yak cheese called chugo, which can come white or brown and smoked.

Churkham keeps very well without refrigeration during Himalayan winters. In the typically warmer and more humid climate in the United States, you should store the cheese in a covered container in the refrigerator. It tends to absorb refrigerator flavors even when well wrapped, so it's best eaten within one month. For use in soups, it helps to first soak the cheese for an hour in slightly warm water.

MAKES ABOUT 8 TO 10 OUNCES

2 quarts plain whole milk yogurt

1 teaspoon salt

Pinch of sugar

Place four layers of cheesecloth in a colander set over a bowl. Add the yogurt and let it drain overnight in the refrigerator.

Mix the drained yogurt with the salt and sugar in a heavy-bottomed saucepan and bring it to a boil over medium-high heat. Gently and continuously stir until the curds separate from the whey, about 5 minutes.

Repeat the layering of cheesecloth in a colander and drain the curds again until cooled to room temperature, about two hours.

Gently press the curds with the back of a spoon to remove excess whey. Discard the whey. Tie the ends of the cheesecloth into a tight knot, making sure that the curds don't spill over. Put the knotted cheesecloth on a plate and place a heavy weight on top, flattening it with the pressure. Place in the refrigerator for 10 to 12 hours.

Untie the cheesecloth and cut the cheese into 1-inch pieces. Traditionally, the cheese is threaded on cotton kitchen string and formed into long garlands, but you can leave it as single pieces. In Tibet, the cheese garlands are sun-dried for 7 to 10 days. Alternatively, you can leave them overnight in a 250°F oven until firm and dry. Cover and store in the refrigerator for up to a month.

Potala Palace. Lhasa, Tibet.

Herd of sheep spotted on way
to Kargil, India.

MEAT

Yak, goat, mutton, and pork are the most frequently consumed meats in the Himalayas. Unlike American meats, those eaten in the Himalayas may be tougher and need to be simmered for hours to tenderize them. To achieve the extra flavor and body that the marrow imparts to their dishes, Himalayans typically cook their meats on the bone, but for our purposes here, I've chosen to use boneless meat and shorter cooking times. If you ever get your hands on some yak meat, by all means try it, but remember that it needs considerably longer cooking time than most American cuts of meat.

Beef with Rainbow Peppers

SERVES 4 TO 6

1 pound boneless beef top round, cut into 1 1/2-inch cubes

1 teaspoon salt

2 tablespoons vegetable oil

1 large red onion, finely chopped

2 cloves garlic, minced

1-inch piece fresh ginger, peeled and minced

1/4 teaspoon Szechuan peppercorns, coarsely ground with a mortar and pestle or in a spice grinder (see page 44)

1 small tomato, finely chopped

1 tablespoon soy sauce

1 teaspoon ground turmeric

1 cup water

1/2 green bell pepper, cut into strips

1/2 red bell pepper, cut into strips

1/2 yellow bell pepper, cut into strips

1/2 carrot, peeled and shredded lengthwise

I still remember the first time I saw photographs of the Tiger's Nest Monastery, one of the most famous in the world. One of the images showed clouds bowing over the monastery, waiting to shower rain over the shimmering gold roof. To make the trip there was a dream come true.

The walk up to the monastery was long and difficult at such a high altitude, but set against a backdrop of the lush green Himalayan mountains, exhilarating and profoundly spiritual. When I finally reached the monastery and took in the breathtaking view of the valley below, I knew it must be one of the world's most beautiful and transcendental places.

Less known to the world is a little café below the monastery on the mountainside. I stopped there on my journey and had this wonderful dish. Traditionally cooked with green chiles, the rainbow assortment of peppers was my extra touch.

Season the beef pieces with the salt, cover with plastic wrap, and let rest for 15 minutes.

Heat the oil in a heavy-bottomed skillet over high heat and sear the beef until evenly browned, 5 to 7 minutes. Remove with a slotted spoon and keep beef warm, covered in a bowl.

Add the onion, garlic, ginger, and Szechuan pepper to the same oil and fry, stirring continuously, until the onions begin to brown around the edges, 3 to 4 minutes. Add the tomato and cook, stirring, until soft. Lower the heat to low and add the browned beef with the soy sauce, turmeric, and water and cook until the beef is cooked through and tender, about 15 minutes. Stir in all the bell peppers and carrot and cook until the vegetables are tender and the sauce has thickened, about 10 minutes. Serve hot.

Paro Taktsang, Tiger's Nest Monastery.
Paro Valley, Bhutan.

Bhutanese Chile-Garlic Beef

SERVES 4

1 pound boneless beef top round, cut into 1 1/2-inch cubes

1 teaspoon salt

2 tablespoons vegetable oil

1 large white onion, sliced

4 cloves garlic, thinly sliced

1/4 teaspoon Szechuan peppercorns, coarsely ground with a mortar and pestle or in a spice grinder (see page 44)

3 dried red chiles

1 cup water

In Bhutan, rather than spend my time eating in restaurants and at roadside stands, I hired a guide and asked him to find people who would be willing to teach me how to cook typical home-style foods. Luckily for me, he found Sonam, a wonderful cook who worked at the Druk Hotel in Thimphu.

When I arrived at Sonam's home, I walked through the rice field to the house and listened to the peaceful sound of prayer flags flapping in the breeze—a sound that reminds some of the clatter of horses' hoof beats. The woman who owned the house was sitting on the roof, turning her prayer wheel and murmuring a mantra. It is important that prayer wheels be turned clockwise to throw the prayers to the wind, so that they may scatter and the prayers be fulfilled around the world.

Not only did Sonam teach me this spicy beef recipe in the few days I spent in her home, she prepared a whole array of other home-style specialties I got to try, such as mushroom stew and butter tea. I was blessed to have such a kind and patient teacher.

Season the beef with the salt, cover with plastic wrap, and let rest for 15 minutes.

Heat the oil in a heavy-bottomed skillet over medium-high heat and sear the beef until evenly browned, 3 to 4 minutes. Remove with a slotted spoon and keep warm, covered, in a bowl.

Add the onion, garlic, Szechuan pepper, and chiles to the same oil and fry, stirring continuously over medium-high heat, until garlic begins to brown around the edges, 2 to 3 minutes.

Lower the heat to low and add the browned beef and water and cook, tightly covered, until the beef is cooked through and tender, about 30 minutes. Check frequently and add a little more water if necessary. Serve hot.

Bhutanese prayer flags.

Bhutanese traditional carving.

Beef with Bean Thread Noodles

SERVES 4 TO 6

5 cups water, divided

4 ounces bean thread noodles (available at Asian groceries)

2 tablespoons vegetable oil

1 onion, thinly sliced

1/4 teaspoon Szechuan peppercorns, lightly crushed with a mortar and pestle (see page 44)

2 cloves garlic, minced

1 pound boneless beef, cut into 1 1/2-inch cubes

1 teaspoon salt

3 potatoes, peeled and cut into 1 1/2-inch cubes

1 tomato, coarsely chopped

1 carrot, peeled, halved lengthwise and cut into 1/4-inch-thick half-moons

1 teaspoon ground turmeric

1 teaspoon ground cumin

1 teaspoon ground coriander

3 tablespoons chopped fresh cilantro

I learned this recipe from Lama Ugen Palden Rongdrol, the brother of my good friend Tashi. Whenever he cooked for us, he'd always make large quantities, ensuring that everyone who came home would be well-fed.

The bean thread noodles absorb the flavors of the beef and spices very well. Vermicelli is a good substitute.

In a pot, bring 2 cups of the water to a boil, add the noodles, and cook until tender and cooked through, 5 to 6 minutes. Drain the noodles and cut them a few times with scissors to make them easier to serve.

Heat the oil in a large heavy-bottomed pan over medium-high heat and cook the onion, Szechuan pepper, and garlic, stirring continuously, until the onions are soft, 2 to 3 minutes. Add the beef and salt and cook, stirring until the beef is evenly browned, 6 to 8 minutes. Increase the heat to high and add the potatoes, tomato, carrots, turmeric, cumin, coriander, and the remaining 3 cups water and bring to a boil. Lower the heat to low and simmer, covered, until the meat is cooked through and tender, about 30 minutes. Stir in the bean thread noodles and serve hot, topped with the cilantro.

Bhutanese-Style Ground Beef

SERVES 6

3 tablespoons vegetable oil

1 white onion, finely chopped

2 cloves garlic, minced

2 pounds ground beef

1 teaspoon salt

2 scallions, coarsely chopped

2 red chiles, coarsely chopped

1 cup water

Cooked Bhutanese red rice, for serving

Flying into Paro Airport in Bhutan is a thrilling if somewhat unnerving experience. The valley in which Paro sits, surrounded by mountains on all sides, is one of the few that actually has enough room for an airport runway. Once you do make it over the last ridge of mountains, you then have to endure a stomach-churning drop into the valley. But after you land, you realize that you have arrived in awe-inspiring Bhutan, a place that makes you believe there really is a Shangri-la.

The first time I was in Paro, in 2007, I felt the need to eat something distinctly Bhutanese. In this way, I am just like my grandfather. He always wanted to eat something local as soon as he arrived at a new destination because he believed that if he did not, he would not have fully arrived. For me, too, the act of eating a local food helps me bond with a new place.

I enjoyed this dish at a little place near the Paro market. Ground beef is actually not the best way to describe the meat in this dish. In Bhutan, the beef would only be hand-chopped, which gives it a coarser texture. Already-ground beef is more convenient, but if you're up for the challenge, by all means hand-chop it.

In a Dutch oven or heavy-bottomed pot, heat the oil over medium heat. Cook the onion and garlic, stirring often, until soft, 5 to 7 minutes.

Add the ground beef and salt and cook, stirring often, and occasionally pressing with the back of the spoon to separate the meat. Cook until the is meat browned, about 4 minutes. Add the scallions, chiles, and water and increase the heat to high. Bring to a boil, and continue to cook until the liquid has evaporated and the meat is cooked, 10 to 15 minutes. Serve hot with the rice.

Pashupati Temple in Nepal.

Dussehra

During the harvest month of Dussehra, a Hindu festival celebrated in India and Nepal, this dish in made in large pots and offered to everyone who comes to your door. Although in India, Dussehra is mainly a Hindu festival, in Nepal, everyone celebrates it regardless of religious background. It's an auspicious time that is supposed to assure good fortune for the year ahead. There is a great deal of visiting back and forth and people come together as one big family. When you go to someone's home, you ask the blessing of the elders, and they give it while marking your forehead with tikka for good luck. Bhutuwa massu is considered a delicacy and is consumed over the ten days of the festival.

Slow-Cooked Lamb with Fried Onions ⇒

Slow-Cooked Lamb with Fried Onions [Bhutuwa Massu]

SERVES 6

2 pounds lean boneless lamb, cut into 2- to 2 1/2-inch cubes

2 teaspoons ground turmeric

2 teaspoons salt

2-inch piece fresh ginger, peeled and coarsely chopped

4 cloves garlic, coarsely chopped

1 fresh green chile (such as serrano), coarsely chopped

6 tablespoons vegetable oil

1 tablespoon ground coriander

1 tablespoon ground cumin

2 red onions, sliced

This dish is typically served with pickled cucumbers (page 373). The essential thing is that the meat must be seared over high heat and then left to finish cooking slowly over a low fire without any added liquid, rendering the flavor highly concentrated.

Generously season the lamb with the turmeric and salt in a bowl; cover and let it rest for at least 30 minutes.

Using a mortar and pestle or mini food processor, grind the ginger, garlic, and chile to a fine paste. To the seasoned lamb add the ginger-garlic paste, 1/4 cup of the oil, the coriander, and cumin and mix until the lamb is well coated. Cover with plastic wrap and let rest in the refrigerator for at least 2 hours, up to 4 hours.

Heat the remaining 2 tablespoons oil in a Dutch oven over high heat. Gently add the marinated lamb and cook until the lamb is evenly browned, 8 to 10 minutes. Lower the heat as low as possible, cover, and cook, stirring occasionally to keep the meat from sticking to the bottom, until the meat is tender, 20 to 25 minutes. Uncover the pan and continue to cook, stirring continuously, until the liquid has evaporated and the oil separates out. Using a slotted spoon, transfer the lamb to a serving dish and keep warm.

To the same oil, add the onions and fry over medium heat until the onions begin to soften and brown, 5 to 6 minutes, stirring continuously. Add a tablespoon of water if needed to keep the onions from sticking to the pan. Top the lamb with the browned onions and serve hot.

Bhutanese Home-Style Beef and Potatoes

SERVES 4

2 tablespoons vegetable oil

1 pound boneless beef top round, cut into 1-inch cubes

2 cloves garlic, minced

3 russet potatoes, peeled and coarsely chopped

3 fresh green chiles (such as serranos), slit lengthwise

1 teaspoon salt

2 cups water

1 teaspoon cayenne pepper

Tashi, the wife of my friend Tenzin Dorji, was one of the most unhurried and yet efficient, skillful, and natural cooks I have ever met. In the village of Balakha near Paro, she managed her household with such a sense of grace and ease that I found myself falling under her spell; I wished never to leave the peace that reigned there.

We did most of our food preparation sitting on the floor. We gathered the ingredients for the dishes we made from her backyard garden. Her granddaughter was sent out to pick chiles from the garden, which she managed with much efficiency. I can say that I will never forget how to make this dish because of the mindfulness with which Tashi taught it to me.

Heat the oil in a heavy-bottomed skillet or a wok and sear the beef over medium-high heat until it is browned evenly, 4 to 5 minutes. Add the garlic, potatoes, chiles, and salt and fry, stirring continuously until fragrant and the potatoes begin to brown on the edges, 4 to 5 minutes. Add the water and bring it to a boil. Lower the heat to low and simmer, covered, until the beef and potatoes are cooked through, about 15 to 20 minutes, adding a little water if the mixture becomes too dry. Stir in the cayenne and serve hot.

Seared Pork Belly with Peppers

SERVES 4 TO 6

2 tablespoons oil

1 pound pork belly, cut into
2- to 3-inch long strips, 1 to 2
inches wide

3 dried whole red chiles

1 teaspoon salt

2 cloves garlic, minced

1/4 teaspoon Szechuan
peppercorns, coarsely ground
(see page 44)

1 teaspoon soy sauce

4 to 6 green Thai chiles or
jalapeños, halved lengthwise
and seeded

1/2 cup water

This is another Tibetan dish that I learned from my friend, Lama Ugen Palden Rongdrol. Searing is a technique of cooking on high heat which seals the juices, making the meat very tender and moist. It's important to be very patient while searing to get the proper brownness on a side before turning.

Heat the oil over medium-high heat in a heavy-bottomed skillet and sear the pork, red chiles, salt, and garlic over medium-high heat until evenly browned, 5 to 7 minutes. Add the Szechuan pepper, soy sauce, and chiles and fry, stirring continuously, until well combined, about 2 minutes. Add the water and bring to a boil. Lower the heat to low and cook, covered, until the pork is cooked through and the liquid has evaporated, 12 to 15 minutes. Serve hot.

Lamb Meatballs in Yogurt Cream Sauce [Wazwan Gushtaba]

My first memory of Kashmir is a cacophony of singing and competing rhythms. I was thirteen years old and the occasion was my cousin Anju's marriage. We had rented a bus to take my sixty family members from Punjab to Kashmir for the wedding celebration.

When we arrived in Kashmir, we stayed at a hotel, and I was happy to discover that our rooms were right next to the kitchens. Cooks were preparing the wazwan, the ultimate Kashmiri feast where up to thirty-six dishes are eaten. The entire feast is orchestrated by the Vasta Waza, the master chef, and his assistants, the wazas. The exciting thing for me was that the Vasta Waza and wazas are highly respected cooking professionals. I was thrilled to see this because I wanted to be a cook and in the rest of the region, cooking is either women's or servants' work. The wazas sing special songs matching the rhythms of hand-chopping the meat for the rishta (301) and this gushtaba, spiced meatballs that traditionally end the meal.

SERVES 4 TO 6

1 teaspoon fennel seeds

1 teaspoon cumin seeds

2 whole green cardamom pods

1-inch cinnamon stick, coarsely broken

2 whole cloves

1 pound ground lamb

3 teaspoons salt, divided

4 cups water

2 dried bay leaves

2 black cardamom pods (see page 40)

1/4 cup ghee (clarified butter) or vegetable oil, divided

1 red onion, sliced

2-inch piece fresh ginger, peeled and minced

1 cup heavy cream

1 1/2 cup plain low-fat yogurt, whisked smooth

1/2 teaspoon ground turmeric

1 teaspoon ground cardamom

In a spice grinder, combine the fennel, cumin, cardamom pods, cinnamon, and cloves and process to a fine powder. In a bowl, combine the ground lamb, 1 teaspoon of the salt, and the spice mixture and mix well with a wooden spoon or your hands. Cover with plastic wrap and let rest for 30 minutes.

Divide the mixture into 16 to 20 balls, about 2 inches in diameter, and keep them covered with a damp kitchen towel.

In a pot with a tight-fitting lid, bring the water to a boil over high heat and add the bay leaves, black cardamom, and 1 teaspoon of the salt. Add the meatballs gently, one by one, and lower the heat. Cover and cook, stirring occasionally, until the meatballs are cooked through, about 5 minutes. Drain the meatballs on paper towels.

Heat 2 tablespoons of the ghee in a heavy-bottomed skillet over medium heat. Fry the onion and ginger, stirring continuously, until golden brown, 4 to 5 minutes. (Add 2 tablespoons water if the mixture begins to stick to the bottom of the skillet.) Remove the onion mixture from the heat, cool, and process to a fine paste in a blender or a food processor. Add a few tablespoons of water if necessary.

In the same skillet, heat the remaining 2 tablespoons ghee over medium heat and add the heavy cream, yogurt, turmeric, ground cardamom, and the remaining 1 teaspoon salt and bring to a boil. Lower the heat, stir in the onion mixture, and gently add the meatballs. Simmer until all the flavors are well combined, about 15 minutes. Serve hot.

Lamb Meatballs in Paprika-Saffron Curry [Wazwan Rishta]

SERVES 4 TO 6

1 teaspoon fennel seeds

1 teaspoon cumin seeds

3 whole green cardamom pods

1-inch cinnamon stick, coarsely broken

2 whole cloves

1 pound ground lamb

1 teaspoon salt

1/4 cup ghee (clarified butter) or vegetable oil

1 red onion, minced

2-inch piece fresh ginger, peeled and minced

5 cloves garlic, minced

1/2 teaspoon ground turmeric

3 teaspoons Kashmiri or Hungarian paprika (see page 43)

2 cups water

1 teaspoon saffron threads, steeped in 1/4 cup warm water

Whenever I think of Kashmir I think of the spices and the aroma of Kashmiri cooking. Kashmir is the place in the Himalayas where a deep, almost maroon-colored variety of saffron is cultivated. Due to the area's abundant rainfall, Kashmiri saffron is cultivated without the need for irrigation.

These meatballs, my version of the legendary Kashmiri dish, are part of the traditional wazwan feast, but can also be enjoyed on their own. The pinch of saffron adds an element of pure Kashmiri exoticism to this recipe. Traditionally, a little extra fat is added to the lamb before it's ground. Try using a fattier cut such as ground lamb shoulder.

In a spice grinder, combine the fennel, cumin, cardamom, cinnamon, and cloves and process to a fine powder. In a bowl, combine the ground lamb, salt, and spice mixture and mix well with a wooden spoon or your hands. Cover with plastic wrap and let rest for 30 minutes.

Transfer to a food processor and process until mixture is very smooth. Divide the mixture into 16 to 20 balls, about 2 inches in diameter, and keep them covered with a damp kitchen towel.

Heat the ghee in a heavy-bottomed skillet over medium heat. Fry the onion, stirring continuously, until golden brown, 3 to 4 minutes. (Add 2 tablespoons of water if needed to keep the onion from sticking.) Add the ginger, garlic, turmeric, and paprika and cook until the mixture becomes fragrant and darker in color, about 2 minutes. Add the water and the saffron-infused water, and bring to a boil. Lower the heat and gently add the meatballs, one at a time, to the sauce. Cover and let simmer, carefully stirring occasionally, until the meat is cooked through and the sauce is thick, about 10 to 15 minutes. Serve hot.

Lhasa Wedding Braised Beef with Daikon

SERVES 4

1 pound bone-in beef chuck, cut into 2-inch pieces

1 pound daikon, peeled and cut into 1/3-inch slices

2 white onions, thinly sliced

2-inch piece fresh ginger, peeled and coarsely chopped

5 cloves garlic, sliced

1/4 teaspoon Szechuan peppercorns, coarsely ground with mortar and pestle or in a spice grinder (see page 44)

1 teaspoon salt, plus more to taste

4 cups water

I was walking around the Tibetan town of Gyantse after visiting its 15th century Palcho monastery. The sun had been surprisingly strong and unforgiving. I was looking for something to drink and a place to rest when I came upon what I thought was a restaurant, even though I hadn't seen a sign for one. I heard a lot of noise, and there were many people, so I peeked in a doorway and discovered to my embarrassment that I had wandered into a wedding ceremony. Just as I tried to back away quietly and go about my business, I was seen by one of the elders who came right over and insisted that I come inside and join them. Others saw me as well, and they too came and pulled me into the celebration. I was now obliged to join in and not rebuff their hospitality. The wedding turned out to be a lovely, friendly ceremony with a lot of singing and dancing to folk music.

The Tibetan wedding is important in both a sacred and secular sense. It is looked upon as the joining of the bride and groom and their two communities. There are rituals for the exchange of food between the families that happen before the ceremony without the bride and groom present. Guests are welcomed with hot butter tea served from multicolored flasks. White silk cloths are tied around all of the serving vessels and kettles for good luck.

This beef and daikon dish is served at nearly every Tibetan wedding, but you don't need a marriage to enjoy it.

Combine all the ingredients in a large Dutch oven or a heavy-bottomed pot. Bring to a boil and let it cook for 10 minutes, skimming the froth as it rises. Lower the heat to low, cover, and simmer, stirring occasionally, and adding extra water if needed until the beef is cooked through and tender, about 1 hour. Add salt to taste and serve hot.

Lamb Rogan Josh

SERVES 4 TO 6

2-inch piece fresh ginger, peeled and coarsely chopped

3 cloves garlic

2 pounds lean lamb, preferably leg, cut into 1- to 1 1/2-inch cubes

1/2 cup plain low-fat yogurt, whisked smooth

2 teaspoons salt

Juice of 1 lemon

3 tablespoons vegetable oil

2 dried bay leaves

One 2-inch cinnamon stick

5 whole green cardamom pods

3 whole cloves

2 onions, finely chopped

2 teaspoons ground coriander

1 teaspoon ground cumin

1/2 teaspoon cayenne pepper

1 tablespoon Kashmiri or Hungarian paprika (see page 43)

3 or 4 dried red chiles, coarsely ground

2 cups water

3 tablespoons chopped fresh cilantro

Rogan josh is now synonymous with lamb curry, especially in India and the United Kingdom. This is a signature dish of the region, perfected by the Kashmiri Vasta Waza; each has his own special way of making it and takes great pride in his own special recipe.

Traditionally, Kashmiri Muslims use dried cockscomb flower to achieve the dish's characteristic deep red color, but in this dish, paprika works in the same way. Vendors can be seen selling the dried cockscomb along with other dried vegetables that become part of the Kashmiri diet in the winter time.

Using a mortar and pestle or mini food processor, grind the ginger and garlic to a fine paste.

In a bowl, combine the lamb, yogurt, ginger-garlic paste, salt, and lemon juice and mix well. Cover with plastic wrap and let rest, refrigerated, for at least 30 minutes, up to 2 hours.

Heat the oil in a heavy-bottomed skillet over medium heat and fry the bay leaves, cinnamon, cardamom pods, and cloves, stirring continuously, until fragrant and darker in color, 1 to 2 minutes. Add the onions and fry until golden brown, 4 to 5 minutes. Add the coriander, cumin, cayenne, paprika, and chiles and cook until well combined. Add the marinated meat and cook, stirring, until the meat evenly turns light brown, 4 to 5 minutes. Increase the heat to high, add the water, and bring to a boil. Lower the heat to low, cover, and simmer until the meat is cooked through and the gravy is thick, 20 to 30 minutes, adding extra water if needed. Adjust the seasoning and stir in the cilantro before serving.

Mustang Lamb Curry with Jimbu

Mustang, which is about 150 miles northwest of Kathmandu, is famous for its celebration of the three-day spring festival Tiji, known as "the chasing of the demons." A magically beautiful place, Mustang has a rich and varied landscape. The cooking in Mustang is distinguished by the frequent use of the herb jimbu, which thrives in this area and is used in this special curry. The jimbu is quickly fried in ghee or oil, but special care must be taken that it doesn't burn. Once fried, it tastes like garlic and onion. Although the cooks in the rest of Nepal only add jimbu to lentils, the cooks in Mustang use it in many different dishes.

This dish is traditionally made with goat or water buffalo, but chicken, pork, or venison can also be used. Like the Bhutuwa Massu (page 290), it is meant to cook in a minimal amount of liquid; just 1 1/2 cups water are used in this recipe, and you let most of it evaporate during cooking. You can add a little more water if it's about to scorch.

Crafting a prayer drum in Nepal.

SERVES 6

2 pounds lean lamb, preferably leg, cut into 1- to 1 1/2-inch pieces

2 teaspoons salt

2-inch piece fresh ginger, peeled and coarsely chopped

4 cloves garlic, coarsely chopped

2 fresh green chiles (such as serranos), coarsely chopped

6 tablespoons ghee (clarified butter) or vegetable oil, divided

2 red onions, sliced

2 teaspoons ground turmeric

1 tablespoon ground coriander

1 tablespoon ground cumin

2 tomatoes, finely chopped

1 1/2 cups water

2 dried red chiles

1/2 teaspoon jimbu (see page 42)

1 teaspoon carom seeds (see page 41)

Generously season the lamb with salt in a bowl; cover and let rest for at least 30 minutes.

Using a mortar and pestle or mini food processor, grind the ginger, garlic, and green chiles to a fine paste.

Line a baking sheet or platter with paper towels. In a Dutch oven, heat 3 tablespoons of the ghee over medium-high heat and sear the lamb until browned evenly on all sides. Using a slotted spoon, remove the lamb and drain the excess fat on the paper towels.

To the fat left in the pot, add the onions and fry over medium heat until golden brown, about 5 minutes. Add the ginger-garlic-chile paste and cook for another minute. Add the turmeric, coriander, and cumin and cook, stirring continuously until fragrant, 2 to 3 minutes. Add the tomatoes and cook until softened, about 3 minutes. Add back the lamb and cook, stirring until the meat is well coated. Add the water and bring it to a boil. Lower the heat to low, cover, and simmer until the meat is cooked through and tender, 40 to 45 minutes.

Uncover and cook over high heat until the sauce is reduced and thickened.

Heat the remaining 3 tablespoons ghee in a small frying pan over medium heat and add the red chiles, jimbu, and carom seeds and fry until darker in color and very fragrant, 5 to 10 seconds. Remove from the heat, and immediately pour the entire mixture into the lamb curry. Stir well before serving hot.

BREADS

Learning to make breads while on the road can be challenging. It is a time-consuming activity, and I can't often spend an entire day making loaves—even when I can find a willing teacher. Luckily for me, I have my friend Tashi and her mother, Cho Lhamo. Cho Lhamo is an expert horsewoman and one of the last in a very long line of powerful women warriors of Tibet, whose history goes back to ancient times.

It was a joy to watch her set up in my kitchen and get down to business. Like very few people I know, she is never in a hurry and her organization and timing are impeccable. Although I could tell she thought I was a little crazy for measuring everything, she was very patient at my insistence on doing so. Somehow she was able to make an entire recipe while we were at the same time styling and taking pictures of another bread. One second she was standing next to us watching as we worked with the camera and styled the shot, and the next she was baking a new loaf. She'd pat me on the arm so sweetly, and would say she could tell I was getting too stressed and needed to calm down. You can't fight the wisdom of such a woman.

Tashi's mother's quiet power is still formidable even now in her seventies. Like my grandmother Biji, who taught me to cook, Tashi's mother is able to put something of her spirit into everything she makes. This is especially true of her bread-making, and it is for that reason that this chapter is dedicated to Cho Lhamo. I am grateful to her for her patience in teaching me so much about the spiritual nature of Tibetan breads.

Lhasa Crispy Bread [Yoshang Paley]

MAKES 8 BREADS

1 1/2 cups warm water

1 teaspoon active dry yeast

1 teaspoon sugar

5 cups all-purpose flour, plus
more for dusting

1 teaspoon salt

8 tablespoons vegetable oil, plus
1/2 teaspoon for oiling the bowl

A few years ago I was on my way from Lhasa to Shigatse in Tibet and decided to stop off and see Yamdrok Lake, a place of great natural beauty and a popular pilgrimage site. Tibetans believe it to be the home of the female goddess-protector of Buddhism. My reason for going to Shigatse was that the first Dalai Lama founded a monastery there, and I wanted to see it for myself. Shigatse has always been the traditional seat of the Panchen Lama. No one knows the ultimate fate of the current Panchen Lama (Gedhun Choekyi Nyima), so I went to Shigatse to make an offering and pray for his safety.

Stopping by the shores of Yamdrok Lake, my driver and I shared a loaf of Tibetan paley while he talked about his desire to travel to New York. In the constant striving for modernity, much is lost, but this paley, a thick, disk-shaped bread, is a reminder of the goodness that still lives in people's hearts.

Pour the water into a small bowl, add the yeast and sugar, and stir to dissolve. Let stand for about 10 minutes, until frothy.

Mix the flour and salt in a bowl and gently add the dissolved yeast. Mix with your hands to form a soft dough, 3 to 4 minutes.

Transfer dough to a floured work surface and knead it for another 3 to 4 minutes, until very elastic. Oil a large nonreactive (glass or stainless-steel) bowl with a 1/2 teaspoon oil and place the dough in it. Cover with plastic wrap. Let rise in a warm place until the dough has doubled in bulk, about 45 minutes.

Divide the dough into 8 balls and gently roll them on a floured surface into 6- to 7-inch disks. Make two even, parallel cuts in every disk.

Heat a small nonstick skillet with a tight-fitting lid over medium heat. Lower the heat to low, place a disk in it, cover, and cook for about 5 minutes. Pour a tablespoon of the oil around the edges of the bread, re-cover, and cook for another 2 to 3 minutes. Flip it onto the other side and cook, uncovered, for another 6 to 7 minutes, until the bread is cooked through and lightly crisp on both sides. Serve hot and fresh.

Tingmo

Tingmo, a lotus-shaped steamed bread, is one of the great street foods of Tibet. It is also very popular in Bhutan and Sikkim, thanks to the many Tibetans who now live there.

I had enjoyed tingmo in the lovely town of Dharamshala many years before, but I hadn't learned its name. When I visited Sikkim in 1995 and saw its many wonders, I ate tingmo again and was finally able to learn its name and how to prepare it.

The amount of water needed in this recipe will vary according to the temperature and humidity, as well as the age of the flour. Older flour is drier and may require a little more water. On a cool, dry day, you may need up to 1 cup. Don't worry if the mixture feels too wet and loose when you begin kneading; the flour will absorb the water as you stretch and fold the dough. Tingmo are especially good with a spicy chile paste or chutney.

Tibetan Steamed Lotus Bread ⟹

Tibetan Steamed Lotus Bread [Tingmo]

MAKES 12 TO 14 BREADS

1 to 1 1/4 cups warm water

2 1/2 teaspoons active dry yeast (1 packet)

1/2 teaspoon sugar

3 cups all-purpose flour, plus more for dusting

1/2 teaspoon baking powder

1/2 teaspoon salt

2 tablespoons vegetable oil or melted unsalted butter

Pour the water into a small bowl, add the yeast and sugar, and stir to dissolve. Let stand for about 10 minutes, until frothy.

Sift the flour, baking powder, and salt into a bowl. Gently add the dissolved yeast and mix with your hands to form a soft dough, 3 to 4 minutes.

Transfer dough to a floured work surface and knead it for another 3 to 4 minutes, until smooth and elastic. Oil a large bowl with 1/2 teaspoon of the oil and place the dough in it. Cover with plastic wrap. Let rise in a warm place until dough has doubled in bulk, about 45 minutes.

On a floured work surface, roll the dough into a rectangle 24 inches long, 8 inches wide, and 1/4 inch thick. Brush with the remaining oil and sprinkle some flour evenly over it. Roll the dough up lengthwise and cut it with a sharp knife into slices 2 inches thick.

Flatten the slices slightly and then twist each evenly around itself at the midpoint. Leave tingmos to rise in a warm place, covered with a damp towel, until doubled in bulk, about 15 to 20 minutes.

Lightly oil a steamer basket and then place some of the tingmos into the steamer, not too many that they overcrowd and stick together. Cover tightly and steam until cooked through, 8 to 10 minutes. Repeat in batches with remaining tingmos.

Amdo paley

His Holiness the Dalai Lama was born in Amdo, Tibet. This paley, named after his home region, is a simple bread, and one of His Holiness's favorites. In 2009, I traveled there for the celebration of Losar, the Tibetan New Year. Both nomads and farmers come together to celebrate this two-week long feast, the biggest of the year.

At the time of Losar, everyone bakes breads. The Amdo paley is particularly important because it's offered to the monks. The first three days of Losar are the most significant of the entire festival. During that period, I accompanied some friends as they took their children around to make proper prostrations to the village elders, bowing to them, touching their feet, and kissing their hands in exchange for holiday blessings. Everywhere I went, incense smoldered, giving off a rich, spicy aroma. Although I could understand little of what people were saying, I could easily comprehend their determination to show gratitude for what they had in life. As the phrase, "tashi delek" (blessings and good luck), was uttered again and again, its meaning moved me profoundly.

As I made my way up a mountain to the Kumbum Monastery in Amdo, I stopped to purchase a bundle of fragrant wood to light as part of a purification ritual. The rising smoke is said to purify the spirit, and there are beehive-shaped ovens all along the trail in which you can burn your wood. I purchased yak butter to light in the lamps of the monastery. There is little fuel in Tibet so any substance that can be used for fuel is a significant part of many religious rituals. While I purchased the yak butter, I bought this delicious Amdo paley, crisp on the outside, soft and chewy on the inside.

Amdo Bread ⟹

Amdo Paley

MAKES ABOUT 4 BREADS

3 cups whole-wheat flour, plus more for rolling

Pinch of salt

2 teaspoons baking powder

1 cup warm water

1 medium egg, lightly whisked

Sift together the flour, salt, and baking powder in a bowl. Mix in the water and the egg. Knead with your hands until smooth and very elastic. Cover with plastic wrap and let rest, 15 to 20 minutes, in a warm place.

Divide the dough into four equal parts and on a lightly floured surface, evenly roll each ball to a 6- to 7-inch disk, about 1 inch thick.

Heat a small nonstick skillet with a tight-fitting lid over medium heat. Place a disk in it, cover, and cook for about 2 minutes. Flip the disk onto the other side and cook for another 2 minutes, uncovered, until the bread is cooked through and lightly crisp on both sides.

Bhutanese Buckwheat Bread [Kepta]

MAKES 2 BREADS

2 cups buckwheat, plus more for rolling (you may substitute whole wheat flour)

1 teaspoon salt

3/4 cup warm water, plus more if necessary

6 tablespoons vegetable oil, divided

When I visited the farmers' market in the Bhutanese capital of Thimphu in 2008, there was more conversation than trading going on. I came to the market not to shop for food, but to meet with Kinley Penjor, a well-known local tour guide, who, I had been told, could find someone to teach me how to make traditional breads. Kinley brought me to his aunt who would become my bread-making teacher. She told me that kepta was her son's favorite. The smile that broke out on Kinley's face was enough to convince me that I should definitely learn this recipe. Although this bread can be made with any roasted flour, it is traditionally prepared with buckwheat, which creates a dark, rich loaf.

In a large pan, gently toast the buckwheat flour over low heat, stirring continuously with a wooden spoon to avoid burning, until very fragrant, 10 to 12 minutes. This roasted flour can be stored in a container for up to a month once cooled.

In a bowl, sift the flour with the salt and add the water a little at a time, kneading the dough until it becomes a firm, smooth ball. Add additional water if necessary. Cover with plastic wrap and let it rest for at least 30 to 40 minutes.

Lightly flour the work surface and knead the dough for another 5 to 6 minutes, until very smooth and firm. Divide the dough in half and use the rolling pin to roll the dough into two 6- to 7-inch disks, about 3/4 inch thick.

In a cast-iron skillet with a tight-fitting cover, heat 3 tablespoons of the oil over medium-low heat and gently fry one disk, covered, until browned and crisp, about 4 to 5 minutes. Turn the bread over, re-cover, and cook until finished, about 3 minutes. The bread is done when it is crisp on both sides and cooked through. Heat the remaining 3 tablespoons of oil in the skillet to make the other bread. Serve hot.

Tibetan Corn Pancakes

MAKES 6 TO 8 PANCAKES

1 cup stone ground cornmeal

1 cup whole-wheat flour, plus
more for dusting

1/2 teaspoon ground turmeric

1 teaspoon salt

1 teaspoon baking powder

1/4 teaspoon baking soda

2 cups water

1/4 cup vegetable oil, divided

Jokhang Temple in Lhasa houses an enormous collection of sacred art dating back to the seventh century CE, including the Jowo Shakyamuni statue of the Buddha, the most holy object in Tibetan Buddhism.

On one visit, after spending many hours absorbing the temple's wondrous artistry, I came across a small shop behind the temple as I was leaving. The shop sold these delicious, freshly cooked corn pancakes. As I ate them, I sat there with a feeling of sublime peace, reflecting on the experience of viewing so many beautiful images, sculptures, and paintings. The cook was quite busy that day, but when I told her how far I had come to see the Jowo Shakyamuni Buddha, she promptly agreed to teach me the recipe. This proved more challenging than I thought because like many cooks, she cooked by feel, not exact measurements, holding out her hand with ingredients and repeating "not too much" or "just a little bit." It took a little while, but the recipe fell in place and now you can enjoy these warm and comforting pancakes, too.

Mix the cornmeal, flour, turmeric, salt, baking powder, and baking soda in a large bowl. Add the water and whisk to a smooth consistency until there are no lumps. Let it rest for at least 30 minutes.

In a nonstick skillet, heat 2 tablespoons of the oil over medium heat and pour in 1/3 to 1/2 cup of batter, evenly covering the base of the skillet. Cook each side until cooked through and golden brown, 4 to 5 minutes. Remove and keep warm. Add 1/2 tablespoon oil and repeat until all the batter is used. Serve hot.

Crispy Fried Cumin Bread [Namki]

MAKES 18 TO 20 BREADS

3 cups all-purpose flour, plus more for dusting

2 tablespoons finely ground semolina

1 teaspoon salt

3 teaspoons cumin seeds

1/4 cup (1/2 stick) unsalted butter

About 3/4 cup warm water

Vegetable oil, for frying

In the Ladakh region of Jammu and Kashmir, I was in a taxi traveling from the city of Kargil to Leh. On the way, it began to rain, and we were forced to stop. The ground is not stable in this region and heavy rain leaves the fragile soil vulnerable to landslides. Luckily for me, the driver pulled over in a place called Khalsi where there is a huge, beautiful sculpture of the Buddha carved right into the face of the mountain. An acquaintance from New York, Amit Shastri, lived in the area and I suggested to my traveling companions that we look him up. When we arrived at Amit's home, he graciously offered us namki and chai. Namki is a fried dough, similar to a fried wonton wrapper, and in this version, seasoned with cumin. In Punjab, you can find mathi, a comparable fried bread seasoned with carom seeds. Fresh Mango Pickle (page 345) makes a great accompaniment to the namki.

Mix together the flour, semolina, salt, and cumin seeds in a large bowl. Add the butter and rub between your hands until the mixture is well combined and very coarse. Add a little water at a time, being careful not to add too much, and knead the dough until the mixture comes together as a firm, but smooth dough. Cover it with plastic wrap and let it rest for 15 to 20 minutes.

Lightly flour the work surface and knead the dough for 5 to 6 minutes, until firm and very smooth. Divide the dough into 18 to 20 balls; keep them covered with a damp kitchen towel. One at a time, flatten a ball with your hand and roll out to a 6- to 7-inch disk, about 1/8 inch thick. Repeat until all the dough is rolled out, keeping the disks separated by waxed paper.

Heat about 3 inches of oil in a large skillet or saucepan over medium heat to 325°F. Carefully fry the disks, pressing them with a slotted spoon to evenly coat them with the hot oil and flipping once, until crisp and golden brown on both sides, about 2 minutes per side. Drain on paper towels before serving.

Namika La Pass between Kargil and Leh
on the Srinagar-Leh highway.

Bodnath Temple Fried Bread [Ajwaini Poori]

MAKES ABOUT 10 BREADS

1 cup whole-wheat flour

1 cup all-purpose flour, plus more for dusting

1 teaspoon salt

1/2 teaspoon carom seeds (see page 41)

2 tablespoons vegetable oil, plus more for frying

About 3/4 cup water

There is a strong community of Tibetans living in exile in Kathmandu where I enjoyed this poori made by an ethnic Tibetan woman named Deepa, who was expecting her first child. She had a stand set up outside the Bodnath Temple, where I made an offering on the baby's behalf. Her poori, dotted with carom seeds, is sliced twice across the top before cooking to let steam escape while it is frying so it doesn't puff up like traditional poori. The layers peel off the top as you eat it.

In a bowl, combine the flours, salt, and carom seeds. Add 2 tablespoons oil and work it into the flour with your fingers until absorbed. Gradually work in 3/4 cup water to form a stiff but pliable dough. Add a few tablespoons of water if necessary. Cover the dough with a damp kitchen towel and let it rest for at least 30 minutes.

Divide the dough into 10 equal balls and keep them covered with the towel. Flatten each ball with your hand and roll out to a 4-inch disk. With a sharp knife, score each poori twice, cutting parallel lines 1-inch apart and 2-inches long in the center of the bread.

Line a baking sheet with paper towels. Heat about 3 inches of oil in a large skillet or wok over medium heat to 350º to 375ºF. Gently slide a disk into the hot oil and immediately start spooning hot oil over the top of the poori with a spatula so that it cooks evenly.

Fry until cooked through and golden brown on both sides, about 1 minute each side. Drain briefly on the paper towels before serving hot. Repeat with the remaining poori dough.

Kashmiri naan

Naan is available everywhere in the Kashmiri city of Srinagar. When it's finished baking, the bread becomes crisp around the edges and stays soft and chewy in the middle. In Indian restaurants in the United States, Kashmiri naan means bread that is filled with raisins and nuts. Imagine my surprise when I saw this naan often being sold in a local shop—no raisins or nuts to be found.

I asked to be let into the kitchen to see how the bakers make their naan. They showed me the tandoor oven, which was in the process of being built by hand out of clay. I watched them prepare the bread and learned how they use well-oiled fingers to etch a few parallel lines in the dough, a distinctively Kashmiri technique.

Kashmiri Naan ⇒

Kashmiri Naan

MAKES 16 TO 20 BREADS

1 cup warm water

1 teaspoon active dry yeast

1 teaspoon sugar

3 tablespoons milk

1 egg, lightly whisked

2 teaspoons salt

4 1/2 cups all-purpose flour

1/4 cup (1/2 stick) unsalted butter, melted

Pour the water into a small bowl, add the yeast and sugar, and stir to dissolve. Let stand for about 10 minutes, until frothy. Stir in the milk, egg, and salt, whisking to combine all of the ingredients.

Place the flour in a large bowl. Gradually add the yeast-milk mixture and knead with your hands to form a soft dough. Remove the dough to a lightly floured surface and knead until smooth and elastic, 6 to 8 minutes. Oil a large bowl (large enough to hold the double volume of the dough) with 1 tablespoon of the butter. Place the dough in the bowl, cover with a damp towel, and let it rest until doubled in volume, about 45 minutes.

Divide the dough into 16 to 20 pieces, roll into balls, and keep covered with the towel. On a lightly floured surface evenly roll each ball into a 5- to 6-inch disk, about 1/4 inch thick.

Evenly brush the disks with a little of the remaining butter and with your thumb tip, gently make a few thin parallel lines, leaving up to 1 inch of space around the edge of the disk.

Heat a griddle to medium-high heat and lightly oil it. Working in batches, place dough disks, buttered side down, on the griddle and cook for 2 to 3 minutes or until puffy and lightly browned. Brush the uncooked sides with butter and turn over. Brush the cooked sides with more butter and cook until browned on the bottom, another 2 to 4 minutes. Remove from the griddle and serve hot. Repeat with the remaining dough disks.

Ladakh Yeast Bread [Khambir]

MAKES ABOUT 20 BREADS

1 1/2 cups warm water

1 teaspoon active dry yeast

1 teaspoon sugar

4 cups whole-wheat flour, plus more for dusting

1 teaspoon salt

2 tablespoons vegetable oil

Looking back on the history of cooking, one of the greatest achievements in food was discovering how to make breads. In Ladakh, as I watched this bread being cooked on a hot stone placed on an open fire, I realized that in spite of the modern times we live in, it is the simplicity and rustic nature of age-old methods and traditions of cooking that create truly heartwarming recipes. This yeast-risen bread made on that day was perfectly crispy and smoky.

Pour the water into a small bowl, add the yeast and sugar, and stir to dissolve. Let stand for about 10 minutes until frothy.

Mix the flour and salt in a bowl. Gently add the dissolved yeast and mix with your hands to form a soft dough, 10 to 12 minutes. Transfer the dough to a floured work surface, and knead it for another 3 to 4 minutes until smooth and elastic.

Oil a large bowl with 1/2 teaspoon oil, place the dough in it, and cover with plastic wrap. Let rise in a warm place until the dough has doubled in bulk, about 45 minutes.

Divide the dough into 20 balls and gently roll them on a floured surface into 4- to 5-inch disks, about 1/3 inch thick.

Heat a nonstick skillet over medium-high heat. Once it is hot, lower the heat to low, place a disk in it, and cook until dark bubbles begin to appear on the bottom, about 2 minutes. Flip the bread onto the other side and cook until cooked through, about 2 minutes more. Lightly brush it with oil and keep it covered. Repeat with the remaining dough disks. Serve hot and fresh.

Tibetan Breakfast Paley

MAKES 12 TO 15 BREADS

3 cups all-purpose flour, plus more for rolling

Pinch of salt

2 teaspoons baking powder

1 1/4 cups warm water

I still remember the last time I left Tibet. It was August 15, 2009 and the flight was number 407 departing, as it so happened, at 4:07 PM. Flights leaving Lhasa are often delayed, but not this one. The plane lifted off, and I experienced the terrible sense of loneliness I always feel when I leave the region.

On my way to the airport that morning I had stopped and purchased a breakfast paley and wondered when I would ever get to taste another one. During my stay in Tibet, I had loved eating paley with chile-garlic paste (page 374) alongside my cup of hot butter tea (page 420). In asking Tibetan people around New York about this paley, I discovered that it was a small bread commonly sold as breakfast food. Laughing, my Tibetan friend Tashi said it was pretty much the Tibetan equivalent of a bagel.

Luckily, I could still have this breakfast paley in New York because Tashi's mother taught me the recipe just before leaving on her own trip home to San Francisco. I could sense that Tashi was already starting to miss her mother though she hadn't departed yet. I could certainly understand. Her mother is as much of an inspiration to her as my own mother is to me.

In a large bowl, sift together the flour, salt, and baking powder. Mix in a little water at a time and knead with your hands until a smooth and elastic dough forms. Cover with plastic wrap and let rest, 15 to 20 minutes, in a warm place.

Divide the dough into 12 to 15 equal parts and on a lightly floured surface, evenly roll each bread into a 3- to 4-inch disk, about 1/4 inch thick.

Heat a large nonstick skillet with a tight-fitting lid over medium heat. Lower the heat to low, place a few disks in it, cover, and let cook for about 2 minutes. Flip onto the other side and let cook, covered, for another 2 minutes until the breads are cooked through and lightly crisp on both sides. Serve hot.

Indian Crisps with Spicy Tomato Salsa [Masala Papad]

SERVES 4

1 ripe tomato, seeded and finely chopped

1 red onion, finely chopped

2 fresh green chiles (such as serranos), coarsely chopped

3 tablespoons coarsely chopped fresh cilantro

2 teaspoons Chaat Masala (page 39)

4 papads (available at South Asian groceries)

Mussoorie is a hill station in the foothills of the Himalayas that I'd visited many times with my sister Radhika during school holidays. In Mussoorie, you can find the remains of the former home and laboratory of the British Surveyor General, Sir George Everest, after whom Mt. Everest was named.

During these summertime visits, one of our favorite snacks was the widely-available masala papad. It is a quick recipe to assemble as papads are readily available in Indian grocery stores. You can add any topping of your choice, but one of my favorites is fresh, ripe tomatoes. In fact, this wonderful pairing is our Indian version of salsa and chips.

In this recipe, the papads are toasted over an open flame burner of a gas stove. If you have an electric stove, heat a dry cast-iron skillet over high heat and toast the papads, one at a time, until bubbles and little black dots form on each side.

In a bowl, combine the tomato, onion, chiles, cilantro, and chaat masala. Cover and let rest in the refrigerator for 10 minutes.

Turn on a flame to medium-high. One at a time, hold a papad with flat tongs right over the flame so that the flame is just touching the papad as it forms bubbles and charred spots. Turn the papad over the flame to ensure even cooking. Let papads cool before serving.

Evenly spread the tomato mixture over the toasted papads. Serve immediately before they become soggy.

Kashmir, India.

CONDIMENTS

The Himalayan people have to be creative in stretching their limited food supply through methods such as preserving and drying, and they must also find ways to heighten the flavors of what can sometimes appear to be rather plain, even austere dishes. Where Himalayan dishes really take flight is in the many intensely flavored condiments—ranging from spicy to sour, pickled to fermented—added to more simply flavored dishes. Condiments are served alongside every meal, even breakfast, to add a burst of flavor to a dish. When the recipe calls for a condiment to be hot, please note that it can be very hot indeed, so use it sparingly.

Note: When fermenting vegetables, make sure the vegetables are fully submerged in liquid. The amount of salt added to the liquid should be about 3 tablespoons per quart of water. The usual temperature range for fermenting is 60-80°F. If you live in a hot region, you should ferment your vegetables in the shade. You will know your vegetables are fermenting because they will begin to bubble after 2 to 3 days. The flavor will continue to develop with a peak happening 7 to 10 days from the start of the process. Always make sure that your vegetables and containers are clean and that you use a trusted water source.

Red Chile Oil Onion Relish

MAKES ABOUT 1 CUP

2 tablespoons sesame seeds

1/2 teaspoon cumin seeds

2 red onions, thinly sliced

1/2 teaspoon salt

Juice of 1 lemon

1/2 teaspoon ground Szechuan peppercorns (see page 44)

2 tablespoons mustard oil (see page 45)

3 dried red chiles

1/2 teaspoon ground turmeric

1/4 teaspoon asafetida (see page 40)

On my way from the tea-growing area of Darjeeling to Nepal, the bus driver stopped in Siliguri just before crossing into Nepal, and I got off briefly with the other travelers to get something to eat. Since traveling from one place to another can take quite a while in this part of the world, there are often food vendors along the way to cater to hungry travelers. Most of these roadside places make only a few simple, seasonal dishes. Since this was near the end of the day, the little shack we stopped at was pretty much out of food. It was raining, as it usually is up in the foothills of tea country, and we gratefully accepted what little he had left. A few chickpeas, some bread, and this bold onion relish were all that remained and it really hit the spot. Try serving it atop flatbread or with your favorite momo.

Heat a small cast-iron skillet over medium heat and roast the sesame and cumin seeds until fragrant and darker in color, about 1 minute. Remove the spices from the skillet and cool. Grind to a fine powder in a spice grinder or with a mortar and pestle.

Combine the onions with the sesame-cumin mixture, salt, lemon juice, and Szechuan pepper in a nonreactive (glass or stainless-steel) bowl.

Heat the oil in a small skillet over medium-high heat until smoking. Add the chiles, turmeric, and asafetida and fry, stirring continuously until the chiles become darker in color, about 1 minute. Immediately pour over the onion mixture and mix well. Serve at room temperature or cover and refrigerate for up to a week.

Fenugreek Gooseberry Pickle

The city of Janakpur in Nepal holds great historical and religious meaning for India's Hindus. It is the legendary birthplace of Sita, the Hindu goddess who was the wife of Lord Rama, the central hero of the Ramayana epic. Indeed, the name Janakpur derives from the name of Sita's father, King Janak.

I was thinking about these spiritual matters when I came across three children vigorously shaking a sturdy tree and laughing with joy as it rained down fruit on their heads. Upon closer inspection, the fruit turned out to be gooseberries, which the children were gathering for their mother who soon came to check on their progress. When I asked her what she planned to do with the berries, she told me that she was going to dry and pickle them. She said she would be proud to share her recipe with me, and her children proceeded to drag me home so that I could see the preparation myself. Naturally, the lesson evolved into tea and bread because in Nepal, you can't invite someone into your home without offering hospitality.

Traditionally, the mustard seeds in this recipe are ground to enhance the sourness of the pickle, but in this case, I have left them whole for visual appeal. Feel free to grind them. Also, piercing the gooseberries helps them absorb the flavors more quickly and evenly. This pickle is especially delicious served with poultry or fish.

A traditonal Nepalese window.

MAKES 2 CUPS

1 pound fresh gooseberries
(available at gourmet groceries
and farmers' markets in season)

Salt

2 tablespoons mustard oil
(see page 45)

1 teaspoon fenugreek seeds
(see page 42)

1 tablespoon brown mustard
seeds

4 to 6 dried red chiles

Pinch of asafetida (see page 40)

1 teaspoon ground turmeric

1 teaspoon Szechuan
peppercorns, coarsely ground
(see page 44)

1 teaspoon cayenne pepper

2 cups water

Wash and dry the gooseberries and gently perforate them with a fork. Sprinkle them with 2 tablespoons salt and let rest for up to 20 minutes.

Heat the oil in a pot over medium-high heat until smoking. Add the fenugreek seeds, mustard seeds, chiles, and asafetida and fry, stirring continuously until fragrant and darker in color, about 1 minute. Add the gooseberries, turmeric, Szechuan pepper, and cayenne and cook, stirring, for 2 to 3 minutes. Add the water and bring to a boil. Lower the heat to simmer and cook, occasionally stirring until the berries are cooked, 15 to 20 minutes, adding more water if necessary to keep the berries from sticking to the pan. Season with additional salt if needed.

Transfer to a clean, sterile, glass container. Let cool, cover, and refrigerate up to a month.

Fresh Mango Pickle with Mustard Oil and Fenugreek

MAKES ABOUT 1 1/2 CUPS

1 1/2 pounds green mangoes, peeled, pitted, and cut into 1-inch cubes (about 4 small fruits)

2 tablespoons light brown sugar

1/2 teaspoon salt

1 tablespoon mustard oil (see page 45)

5 dried red chiles, crushed

1 1/2 tablespoons cumin seeds

1 teaspoon fenugreek seeds (see page 42)

1 teaspoon ground turmeric

2 cups water

Every family has its own recipe for mango pickles, and they are all different. True family heirlooms, these recipes tell much about a family's history and this one was a treasure handed down to me from my Aunt Sunita. This grand, elderly lady is my friend's mother, and she lives in Jammu across the street from a temple where the bells are rung by hand all day long (Jammu is known as the City of Temples).

Aunt Sunita made this pickle with green mangoes from her front yard. Green mangoes are not picked; instead, traditionally, you gather them when they drop from the trees and are not yet ripe. In the United States, you can buy them online or in specialty stores. Using green mangoes, which are very firm, unripe, and tart, rather than sweet, ripe mangoes is key.

Every time I make this pickle, I can almost hear the bells of Jammu ringing and Aunt Sunita's stern directions for making the pickle exactly the right way.

In a nonreactive (glass or stainless-steel) bowl, combine the mango, sugar, and salt and mix well. Let rest for 20 to 30 minutes.

Heat the oil in a large skillet over medium-high heat just until smoking. Reduce the heat to low and add the chiles, cumin, and fenugreek seeds and fry, stirring continuously until golden brown and fragrant, about 1 minute. Add the mangoes and turmeric and cook, stirring occasionally until the flavors are well combined, 4 to 5 minutes. Add the water and bring it to a boil. Lower the heat to low and simmer until the mangoes are tender and the liquid has evaporated, about 10 minutes.

Cool to room temperature before transferring to a clean, sterile, glass jar. Store, tightly covered, in the refrigerator for up to a month.

Spicy Asafetida Tomato Chutney

MAKES ABOUT 1 1/2 CUPS

2 tablespoons vegetable oil

2-inch piece fresh ginger, peeled and finely chopped

6 cloves garlic, coarsely chopped

4 to 6 dried red chiles

1/2 teaspoon asafetida (see page 40)

1 teaspoon ground turmeric

4 tomatoes, coarsely chopped

10 fresh green chiles (such as serranos), thinly sliced

2 tablespoons white vinegar

1 teaspoon salt

This chutney is very common in Nepal and is usually served with dumplings, but I love to serve it with just about any meal or even as a spread for breads.

Asafetida is a powerful-smelling spice and must be used sparingly. When cooked, it smells of garlic and onions. It is ground from the dried resin that comes from the stems and roots of a large fennel-like plant. My grandmother Biji used to soak a piece of asafetida resin in water and would then use the flavored water to deglaze pots after she cooked onions.

Heat the oil in a stainless-steel wok or skillet over medium-high heat and fry the ginger and garlic, stirring continuously, until golden brown, about 2 minutes. Add the red chiles, asafetida, and turmeric and fry until the chiles become darker, about 1 minute.

Add the tomatoes, green chiles, vinegar, and salt and cook, stirring until the ingredients are well combined. Cover and lower the heat to low and cook, occasionally stirring, until the chutney becomes thick. Serve it warm or at room temperature. Store tightly covered in the refrigerator for up to a week.

Nepalese Lemon Pickle

MAKES 1 QUART

1 teaspoon carom seeds
(see page 41)

2 tablespoons brown mustard
seeds

1 teaspoon fenugreek seeds
(see page 42)

1 tablespoon fennel seeds

1 pound lemons (about 8), plus
juice of 2 lemons

1/2 cup salt

1/4 cup sugar

Pinch of asafetida (see page 40)

1 teaspoon jimbu (see page 42)

3 dried red chiles, coarsely
broken

2 teaspoons cayenne pepper

6 to 8 whole cloves

2 tablespoons vegetable oil

After a three-hour bus trip traveling northwest from Kathmandu to the Pokhara Valley, I reached a fantastic cluster of houses nestled in the foothills above the valley. The houses wound along a maze of streets, and there were no signs to help me find the guesthouse where I was to spend the night. My gut told me to follow the prayer flags waving gently in the wind and finally, there it was.

Once there, I met my Sherpa friend who was chewing on a lemon pickle he had bought from the corner store. Naturally, as is customary in that part of the world, he asked me to share it with him. It was one of the most flavorful pickles I have ever tasted. Please note that the recipe needs at least 3 weeks of pickling time. Regular lemons will do beautifully, but if you're able, use Meyer lemons for transcendent results.

Heat a small skillet over medium heat and toast the carom, mustard, fenugreek, and fennel seeds, shaking occasionally, just until they begin to pop and become darker, 3 to 5 minutes. Remove from the skillet and cool. Grind to a fine powder in a spice grinder.

Trim the stem ends of the lemons, quarter the lemons lengthwise, and discard any obvious seeds. Place the lemons in a large bowl and stir in the salt and sugar. Stir in the ground spice mixture, asafetida, jimbu, chiles, cayenne, cloves, oil, and lemon juice.

Transfer the lemon mixture to a clean, sterile 1-quart jar. Gently press on the lemons with a clean spoon to immerse them in the juice. Top it with the vegetable oil. Seal the jar and place it in the sun or a warm place for at least 3 weeks for the lemons to soften and the flavors to blend. Occasionally press the lemons down to submerge in the liquid and shake well. Store, tightly covered, in the refrigerator for up to six months.

Chiles in Vinegar and Himalayan Salt

MAKES ABOUT 1 1/2 CUPS

1 1/2 cups rice vinegar

1 tablespoon sugar

2 teaspoons Himalayan pink salt (see page 42)

1 cup coarsely chopped fresh green chiles (such as serranos)

Juice of 1 lemon

Himalayan salt is now "de rigueur" in the kitchens of not only professional chefs but many serious home cooks as well. This particular type of salt, which was left behind at the time the Himalayas were formed about 70 million years ago, was an important trade item along the Silk Road, a series of trade routes that connected China with the Himalayas, South Asia, the Middle East, and Europe. Many extravagant claims are made about Himalayan salt's healthful benefits, but its main virtue is that it has an earthy flavor without any off-tasting iodine. The pink color of the salt comes from iron oxide and it contains many other desirable trace minerals.

You could, if you wish, use regular salt for this recipe, but why would you, now that you know how great Himalayan salt is?

In a nonreactive saucepan, bring the vinegar, sugar, and salt to a boil. Lower the heat to medium and simmer to a light syrup, 6 to 8 minutes. Remove from heat and let cool for 10 minutes.

Add the chiles and lemon juice and let it cool to room temperature.

Transfer to a clean, sterile jar with a tight-fitting lid and place it in the sun or warm place for at least 3 days until the chiles soften and the pickle is ready. It keeps well for up to 3 weeks in the refrigerator.

Pepper Brined Garlic and Star Anise

MAKES 1 PINT

1/2 cup white wine vinegar

1 cup water

3 tablespoons black peppercorns

2 dried bay leaves

1 whole star anise

1 tablespoon sugar

1 tablespoon salt

1 cup peeled garlic cloves

This pickled garlic and its brine are both wonderfully versatile. I often use the brine puréed with fresh ginger to marinate fish and chicken for grilling or add a few spoonfuls of it to curries. The garlic makes an excellent addition to soups when smashed with the flat side of a chef's knife or minced and then added to a salad dressing.

Combine the vinegar, water, black peppercorns, bay leaves, star anise, sugar, and salt in a nonreactive saucepan and boil for 5 minutes over high heat. Lower the heat, add the garlic, and simmer until the mixture becomes fragrant, about 2 minutes.

Transfer the mixture to a clean, sterile jar with a tight-fitting lid, filling it to within 1/2 inch of the top. Let cool to room temperature and store in a cool, dark place for about a week until garlic is pickled.

Keep refrigerated for about a month once the jar is opened.

Dal Lake floating vegetable and saffron market. Srinagar, Kashmir.

In Srinagar, a city known for its gardens, lakes, and houseboats, there is a beloved daily floating market in Dal Lake where boats gather together in a kind of flotilla to sell their goods.

It was so peaceful as the boatmen gathered together among the floating lotus before sunrise that I found myself getting lost in a daydream of perfect beauty. I almost forgot about buying bitter gourd for my friend Suneet's mother who had promised to teach me her wonderful pickle recipe.

The market was breaking up, and in a panic I wound up overpaying for the gourd. I fibbed about the price to Suneet, and he still frowned, saying it was too much but not bad for a foreigner. I just managed to catch the slightest wink pass between him and his mother, but wisely pretended not to notice.

Kashmiri Bitter Gourd Pickle ⟹

Kashmiri Bitter Gourd Pickle

MAKES ABOUT 1 1/2 CUPS

3 bitter gourds (available at
South Asian groceries), washed
and dried

Salt

1 tablespoon ground turmeric

3 tablespoons mustard oil
(see page 45)

2 tablespoons fennel seeds

1 tablespoon cayenne pepper

1/2 teaspoon asafetida
(see page 40)

2 tablespoons tamarind paste
(see page 45)

2 tablespoons mango powder
(see page 45)

1 tablespoon coriander seeds,
coarsely crushed

2 tablespoons black mustard
seeds, coarsely crushed

3 dried red chiles

1 teaspoon Kashmiri Garam
Masala (see page 39)

Cut off the stems and 1 inch from the bottom of the bitter gourds. Halve them lengthwise and remove all the seeds. Cut into 1-inch slices.

Gently rub the bitter gourds with 2 teaspoons salt and the turmeric and set aside in a nonreactive (glass or stainless-steel) bowl for at least 30 minutes to extract some of the bitterness.

Squeeze the juice from the bitter gourds with your hands and rinse with fresh water.

In a skillet, heat the oil over medium heat and add the fennel seeds, cayenne, and asafetida and cook, stirring continuously, for 1 minute. Stir in the bitter gourd, tamarind paste, mango powder, coriander seeds, mustard seeds, dried chiles, and garam masala. Add 2 to 3 tablespoons water and cook until the bitter gourd is tender and all the flavors are combined. Season with more salt if necessary.

Cover and let stand for an hour. Serve warm or at room temperature. Store, tightly covered, in the refrigerator for up to 2 weeks.

Daikon-Cilantro Relish

MAKES ABOUT 2 CUPS

2 cups coarsely grated
daikon radish

1 small carrot, julienned

2 fresh green chiles (such as
serranos), finely chopped

1/4 cup white vinegar

1 teaspoon salt

1/4 teaspoon Szechuan
peppercorns, coarsely crushed
with a mortar and pestle
(see page 44)

2 tablespoons fresh
cilantro leaves

I've enjoyed this relish many times at roadside stands throughout the Himalayas and this recipe, from one such Tibetan stand, is my favorite. Daikon is one of the most important vegetables in Tibet as it can grow at high altitudes and withstand temperature extremes. This relish can be served with any dish, especially momos (page 94), a traditional Himalayan dumpling. The relish may also be dried in the sun to preserve it. I have added cilantro, which is not traditional, to give this relish a light fresh flavor.

In a bowl, combine all of the ingredients and mix well. Store in the refrigerator for up to 3 days.

Cleaning daikon.

Cabbage, Chile, and Carrot Pickle in Mustard Oil

MAKES ABOUT 3 CUPS

1 tablespoon black or brown mustard seeds

1/2 teaspoon fenugreek seeds (see page 42)

1 tablespoon ground turmeric

2 teaspoons cayenne pepper

2 tablespoons salt

5 tablespoons mustard oil (see page 45) or vegetable oil, plus more as needed

1 small head green cabbage, cored and coarsely chopped

1/4 pound green beans, trimmed and coarsely chopped

1 carrot, peeled and coarsely chopped

I have traveled in Nepal during many phases of my life: as a poor student, an unemployed cook, an affluent traveler, and a spiritual seeker. The mountains have always sheltered and nurtured me, and I feel a special connection to this sacred land of Hinduism and Buddhism. It has been a great privilege during these trips to have been able to live with local families rather than in hotels. Choosing home stays over hotel lodgings meant that I could learn local recipes and food customs firsthand.

Recipes are often seasonal, but this one is seasonal in a counterintuitive way. This Nepali pickle, made of winter vegetables, is often made in the spring when the spring planting has been completed. New vegetables will be harvested soon, so it's time to get rid of the old winter ones that have been kept in storage all winter long. Out of the root cellars come the wrinkled, sweet carrots and the softened heads of cabbage. They lend themselves particularly well to making this pickle; in the spring, the sun is at the perfect angle for fermenting the pickle in the open air. When you open the jar after the fermentation is completed, you will be rewarded with a wonderful, heady aroma.

In a spice grinder or with a mortar and pestle, combine the mustard and fenugreek seeds and grind to a fine powder.

Combine the spice mixture with the turmeric, cayenne, salt, and 5 tablespoons mustard oil and mix well. Pour the mixture over the vegetables and using clean hands, evenly coat them with the spice mixture.

Place the mixture in a clean, sterile jar, large enough to hold all the vegetables. Add additional oil until the vegetables are fully submerged. Tightly close the lid and place the jar in the sun to ferment until slightly sour, at least 2 or 3 days. You can also ferment it in a warm area indoors, which generally takes 3 to 4 days for the pickle to be ready. Store in the refrigerator for up to 3 weeks.

Sweet Green Chile and Ginger Pickle

MAKES ABOUT 1 CUP

8 to 10 cubanelle peppers

2 tablespoons black or brown mustard seeds

2 tablespoons cumin seeds

2 tablespoons coriander seeds

1 tablespoon fennel seeds

1/2 teaspoon fenugreek seeds (see page 42)

1/2 teaspoon Szechuan peppercorns (see page 44)

1/4 cup mustard oil (see page 45)

4-inch piece fresh ginger, peeled and julienned

2 teaspoons salt

1 1/2 teaspoons ground turmeric

Juice of 1 lemon

1/4 cup white vinegar

3 tablespoons jaggery (see page 44) or dark brown sugar

Ilam, famous for the great flavor of its eponymous tea, is a small hilly town with pristine landscapes of sloped tea gardens, thick natural forests, and holy sites. It is a special part of the Himalayas with a gorgeous backdrop of mountains where people and nature peacefully coexist. An almost two-hour walk from Ilam is Jasbire, a small slice of heaven in the far eastern corner of Nepal. The walk to Jasbire is beautiful, but if you get lucky, you can catch a ride with locals or with trucks filled with fresh farm produce on their way to the markets.

After riding in the back of one of those trucks to Jasbire, I stopped at a small vegetarian café and had this pickle with a dish of plain lentils. Cubanelle (or Cuban) peppers are long, light green, mildly hot peppers. If you cannot find them, substitute poblano peppers.

Rinse and dry the peppers and cut them into 1- to 2-inch lengths.

Heat a small cast-iron skillet over medium heat and toast the mustard, cumin, coriander, fennel and fenugreek seeds, and Szechuan pepper until darker in color and very fragrant, 1 to 2 minutes. Let the spices cool and grind them into a coarse powder in a spice grinder.

In a heavy-bottomed nonreactive skillet, heat the oil over medium heat until faintly smoking, about 2 minutes. Lower the heat to low and add the peppers, ginger, salt, turmeric, and spice mixture and cook, stirring continuously, until very well combined, 4 to 5 minutes. Stir in the lemon juice, vinegar, and sugar and cook for another 2 minutes, until dry.

Remove from the heat and let it cool before transferring to a clean, sterile, airtight jar. Let it sit in a warm place in the kitchen until very flavorful, about 2 days. Store in the refrigerator for up to one month.

Kashmiri Turnip, Spinach, and Carrot Pickle

MAKES ABOUT 2 1/2 CUPS

1 teaspoon ground turmeric

2 teaspoons cayenne pepper

1 tablespoon Kashmiri or Hungarian paprika (see page 43)

2 tablespoons salt

2 carrots, peeled and cut into large cubes

2 turnips, peeled and cut into large cubes

10 spinach leaves

1 teaspoon fenugreek seeds (see page 42)

1 tablespoon fennel seeds

1 tablespoon black mustard seeds

2 tablespoons mustard oil (see page 45), plus more as needed

1 tomato, cut into wedges, for garnish when serving

Bishamber ji is a cook who spent twenty years cooking in Srinagar, Kashmir. From him, I learned a great deal about how spices are used in the mountainous areas.

When he and his family moved to Amritsar in 1990, I hired him as cook for my Lawrence Gardens catering company. I felt lucky to have him as he was a talented cook with a fine sense of humor and an even temperament that made him ideal for working in the high-pressure catering business.

In this versatile recipe, as is traditionally done in Punjab, the vegetables are fermented (Bishamber ji would boil them in vinegar instead). However, the spicing is pure Kashmiri-style, learned from him.

In a large nonreactive (glass or stainless-steel) bowl, sprinkle the turmeric, cayenne, paprika, and salt over the carrots, turnips, and spinach and let rest for at least 15 to 20 minutes.

In a small cast-iron skillet, dry-roast the fenugreek, fennel, and mustard seeds over medium heat until fragrant and dark in color, about 1 minute. Let the spices cool and grind them to a fine powder in a spice grinder or with a mortar and pestle. Mix the ground spices well with 2 tablespoons of the mustard oil and combine it with the seasoned vegetables.

Place everything in a clean, sterile jar large enough to hold all of the vegetables. Add additional oil until the vegetables are fully submerged. Tightly close the lid and place it in the sun to ferment until slightly sour, at least a week. You can also ferment it in a warm area indoors, which generally takes about 10 days. Store in the refrigerator for up to 1 month.

Gulmarg Tamarind Onion Relish

MAKES ABOUT 1 CUP

2 red onions, coarsely chopped

1 teaspoon Kashmiri or Hungarian paprika (see page 43)

1/2 teaspoon cayenne pepper

2 tablespoons tamarind paste (see page 45)

1 tablespoon finely chopped fresh cilantro

1/2 teaspoon salt

This chutney was a signature recipe of my aunt Sarita who lived in Gulmarg. Gulmarg, also known as the "Meadow of Flowers," is a popular hill station and skiing destination in the state of Jammu and Kashmir.

Kashmiri paprika adds a subtle pungency and vibrant red color to this dish. Sometimes if I'm in the mood for a less pungent relish, I add a tablespoon of honey, which smooths out the heat of the cayenne pepper and the acidity of the tamarind. I love adding a tablespoon of this chutney to plain yogurt to create a unique tamarind raita.

Mix all of the ingredients in a nonreactive (glass or stainless-steel) bowl and let rest for 3 to 4 minutes before serving.

Store in the refrigerator for up to 2 weeks in a tightly covered, clean jar.

Gulmarg. India.

Red Chile Onion Chutney [Ezzy]

MAKES ABOUT 1 CUP

8 to 10 dried red chiles

1 red onion, thinly sliced

1 tomato, seeded and coarsely chopped

1/2 teaspoon salt

I arranged through a local guide to go and see dha, or traditional archery, at the Changlimithang Stadium in Thimphu, the capital city of Bhutan. Archery is the national pastime and the place to see it is in Thimphu. While Olympic archers compete from a distance of fifty meters, the Bhutanese compete at a distance of one hundred and forty meters. Luckily for the Olympians, the Bhutanese aren't interested in participating in close-range competitions.

I had intentionally skipped breakfast so that I could enjoy a traditional breakfast of Bhutanese red rice with ezzy. Ezzy is a very hot condiment and should be handled with care. While I could only manage a little bit of the ezzy on my rice, a two-year-old boy sitting next to me heaped it on with great happiness.

In a heavy skillet, dry-roast the chiles over medium-low heat until very fragrant and slightly charred, about 2 minutes. Coarsely chop them and transfer to a bowl. Add the onion, tomato, and salt and mix well. Store, tightly covered in a clean jar, in the refrigerator for a week. Let it come to room temperature before serving.

Nepalese Tomato Chutney [Golbheda Ko Achaar]

MAKES ABOUT 1 1/2 CUPS

2 tablespoons vegetable oil

4 cloves garlic, thinly sliced

2 pounds ripe cherry tomatoes

1/3 cup water

1 fresh green chile (such as serrano), very coarsely chopped

2 teaspoons salt

1/8 teaspoon ground Szechuan peppercorn (see page 44)

1 tablespoon fresh lemon juice

1/4 cup tightly packed, finely chopped fresh cilantro

The smells of bakeries, delicious curries, and incense were always wonderful to wake up to when I stayed at a small guesthouse in Thamel, the center of tourism, entertainment, and food in Kathmandu. The reflection of a nation is always best seen through its cuisine and art and they are both available in abundance on the busy winding streets of Thamel.

I first tasted this spicy tangy chutney while sitting in a pleasant garden restaurant in Thamel surrounded by Nepali music and travelers and trekkers from all around the world. Pan-roasting the tomatoes and garlic helps create the layers of deeper flavors in this dish.

Heat the oil in a heavy-bottomed pan over medium-high heat and fry the garlic until golden brown, about 2 minutes, stirring continuously. Add the tomatoes and fry until very soft and the skins separate easily from the pulp, 3 to 4 minutes.

Add the water, chile, salt, and Szechuan pepper and let it boil, pressing the tomatoes with the back of the spoon. Lower the heat to low and cook until the mixture is well combined, 3 to 4 minutes.

Let cool for 5 minutes. Transfer to a blender, add the lemon juice and cilantro, and pulse to a coarse paste. Refrigerate in a clean jar for up to 2 weeks.

Sun-Fermented Cucumber Pickle [Khalphi]

MAKES ABOUT 1 PINT

1 large Nepali cucumber or 4 regular cucumbers, scrubbed to remove any wax

1/4 cup black or brown mustard seeds, finely ground with a mortar and pestle or in a spice grinder

2 tablespoons salt

1 jalapeño chile, seeded and finely chopped

1 tablespoon ground turmeric

5 tablespoons mustard oil (see page 45) or vegetable oil, plus more as needed

During the harvest month of Dussehra, a Hindu festival celebrated in India and Nepal, it's traditional to serve this pickle with the Nepalese dish Bhutuwa Massu (page 290). Of course, when making this pickle at home, you should feel free to enjoy it at any time and for any occasion.

If using Nepali cucumber, halve the cucumber lengthwise and scoop out and discard the mature seeds. Halve each cucumber-half lengthwise and cut the quarters into 2- to 3-inch-long pieces. If using regular cucumbers, trim the ends, quarter the cucumbers lengthwise, and trim off the seedy core. Place the cucumber pieces in a large nonreactive (glass or stainless-steel) bowl.

In a small bowl, mix the mustard seeds, salt, jalapeño, turmeric, and 3 tablespoons of the oil into a smooth paste. Pour the mixture over the cucumbers and evenly coat them with the spice mixture using clean hands.

Place them in a clean, sterile jar large enough to hold all the cucumbers. Push them with your hands to tightly fit in all the pieces. Top it with the remaining 2 tablespoons oil. If necessary, add additional oil until the vegetables are fully submerged. Tightly close the lid and place it in the sun to ferment until slightly sour, at least a week. You can also ferment it in a warm area indoors for 10 to 12 days.

Store in the refrigerator for up to 2 to 3 weeks.

Tibetan Chile-Garlic Paste

MAKES ABOUT 1/2 CUP

20 dried red chiles, stemmed

4 cloves garlic

3 tablespoons vegetable oil

3 tablespoons white wine vinegar

Salt

This blazing hot condiment is obligatory at mealtime in Tibet. There is no meal that you sit down to in Tibet, including breakfast, where this is not served and stirred into just about anything. It's quite spicy so be sure to warn your guests to exercise caution.

Heat a large, heavy-bottomed skillet over medium heat. Dry-roast the chiles, stirring continuously, until they become very fragrant, about 2 minutes.

Transfer the chiles, garlic, and 2 to 3 tablespoons water to a mortar and pestle, and grind to a coarse paste.

Heat the oil in a skillet over medium heat, add the chile-garlic mixture, and stir well. Add the vinegar and salt to taste and cook until very fragrant, about 2 minutes.

Let cool. Transfer the chile paste to a clean, sterile, dry jar with a lid. Store in the refrigerator for up to 4 months.

Lhasa, Tibet.

Mili Dana (page 416) from a
street vendor in Kolkata.

DESSERTS

Himalayan desserts are like the rest of the region's cuisine: simple and unpretentious. In fact, people often choose to eat dried or fresh fruit, or a piece of rock sugar for dessert. Moreover, no real tradition of eating desserts after a meal has ever developed in the region; Himalayans mostly prefer sweet treats with afternoon tea or as a midday pick-me-up. That said, there's no reason why you can't serve any of these desserts after a meal. Some desserts, such as the roth cookies (see page 378), are eaten during religious festivals or auspicious occasions.

Roth and rituals

When I was putting this book together, I was seized with the impulse to run to the Brooklyn Mini Storage where I had stored Sheela Auntie's recipes. I still remember the damp smell of the storage facility and searching feverishly through boxes and trunks until I found her recipe book, grandly titled My Kashmir.

I should have gone back into the city because I had many other things to do that day, but I just couldn't stop reading. Soon, I migrated to a corner of the storage facility and read through the whole thing. Sheela Auntie possessed great style and was as much admired among her peers for her sense of fashion as for her delicious cooking. Every recipe was in some way a document of her life. It was one of those moments that made me travel back in time to an era of perfect happiness in my youth when we would eat her cooking. This little gem of a story is from her notes about roth, a type of poppy seed cookie. It is an old story, often told in the past but now frequently forgotten, that emphasizes the importance of belief and faith. It does not withstand the onslaught of logic, but it affirms that the power of faith can create miracles.

Roth has cultural and religious significance for Kashmiri Hindus and is usually prepared at the time of the Kashmiri festival, Pun, in September. Puja is performed to invoke gods for blessings for prosperity and good luck. Traditionally, an elder family member relates a folk story such as this one.

In this story, prasad means a sacred offering, frequently a sweet of some sort. Dakshina is a monetary offering to compensate a priest for spiritual services.

THE LEGEND OF THE ROTH POOJA

Many years ago there lived a very poor Brahmin family, a husband, his wife and their beautiful daughter. The husband fed the family by begging alms, the daughter collected firewood from the forest. Once, on the fourth day of the month of Bhadoon Shakula Paksh, she saw something miraculous—a group of Devis descending from the heavens! Curious, she hid herself behind a tree to watch. They selected and prepared an area to make roth and began kneading together flour, ghee, sugar and cardamom and baking them on a hot plate. They could not complete their puja without a girl. Seeing her hidden behind a tree, they brought her out, bathed her and gave her a new dress to wear. After completing the puja, they gave her the roth as prasad and some money as dakshina. Once this was done, the Devis left and returned to their place in the heavens. Upon returning home the girl's parents did not believe her story. They beat her for being a thief even though she protested her innocence.

On the same day of the following year, the Brahmin girl was determined to repeat the ceremony performed by the Devis. Having no money, she collected cow dung and separated the undigested wheat, which she ground into flour. She had no ghee or sugar, so had to make do with water. Just as she had seen the Devis do, she cleaned the area of the previous year's celebration and baked her poor cakes on the hot rocks. The Devis were so pleased by her demonstration of faith that they decided to reward her. After she had covered her cakes with a cloth and completed her meager puja, she removed the cloth covering and was astonished to find that her cakes had been turned into gold. She offered thanks to the Devis and ran home to share the good fortune with her parents. But as before, they did not believe her and assumed she had committed some even greater crime this time. She was vigorously punished and sent to bed wailing. The Devis, seeing that injustice was being done to the girl came to her parents in a dream to reassure them that they had rewarded her faith. Upon waking, the girl's parents showered her with love and affection. Ever after, the family faithfully performed the roth puja and their good fortune steadily increased.

Some years later, the king was passing through on his way home from a hunting expedition and his eyes happened upon the Brahmin girl who was now a beautiful young woman. In the way of such things, the king was taken with the girl and asked her father for her hand in marriage. The marriage was made and that is how the poor little Brahmin girl became the queen.

This, however, is not a story of easy happy endings. As the time grew near for the roth puja, the new queen asked her husband for everything she needed to make the proper offering. The king's minister, a jealous man, told the king that the queen's requirements were exorbitant and unnecessary, that she was being greedy asking for all of this material for a puja he had never even heard of. The king agreed and refused her request. Naturally, the queen was terribly upset and begged the king to reconsider. When he would not, she went to the puja room to beg the Devis to pardon her. The Devis heard her and sent messages to the king in his dreams warning him that he would lose his kingdom for not performing the puja.

The very next day, the king from the neighboring country invaded and conquered his kingdom, his soldiers abandoned him and he was sent into exile with his wife. Now in dire straits, the king begged pardon from his wife. She, in turn, advised him that he must ask forgiveness from the Devis. The king prayed for the Devis to forgive him, which they did, but only after he promised to properly perform the puja. So he did, whereupon his soldiers returned to his side and they recaptured the kingdom in a great victory. Ever since then, the entire kingdom performed the roth puja faithfully.

Concluding prayer: Let us now pray to the Almighty that he will bless us as he did the little Brahmin girl and may he give us strength to remain strong and dedicated in our observance of the puja.

Kashmiri Poppy Seed Cookies [Roth]

MAKES ABOUT 20 COOKIES

2 cups all-purpose flour

1/4 cup semolina flour

1 teaspoon salt

1/2 teaspoon baking powder

1/4 cup ghee (clarified butter) or vegetable oil

1/2 cup water

1/4 cup white poppy seeds (may substitute black poppy seeds)

Vegetable oil, for frying

"The Legend of the Roth Pooja" (page 379) teaches me that having faith in doing the right thing and following up on it will be rewarded. I make a careful inventory at the end of each year to try to fulfill any promises I may have left undone. It allows me to go into the next year with a feeling of wholeness and completion.

Traditionally, roth is made with white poppy seeds, but black poppy seeds work just as well.

Sift the flour, semolina, salt, and baking powder into a bowl. Add the ghee and rub between your palms until crumbly. Gradually add the water (you may not need it all, or you may need more) and mix well, using your hands, into a firm and pliable dough. Cover with a damp kitchen towel and let rest for at least 30 minutes.

Divide the dough into 20 balls and roll out each into a 3-inch disk, 1/2 inch thick. Sprinkle the poppy seeds evenly over them and press to make them adhere.

Line a baking sheet with paper towels. Heat 3 inches of oil in a deep skillet over medium heat to 325°F. Carefully fry the disks a few at a time until crisp and golden, 5 to 7 minutes.

Remove with a skimmer or slotted spoon, drain on the paper towels, and serve with hot Kashmiri Tea (page 423).

Saffron Rice Pudding [Zaffran Zarda]

SERVES 6

5 cups water

1 cup basmati rice

1 tablespoon ghee (clarified butter)

10 whole cashews

10 shelled pistachios

4 whole green cardamom pods

2 tablespoons unsweetened dried coconut flakes

2 cups whole milk

1 teaspoon saffron threads

3/4 cup sugar

My dear childhood neighbor, Saroj Auntie, taught me this recipe for zarda. We lived next door to each other and the mail carrier would often deliver her letters to our house, and ours to hers. Whenever we received a piece of her mail, I confess that I would be eager to drop it off to her, hoping to get a small serving of her zarda as a reward for my delivery service. I was seldom disappointed.

Bring the water to a boil in a pot. Add the rice, lower heat to medium, and cook, uncovered, until the rice is cooked but still firm, about 15 minutes. Drain.

In a heavy-bottomed skillet, heat the ghee over medium heat. Add the cashews, pistachios, cardamom pods, and coconut and cook, stirring, until darker in color and fragrant, about 2 minutes.

Add the milk, saffron, and sugar and bring to a boil. Gently stir in the rice until well coated. Lower the heat to low and simmer, covered, until most of the liquid is absorbed and all the flavors are well blended, about 10 to 15 minutes. Let cool to room temperature before serving.

Jaggery Rice Pancakes [Til Pitha]

Jaggery

These pancakes are the perfect example of a dish that doesn't belong to anyone, yet belongs to everyone. I was in a barbershop in Assam, sitting for a shave and a haircut when the barber asked me what I was doing in the area. I replied that I was learning about Assamese food for a cookbook. The barber declared, "You must write about my grandmother's pitha. It's the best one you will ever have." He told me that her til pitha were small, the size of a kneecap (which gives them their name) and were made with jaggery, a sweetener made from sugar cane and the sap of the date tree.

Suddenly, another voice piped up. "My wife makes til pitha," announced a man to my left. He explained that his wife's pitha, which he claimed were certainly the best, were made with sesame, orange rind, coconut, and jaggery.

"It's too bad you've never tried the one my mother made," I heard a third man say. I said that he must have been lucky to have such a good cook for a mother. "Mother always made them with nuts and salt," he added fondly.

Before I knew it, everyone in the barbershop had offered a different version of pitha, and I had more invitations to try them than I had days left in Assam.

This recipe is my version of til pitha and is a tribute to the wonderful people of Assam. Pitha are fried pancakes made of bora rice flour (an Assamese glutinous rice) and filled with a mixture of sesame seeds and jaggery. They are generally served during Bihu festivals in Assam. People in villages start preparing these long before the festival begins. The rice is soaked and dried for two nights before being ground, combined with different flavorings, and fried in oil on a hot griddle. Pitha are also an inseparable part of jolpan, snacks that are generally served at breakfast. As you can tell from my experience at the barber's, pitha can be filled with many combinations of nuts, spices, and citrus rind. Experiment with your favorite flavors to find the one you like best. The rice requires soaking, so plan ahead.

SERVES 6

1/4 cup glutinous rice

3/4 cup basmati rice

4 1/4 cups water, divided

2/3 cup black sesame seeds (available at Asian groceries) or white sesame seeds

1/4 cup jaggery (see page 44) or date palm sugar

1/4 cup ghee (clarified butter) or vegetable oil

Combine the glutinous rice and basmati rice in a fine-mesh strainer and rinse under cold running water until the water runs clear. Transfer the rice to a bowl, cover with 4 cups water, and soak for 6 hours or overnight.

Drain the rice and transfer to a blender. Process the soaked rice to a smooth, fine paste, similar to the consistency of thick pancake batter, adding a little more water if necessary. Transfer to a bowl, cover, and refrigerate until ready to use.

In a heavy-bottomed skillet, dry-roast the sesame seeds over medium heat, stirring continuously, until fragrant, 2 to 3 minutes. Transfer to a blender, add the jaggery and 1/4 cup water and process to a fine paste.

Heat the ghee in a heavy-bottomed pan over medium-high heat and lower the heat to medium-low. Spoon in 3 tablespoons of batter and gently spread it to a thin crêpe. Let it cook until darker in color and lightly crisp, about 2 minutes. Remove the pancake from the pan and spread 1 tablespoon of the jaggery mixture in the middle. Roll it up tightly like a cigar to enclose the jaggery. Repeat with remaining batter. Pitha can be served warm or at room temperature.

Nepalese Steamed Sweet Dumplings [Yomari]

Traditional Nepalese door.

When I trained at the Soaltee Oberoi Hotel in 1993, my Newari friend invited me to his home for a birthday party for his son. The Newar people are indigenous to the Kathmandu Valley and are known for their hospitality.

My friend told me that only family and friends would be attending, so I was a little surprised when the house was packed with at least a hundred people. Were there twenty different dishes? Thirty? A hundred? I couldn't tell you. All I know is that the hospitality of the Newar—and their passion for cooking—perhaps cannot be matched anywhere else in the world.

I particularly enjoyed the yomari, rice flour dumplings stuffed with a sweet milk-based filling. At the time, I didn't know what they were called nor could I find anyone in Nepal who could tell me. The taste, dough, and steaming process of yomari surprisingly reminded me of one of Mumbai's favorite desserts, modaks. When I got back to the U.S., I tried Googling the dish with as many different search terms as I could think of, but no luck.

One day, during Diwali, the five-day Hindu "festival of lights," I was in Jackson Heights, Queens at the Patel Brothers Indian grocery store and ran into my Newari friend Sunita Shreshta. When I asked her what she was planning to cook for Diwali, she named about a dozen dishes. I knew most of them, but the dish yomari was unfamiliar. She described how it looked, and I knew I finally found the dumplings I had so enjoyed in Kathmandu.

At her family's Diwali celebration, she made very simple dumpling-like shapes, explaining that when her grandmother used to make them, all the kids in the family helped in the process. Eating them brought me right back to Kathmandu.

SERVES 4 TO 6

2 cups very fine rice flour, plus more for kneading

Pinch of salt

About 1 cup warm water

3 tablespoons sesame seeds

1 cup Khoya (recipe follows)

1/4 cup sweetened shredded coconut

1/4 cup jaggery (see page 44) or dark brown sugar

Vegetable oil spray

Add the flour and salt to the bowl of a food processor. Gradually add the water and process until a smooth dough forms.

On a lightly floured work surface, knead the dough with your hands until pliable and very elastic, 4 to 5 minutes. Add a tablespoon of water if necessary. Cover with plastic wrap and let rest for at least 20 to 30 minutes.

Heat a heavy-bottomed skillet over medium heat and roast the sesame seeds until fragrant, continuously stirring to ensure even cooking, about 2 minutes.

In a bowl, combine the sesame, khoya, coconut, and jaggery and mix well, using a wooden spoon, until smooth.

Knead the dough again on a lightly floured work surface until soft and smooth, 2 to 3 minutes. Divide the dough in 12 balls and keep them covered with a damp kitchen towel. Roll each ball into a 2-inch-long oval and lightly wet the edges of the oval with water. Form each into a cone with a pocket and place 2 tablespoons of the filling in it. Pressing with finger and thumb, tightly pinch it, sealing in the filling. Cover the filled cones with a damp kitchen towel to avoid drying out and cracking.

In a saucepan, bring 1/2-inch water to a rolling boil. Reduce heat to medium and simmer. Lightly grease a steamer tray or basket and place as many cones that can fit into it.

Place the steamer basket in the saucepan, cover, and steam until all cones are cooked through, 6 to 8 minutes. Remove and serve either warm or at room temperature.

Milk Cheese Filling [Khoya]

MAKES ABOUT 1 CUP

1 tablespoon ghee (clarified butter) or vegetable oil

1 pound whole milk ricotta cheese

Khoya is one of the key ingredients in South Asian dessert recipes. Chefs (halwais) stir the khoya mixture nonstop in heavy-bottomed woks placed over low flames of charcoal grills. The mixture is cooked until most of the liquid is evaporated and only milk solids remain. The traditional process of making khoya can take up to three hours and requires complete concentration and attention to prevent the milk from burning. The halwais will not look away from their pots for even a second as the completion time draws near. Burning the khoya at that point means a large financial loss and a great deal of time wasted.

Many times you will find khoya being sold in markets in two ways, sweetened or unsweetened. I prefer unsweetened because the sugar can always be added later and the added weight of the sugar in the sweetened version makes it unnecessarily more expensive. Using ricotta, I've created a pseudo-khoya that makes a fine substitute in just a fraction of the time it takes to create the traditional khoya.

Heat the ghee in a heavy-bottomed skillet over medium heat. Swirl to evenly coat the bottom of the pan. Lower the heat to medium-low and add the ricotta. Cook, stirring continuously, until most of the water is evaporated and the cheese seems dry, about 10 to 12 minutes.

Remove from the heat and let cool. Transfer to a clean jar, cover, and refrigerate for up to a week.

Nepalese Fried Cookies [Jeri]

Jeri, also known as jalebi, is one of the most popular desserts from the Nepalese region and always seemed to me like the work of an artist with its intricate and tangled structures floating in sizzling hot oil.

One of my fondest childhood memories involves these lovely cookies. I was totally unprepared for final exams at school so I pretended to be sick. My grandmother dipped some jeris into hot milk and gave them to me to help speed my "recovery." They were certainly a comforting food, but they came with a steep price tag. I had to live for a while with the guilt of lying.

The key to this dessert is the batter. In Kathmandu, jeris are very intricate and thin. For this home version, I simplified the process, but it's still very delicious. Please note that the batter must be made at least 6 hours ahead or the night before cooking.

SERVES 4 TO 6

1 cup all-purpose flour

1 1/2 tablespoons cornstarch

1 1/2 teaspoons baking powder

1/2 teaspoon vegetable oil, plus more for frying

1 tablespoon low-fat plain yogurt

1/2 teaspoon orange food coloring (optional)

1 1/2 cups water, divided

1 cup sugar

4 green cardamom pods, crushed opened

1 tablespoon rose water (optional)

Sift together the flour, cornstarch, and baking powder into a bowl and give it a little whisk to ensure that it's mixed well.

Add 1/2 teaspoon oil, the yogurt, and food coloring and gradually add about 1 cup water, whisking continuously to avoid lumps. The batter should be smooth and the consistency of thick pancake batter. Cover the bowl with plastic wrap, and let it rest at room temperature for at least 6 hours or overnight to ferment slightly.

In a pot, combine the sugar, cardamom, rose water, and the remaining 1/2 cup water and bring to a boil over medium heat, stirring continuously. Lower the heat and cook until the sugar is dissolved and reaches a one-thread consistency (a thin string should form when poured with a spoon). Keep warm over very low heat.

In a heavy skillet, heat at least 2 inches of oil over medium heat to 325°F. Mix the fermented batter with a wooden spoon and pour into a heavy plastic bag or a squeeze bottle. To test for the right oil temperature, drop a small amount of batter into the oil. If it sizzles and gradually rises to the top, the oil is hot enough. If it rises immediately, the oil is too hot.

Once the oil is ready, make a small hole at the end of the bag and press the batter cautiously over the hot oil, keeping the tip about 3 to 4 inches from the surface. Move your hand in a circular motion, from inside to outside, keeping the circle about 3 inches wide. It might take a few tries before you get it just right, but it's okay if the shape isn't perfect. Adjust the heat as you fry to maintain the correct oil temperature.

Fry until light golden at the edges, 1 to 2 minutes. Gently turn over using a slotted spoon and fry until completely golden and crispy.

Remove with a slotted spoon and immediately dip in the sugar syrup for a minute or until well soaked. Let the excess syrup drain back into the bowl. Serve warm or at room temperature.

Jammu Sweet Pancakes [Malpura]

SERVES 6

1 cup Khoya (page 389)

1 cup all-purpose flour

Pinch of salt

1/2 cup milk

1 cup sugar

2 teaspoons ground cardamom

1 teaspoon saffron threads

1/2 cup water

Ghee (clarified butter) or vegetable oil, for frying

When I'm travelling, I like to find a sense of rootedness by revisiting people whom I have met before and places that I've enjoyed. But at the same time, I worry that I'm missing out on making new discoveries. In the case of this malpura recipe, my repeat visits to a tea shop in Jammu did pay off. It took me awhile and many visits, but I finally bonded with the shop owner enough to ask him for the recipe for his delicious version of malpura. In Peshawar, during Ramadan, you can find a version made with semolina flour that's denser but just as delicious.

My favorite time to eat these comforting syrup-dipped pancakes is the beginning of monsoon season. When it rains, it's time for malpuras.

Combine the khoya, flour, and salt in a bowl. Gradually whisk in the milk to make a smooth, thick batter. If the khoya is very grainy and makes the batter lumpy, you might have to blend the mixture in a food processor.

In a pot, combine the sugar, cardamom, saffron, and water and bring to a boil over medium heat, stirring continuously. Lower the heat and cook until the sugar is dissolved and reaches a one-thread consistency (a thin string should form when poured with a spoon). Keep warm over very low heat.

Heat enough ghee or oil to a depth of about 1 inch in a heavy-bottomed skillet, preferably nonstick, over medium heat. Lower the heat to medium-low, add 3 tablespoons batter, and spread it with the back of the spoon into a 3-inch disk. Let it cook until the edges begin to brown. Turn to the other side and let it cook until golden, about 2 minutes. Remove to a plate and keep warm.

Add more ghee to the pan as needed and repeat with the remaining batter. Dip the cooked malpuras in the sugar syrup to evenly coat and remove with a slotted spoon. Serve warm or at room temperature.

Tibetan Sweet Pasta with Tsampa [Bhatsa Marku]

Tsampa cart.

Before my first visit to Tibet, I had made sure to memorize the names of several dishes that I was anxious to learn and bhatsa marku, a sweet pasta dish, was high on my list. Tenzing, my guide in Tibet, was surprised when I told him that I'd eaten it in a Tibetan restaurant in New York, and insisted that we try a proper version. It turned out to be everywhere in Tibet. Tenzing announced to nearly every person we encountered that I loved bhatsa marku. Of course, I was constantly offered it and found myself eating it almost non-stop on the trip.

This recipe was inspired by Tsering Wangmo's simple version in her wonderful book, The Lhasa Moon Tibetan Cookbook. *When we were testing recipes for this book, her version was a touchstone for what follows.*

Cooks often add chuship cheese (page 266) to their bhatsa marku, but for serving guests, a lighter version without the cheese may be preferable. Any version tastes great with hot butter tea (page 420).

SERVES 6 TO 8

2 cups all-purpose flour, plus more for kneading

Pinch of salt

1 1/3 cups water

1 cup (2 sticks) unsalted butter

1/2 cup tsampa (see page 46)

1/2 cup dark brown sugar

Combine the flour and salt in a bowl. Gradually add the water and mix to form a soft dough. Knead the dough until very elastic, 3 to 4 minutes. Cover the dough with plastic wrap and let it rest for up to an hour.

Knead the dough again on a lightly floured work surface until elastic and smooth, 2 to 3 minutes. Roll the dough into a 1/4-inch-thick disk. Cut the disk into 1-inch-wide strips with a sharp knife. Gently tear each strip into 1/2-inch pieces. Rub each piece around your thumb to shape the dough into shells.

Fill a large pot with water and bring it to a boil over high heat. Add the pasta to the water and cook until al dente, about 2 minutes. Drain.

Melt the butter in a heavy-bottomed skillet over medium heat and stir in the tsampa and sugar. Add the pasta and cook until well coated, carefully stirring. Serve at room temperature or cold.

Nepalese Sweetened Yogurt with Fruit [Srikani]

SERVES 4 TO 6

6 cups plain whole milk yogurt or 3 cups plain full-fat Greek-style yogurt

2 cups sugar

1 cup mixed fruits (optional)

4 green cardamom pods, coarsely crushed

Pinch of saffron threads (optional)

Bael fruit.

A friend of mine was on his way to Bhaktapur, a historic town in Nepal, to research a story he was writing about bael that turned out to be so fascinating, it ended up distracting me from my own mission. Bael (or bel) is a pear-shaped fruit found throughout India. It has a woody exterior and sweet, yellow-orange pulp inside. Young girls in Bhaktapur are symbolically married when they are between five and eleven years old to the bael, which symbolizes Lord Shiva. It is thought that one reason for this unusual marriage practice is that it allows women to circumvent the practice of sati, which people in Bhaktapur oppose. Sati is a tradition in which a widow is expected to leap on her husband's funeral pyre if he predeceases her. The traditional baelbyah assures that every girl is married to the bael fruit and therefore will never become a widow.

Srikani is a thick yogurt dessert with a velvety body punctuated by nuts and fruits. Every house has its own version and the one I had in Bhaktapur included bael in the mix. If you cannot find bael, feel free to use chopped apples.

If using regular yogurt, line a colander with a double layer of cheesecloth and place it over a large bowl. Place the yogurt in the cheesecloth and let it drain overnight in the refrigerator. Periodically drain off the liquid. (You should yield about 3 cups of strained yogurt with a thick, sour cream–like consistency.)

Transfer the strained yogurt or the Greek yogurt (if using) to a bowl. Add the sugar and beat until light and creamy. Add the fruits and mix to combine. Top with the cardamom and saffron and serve chilled.

Bhutanese Cookies [Khurma]

Karwa Chauth is a Hindu festival in which married women fast from sunrise to moonrise for the longevity and prosperity of their husbands. This holiday holds fond memories for me. I can recall my mother fasting before the start of Karwa Chauth. There was always a platter of ritual foods ready for when she broke her fast. Almonds, halwa, and meethimathi, a kind of fried cookie very much like these Bhutanese khurma, were some of the foods she was served. When many years later I sampled these khurma in the town of Paro, I flashed back in my mind to my mother holding up a sieve through which, as part of Karwa Chauth, she had to catch her first glimpse of the moon to break the fast. As the rest of the family all waited outside for that glimpse of the moon, I would steal these cookies from her platter while she pretended not to notice.

MAKES ABOUT 15 COOKIES

2 cups all-purpose flour, plus more for dusting

1 teaspoon orange food coloring (optional)

1/4 cup (1/2 stick) unsalted butter

1/2 cup warm water

1/2 cup sugar

1/2 cup water

Vegetable oil, for frying

Mix together the flour and food coloring (if using) in a large bowl. Add the butter and rub between your hands until the mixture is well combined and very coarse. Add a little warm water at a time, up to 1/2 cup, and knead the dough until the mixture comes together as a stiff ball. Cover with plastic wrap and let rest for at least 15 to 20 minutes.

Bring the sugar and 1/2 cup water to a boil in a small saucepan over high heat. Lower the heat to medium and cook until the sugar is dissolved and mixture becomes a thick syrup. Keep warm over very low heat.

Lightly flour the work surface and knead the dough for another 5 to 6 minutes, until firm and smooth. Divide the dough into 15 balls and keep them covered with a damp kitchen towel. Flatten each ball with your hand and roll out to a 6- to 7-inch-long rectangle, 2 inches wide and 1/4 inch thick.

Line a baking sheet with paper towels. Place a wire rack over another baking sheet. Heat about 3 inches of oil in a large skillet or saucepan over medium heat to 325ºF. Turn the heat to low and carefully fry the rectangles a few at a time, pressing them with a slotted spoon to evenly coat them with hot oil. Turn the rectangles once and fry until crisp and golden brown on both sides, about 2 minutes each side.

Remove with a slotted spoon and drain the excess oil on the paper towels.

Carefully dip the pastries in the syrup and let dry on the wire rack. Store, refrigerated, in an airtight container for up to a month.

Semolina Sweets [Halwa]

SERVES 4

1 cup sugar

2 1/2 cups water

1 teaspoon ground cardamom

1/2 cup (1 stick) unsalted butter

1 cup finely ground semolina or Cream of Wheat

Smell is such a powerful component of food memory for me. One of my most indelible memories dates from my childhood when I was staying with my auntie, Mrs. Shreshta, during the fall Tihar Festival, also known as Deepawali. I was lying in bed upstairs in a state between sleeping and wakefulness when the smell of the semolina halwa wafting up from the kitchen carried me back in a dream state to when my grandmother made this dessert when I was a child.

The scent of halwa cooking is one that warms and comforts me more than any other I can think of. Perhaps one of the reasons I have such warm memories of this treat is that my Biji never failed to make me semolina halwa for my birthday. Most memorably, on my sixth birthday, I went down to the kitchen where my Biji was cooking the halwa and she surprised me with a pair of brand new shoes. Needless to say, I was thrilled.

Mix sugar, water, and cardamom in a pan and heat over low heat, stirring continuously until dissolved.

Melt the butter in a heavy-bottomed saucepan over medium-low heat. Add the semolina and cook, stirring continuously, until darker in color and very fragrant, 6 to 8 minutes. Add the sugar syrup and mix with a whisk to avoid any lumps. Increase the heat to high and bring to a boil. Lower the heat to low and simmer until all the water is absorbed, about 5 minutes. Serve hot.

Kashmiri Vermicelli with Milk [Seviyan]

SERVES 4 TO 6

2 tablespoons ghee (clarified butter) or unsalted butter

1/4 cup raisins

2 ounces Indian vermicelli (seviyan, available at South Asian groceries)

1 teaspoon ground cardamom

2 cups whole milk

1/4 cup sugar

Pinch of saffron threads

3 tablespoons chopped pistachios

This is a sweet dish made from seviyan (Indian vermicelli) and milk and is enjoyed by many throughout India. It is traditionally eaten on the occasion of Eïd al-Fitr, which celebrates the end of Ramadan.

Everywhere you go during Ramadan, in places like the town of Srinagar, you can see piles of seviyan, which is made from wheat flour and has an earthy, nutty taste. Italian vermicelli would not make a good substitute.

Heat the ghee in a heavy-bottomed pan over medium-low heat and cook the raisins until they swell, about 1 minute. Add the vermicelli and cook, stirring gently until evenly light brown, 3 to 4 minutes.

Bring the milk and sugar to a boil over high heat in a pot. Add the milk mixture to the vermicelli and mix well. Cook, stirring until the vermicelli is soft, 2 to 3 minutes. Stir in the saffron and top with the pistachios. Serve hot or cold.

Bhutanese Sweet Rice [Mehtak]

SERVES 4

1/2 cup (1 stick) unsalted butter, divided

1 cup long-grain rice, preferably basmati

2 cups water

5 tablespoons sugar

1/4 cup raisins

1 cup Chinese dates (available at Asian groceries) or other favorite dried fruit

This dish, studded with Chinese dates, is commonly served during the religious festival Losar and other special occasions. Imported from China to the Himalayas, Chinese dates come in red and black varieties and can be eaten fresh or dried, as a snack or cooked into a sweet. They are also called "jujubes" and are available at Asian grocery stores or online. In Bhutan, date leaves are also used as potpourri for the home.

It is said that dates nourish the blood and calm the mind. I don't know if this is true, but I encourage you to try them nevertheless just for their wonderful flavor.

Heat 2 tablespoons of the butter in a skillet over medium-high heat. Cook the rice until it becomes translucent, about 2 minutes. Add the water and sugar and bring to a boil. Cook until almost all of the water has been absorbed, 8 to 10 minutes. Reduce the heat to low, cover with a damp kitchen towel and then with a tight-fitting lid, and cook for another 5 minutes.

Fluff the rice with a fork and mix in the remaining 6 tablespoons butter, raisins, and dates. Serve at room temperature.

Tibetan Celebration Sweets

MAKES 8 COOKIES

1 cup ricotta cheese

1/4 cup sugar

1/4 cup golden raisins

When I went to a party for my Tibetan guide's daughter, I learned to make these sweets in addition to chicken meatballs (page 248). I was surprised when my guide's wife told me that these cookies only contained three ingredients and was doubtful until I made them myself. As it turned out, the recipe really was that wonderfully simple.

Traditionally, churu (page 268) is used in this recipe. In this adapted version, I use full-fat ricotta instead.

Heat a heavy-bottomed wok or a skillet over medium heat. Cook the ricotta cheese, stirring continuously until the cheese begins to darken and dry, 6 to 8 minutes. Remove from heat and let cool for 10 to 15 minutes, until just warm.

Add the sugar and raisins and mix well until it resembles coarse flour. Mold into your favorite shapes, such as small rounds or pyramids, and serve cold.

Tibetan Rice Pudding

SERVES 4

1/2 cup broken basmati or short-grain rice

1 tablespoon unsalted butter

3 cups whole milk

1 cup water

1/4 cup sugar or grated jaggery (see page 44)

Pinch of salt

1/4 cup raisins

8-10 green cardamom pods, lightly crushed

I use broken rice rather than whole rice when I make this pudding because it releases more starch and creates a thicker consistency. To make your own broken rice, place the rice in a blender or food processor and pulse a few times until the rice is broken up. If you're serving this dish cold, add a little more sugar; chilled rice pudding tastes less sweet than when hot.

Rinse the rice well and soak in water, covered by 2 inches, for at least 30 minutes. Drain.

Melt the butter in a heavy-bottomed saucepan over medium heat and stir in the rice. Cook until the rice turns translucent. Add the milk and water and bring to a boil. Lower the heat to low and simmer, covered, stirring continuously to prevent scorching. Cook until the milk is reduced by half, about 10 to 15 minutes.

Add the sugar, salt, and raisins and cook, stirring continuously, for another 2 to 3 minutes.

Serve warm or cold, topped with the cardamom. If serving cold, let cool to room temperature before refrigerating.

Droma

SERVES 4

1 large sweet potato, diced small

3 tablespoons unsalted butter

1/4 cup sugar

I had been told that traveling in Tibet means never having to worry about getting lost, and it turned out to be true. On one trip, driving from Lhasa to Churkha, our car broke down in the middle of nowhere just as the sun was setting. The driver patted my shoulder to reassure me and said that there was a light to the east of us. I expressed concern about being welcome at a stranger's house, and he just smiled and said that it was not like that in Tibet. And indeed it was not. After a long walk, we were given a kind welcome and a place to sleep for the night.

The grandmother who was in charge of the kitchen showed us a basket of what turned out to be droma, a small sweet potato-like root that I had never tasted before. The children had dug them up from the surrounding hillside that morning. I helped her in the kitchen as she prepared the droma.

I was happier with that dessert than just about any other I have ever tried. She served it to us in simple wooden bowls that carried a whiff of the fireplace from the smoke-infused wood. I understood that in exchange for the family's hospitality, I was expected to share some information about myself so I told them stories about my first trips to the mountains with my grandfather. Stories and news from the outside world are still valuable currency in places like Tibet where travel and communication are difficult.

There are generally two harvests of droma, one in the fall and one in the spring when they are sweeter. I wish someone could freeze and bring them to the markets in America. They are not easy to get, but are so special and evocative of Tibet that I had to include the recipe here with sweet potatoes as their stand-in.

Fill a medium saucepan with water and bring to a boil over high heat. Add the diced sweet potato and cook until tender, but still firm, about 10 minutes. Drain.

Melt the butter in a skillet over medium heat. Add the sweet potato and sugar and cook until the sugar dissolves and the mixture is syrupy. Serve warm or cold.

Tibetan Walnut Fudge

MAKES 1 1/2 POUNDS

2 cups walnut pieces

1/2 cup water

1/4 cup (1/2 stick) unsalted butter

3/4 cup dark brown sugar

2 cups whole milk

I learned this recipe in Tibet from a carpet maker's wife. It turned out that the dye for the wool used to weave his rugs was made from the skins of the walnuts his wife used to make this delicious fudge.

Combine the walnuts and water in a blender or a food processor and purée to a coarse mixture.

Melt the butter in a large saucepan or skillet over medium heat. Add the ground walnuts and cook, stirring continuously, until fragrant, 3 to 4 minutes. Add the sugar and cook until well combined and the sugar is dissolved, 8 to 10 minutes. Add the milk and bring to a boil, lower heat to medium, and simmer about 4 minutes. Continue to cook until the fat separates out and the mixture is thick and smooth. Pour off the fat, let fudge cool, and serve at room temperature. It will remain soft and is best eaten with a spoon.

Store in the refrigerator for up to one week.

Indian Cardamom Ice Cream [Kulfi]

MAKES 1 DOZEN KULFI

2 cups evaporated milk

1 can (14 ounces) sweetened condensed milk

1 cup heavy cream

1 tablespoon ground cardamom

Kulfi is one of the most beloved desserts in all of India and tastes like a combination of Popsicles and ice cream. As children, we almost never tasted a completely frozen kulfi because we would keep opening the freezer door to check to see if it were ready and so it would never set properly. Often, we would just drink the kulfi as slushy flavored milk, and we loved that, too.

Combine all the ingredients in a bowl and whisk until the condensed milk is well incorporated.

Pour into 12 small Popsicle molds or 12 plastic Dixie cups with a Popsicle stick for each one and freeze overnight. Or, pour the mixture into a 9 by 13-inch metal baking pan and freeze for 8 hours or overnight. Cut with a sharp knife into 2-inch cubes and serve.

Sweet Chickpea Crisps [Mili Dana]

To show respect to our elders in traditional Hindu families, we touch their feet and then our foreheads, indicating our desire to benefit from their wisdom. In turn, our elders reach out to us and touch our foreheads to confer their blessings upon us. In this way, the mutual respect and love between generations is renewed every day.

On a trip to Kolkata in 2007, I came to the foot of the River Ganges and dipped my hands in its waters and carried it to my forehead, much as I do with my elders. It seemed a fitting way to honor the way this most sacred river gives life to millions. Kolkota is the end of the River Ganges' journey from the Himalayas. It is where the river empties its sacred waters into the Bay of Bengal and the cycle of water and the cycle of life begin anew.

I was thinking this over when I found a street vendor in Kolkata selling mili dana, weighing them with his handheld scale, surrounded by people who had lost a dear one or, as they put it, had arrived at the "end of the journey of one life." Kolkata is where millions of Indians come to remember their dead and release the ashes of their loved ones into the delta so that the soul may be reincarnated or find its way to heaven. These sweet crisps were the last dessert I ate on this trip to Kolkata.

SERVES 4 TO 6

1 cup chickpea flour
(see page 44)

1/2 cup lukewarm water

1 1/2 cups sugar

1 teaspoon ground cardamom

1 cup water

Vegetable oil, for frying

In a bowl, combine the chickpea flour and lukewarm water and lightly whisk to make a smooth thick batter. Let rest for 4 to 5 minutes.

In a pot, combine the sugar, cardamom, and 1 cup water and bring to a boil over medium heat, stirring continuously. Lower the heat and cook until the sugar is dissolved and reaches a one-thread consistency (a thin string should form when poured with a spoon). Keep warm over very low heat.

Heat 3 inches of oil in a large, deep skillet over medium heat to 325°F.

Stir the batter. The batter must drop through the skimmer in droplets so it's important that it's not too thick or thin. Add another tablespoon of water if it seems too thick. Hold a perforated skimmer 2 to 3 inches above the oil and pour 2 tablespoons of batter over the skimmer. (A 8-inch-diameter stainless-steel skimmer works perfectly.) The skimmer should be high enough for the batter to separate into droplets, but low enough so that it doesn't cause the oil to splash. Press the batter on top of the skimmer gently with your other hand in a circular motion to continuously drop it in the oil. Use enough batter to fill the bottom of the pan in a single layer of droplets, being careful not to overcrowd.

Fry, stirring gently to ensure even cooking, until it turns golden brown, 3 to 4 minutes.

Remove the fried batter with a slotted spoon and add to the sugar syrup. Continue to cook all the batter and let it soak in sugar syrup for at least 5 minutes, until all the syrup is absorbed.

Let it cool and serve at room temperature. Store in the refrigerator, covered, up to 2 weeks.

Green tea counter outside mosque
in Srinagar. Kashmir. India.

BEVERAGES

These beverages are typical of the drinks consumed in the Himalayas. In recent years, traditional drinks have taken on flavors from neighboring countries such as India and China; drinks such as lassi and masala chai are becoming great favorites.

Tea is the most popular beverage in the region, and there is a prescribed etiquette for drinking it. To sip the tea, first blow on the surface, sending any floating yak butter foam off to the far side of your cup. You must take at least two sips. Your cup will always be refilled. When you have had enough tea, saying you have had enough is simply not done. Instead, simply stop drinking and leave your cup full.

Tibetan Butter Tea [Poecha]

MAKE 4 CUPS

6 cups water

3 tablespoons loose Tibetan tea
or any good-quality dark tea

1 cup whole milk

1 pinch baking soda (optional)

1/2 teaspoon salt

2 tablespoons unsalted butter

Traditional butter tea, famously made with yak butter, is an acquired taste—but if you do acquire it as I did, you'll really get hooked. You may be able to try the real butter tea with yak butter if you have Tibetan friends or if you're lucky enough to travel in the region. Otherwise, this recipe, which calls for unsalted cow's milk butter, is a pretty close approximation.

One important trick I learned in Tibet to retain the beautiful earthy color of this tea is to simply add a pinch of baking soda. Tibetans also believe that whisking the tea aerates it and improves the flavor; try it and see what you think.

Boil the water. Add the tea and bring to a boil again. Lower heat to medium and let simmer 12 to 15 minutes, stirring occasionally with a whisk.

Add the milk and baking soda (if using) and bring to a boil again.

Remove from the heat and let rest for 2 minutes for tea to be totally infused. Strain the tea into a large container with a good lid, and with a wooden spoon, mix in the salt and butter until well combined (you may also combine all the ingredients in a blender). Serve hot.

Kashmiri Tea [Kawha]

SERVES 6

6 teaspoons loose Kashmiri
green tea

2-inch cinnamon stick

2 green cardamom pods, slightly
crushed open

2 whole cloves

1/4 cup sugar

3 1/2 cups water

1/2 teaspoon saffron threads

10 to 12 blanched almonds,
coarsely chopped

I must have been twelve years old when I first saw a samovar. I was at my cousin's wedding in Kashmir and there was a beautiful samovar in the hotel lobby that I fell in love with and never forgot. I had never seen so much intricate art applied to a piece of kitchen equipment before, and I couldn't wait until I had enough money to buy one of my own.

A year before I left Amritsar to come to New York, I was hired for a high-end catering job where the customer wanted a celebration that was truly exotic and out of this world. As I spoke with my client, my mind flashed back to my cousin's wedding (page 298) and its wazwan feast, a traditional Kashmiri banquet. When I proposed the idea of a thirty-six-course feast, his eyes got large as if in a dream and he immediately insisted on it. We arranged for the same Vasta Waza, or master chef, who had prepared my cousin's wedding feast to come from Srinagar with his retinue of cooks. They brought their samovar from which they drank kawha all day long (which, unlike chai, is never with milk).

As they were preparing to leave after the feast, I approached one of the Vasta Waza's assistants to see if I could make an offer to buy the samovar. I was shocked when the Vasta Waza himself came to me and insisted on giving it to me as a gift. He had not forgotten me from my cousin's wedding and was pleased to see that I had become a chef and had not forgotten him either. I have to confess that the gift made me tear up a bit.

Combine the tea, cinnamon, cardamom, cloves, sugar, and water in a medium heavy-bottomed pot and bring to a boil over high heat. Lower the heat to low, cover, and simmer until all the flavors are well combined, 3 to 4 minutes. Remove from heat and let it infuse for another 2 minutes.

Strain. Stir the saffron into the tea. Serve a half-cup per person, topping each with almonds.

Tsampa Water with Lemon [Sattu]

SERVES 4

6 cups cold water

6 tablespoons tsampa (see page 46)

2 tablespoons sugar

1/2 teaspoon salt, or less to taste

Juice of 1 lemon

Pulchand and Gulabi, our family's caretakers since the day I was born, were country people from a Himalayan village near Nainital in northern India. When they went on vacation back to their village, they would always bring back sattu, the Nainital version of tsampa. To them, tsampa meant any grain that was toasted and then ground. They made this beverage from sattu and told me that it was the only beverage that could beat the heat in the summer. If you're trying this for the first time, try adding just a half pinch of salt to start.

Combine all the ingredients in a blender and pulse until well combined. Serve chilled over crushed ice.

Lassi or Tara

SERVES 6

1 quart plain low-fat yogurt

6 tablespoons brown sugar

10 ice cubes

1/2 cup buttermilk

Pinch of salt

The growing popularity of lassi among Tibetans reflects the Indian cultural influences on the Tibetan exile community. Tara, a more traditional Tibetan drink, is made from buttermilk, not yogurt, and is never sweet. This recipe is for a hybrid lassi-tara drink.

In the Himalayas, people drink lassi as a cooling beverage during the hot summer days. It is made with whole milk yogurt rather than the low-fat kind common in America. The whole milk yogurt used in India is not homogenized so the cream rises to the top and can be enjoyed separately. Sweet lassi may be made with fruit purées, such as mango, a type of lassi you find served much more often in Indian restaurants in America than in India itself. Some lassi recipes, such as this one, call for brown sugar, which imparts a more distinctly Tibetan flavor. Savory lassi is usually made with dry-roasted cumin.

Blend all the ingredients in a blender on high speed until smooth and frothy. Serve chilled.

Lhasa River.

Kashmiri Salty Fennel Tea [Suja]

SERVES 4

4 cups water

2 teaspoons fennel seeds

1/4 cup loose Kashmiri tea or black tea

1 cup whole milk

1 pinch baking soda

1/2 tablespoon salt

In Kashmir, it is traditional to say "sheen mubarak" ("blessed snow") to mark the first snowfall. Everyone then goes out on a flurry of home visits and trades phone calls. People share foods, typically their favorite dishes, in quickly thrown together parties. I first tried suja at one such party. It was wonderfully soothing, fennel flavored, and a little salty. I clearly remember sitting wrapped in a traditional warm Kashmiri pheran, a coat resembling a large blanket with sleeves woven with Kashmir wool, and sipping this suja while watching the snow falling on my aunt's garden.

Combine the water, fennel seeds, and tea in a pot and bring it to a boil over high heat. Lower the heat to low and simmer for 2 minutes, until all the flavors are well combined.

Add the milk and baking soda and let it brew for another 3 to 4 minutes. Stir in the salt and serve hot, passed through a tea strainer if you prefer.

Ramadan Sweet Milk

SERVES 4

2 cups whole milk

1 1/2 cups water

3 tablespoons sugar

1/4 teaspoon rose water (optional)

3 tablespoons basil (tulsi) seeds
or chia seeds, soaked in 1/2 cup
warm water for 10 minutes

Ice cubes, for serving

It is traditional when breaking the daily fast during Ramadan to eat dates and drink some sort of sweetened milk. During Ramadan in Kashmir, every Muslim shopkeeper carries a bucket of this milk with him to work. When the time comes to break the fast, the merchants come out of their stores to share the milk with one another and with passersby. It is a drink that symbolizes unity and prosperity for all.

In this recipe, whole cow's milk is scented with rose water and basil seeds. This drink is perfect served with a handful of dates. The basil seeds in the recipe refer to tulsi (not Italian basil) and are available at South Asian or Indian groceries. You may also use chia seeds, which are now more readily available.

Combine all the ingredients in a bowl or pitcher, and stir until well combined. Pour into glasses over ice cubes and serve.

Spiced Limeade [Masala Nimbu Paani]

SERVES 6

3/4 cup sugar

Juice of 4 limes

5 cups cold water

1 tablespoon Chaat Masala (page 39)

Pinch of salt

Ice cubes, for serving

One of my favorite places to enjoy nimbu paani is one of the many food stalls in Rishikesh in the foothills of the Himalayas. Rishikesh is sacred to Hindus because it is where the Ganges leaves the mountains, and Lord Vishnu is said to have appeared there. There are many Americans and other Westerners there, which at first puzzled me as a child because I didn't know about the Beatles and their visit to the town in 1968. My grandfather did, of course, as there was nothing important going on that he didn't know about. The Beatles visited the ashram of Maharishi Mahesh Yogi, and it is still a favorite destination for nostalgic American visitors and devoted Hindus alike.

Mix all the ingredients except the ice in a large container and chill in the refrigerator. Serve cold over ice.

Nepalese Goli Wali Bottle Limeade

SERVES 6

Juice of 4 limes

5 cups seltzer

1 tablespoon black salt, or to taste (see page 40)

Ice cubes, for serving

On most street corners in Nepal, you can find stands selling long glass bottles with little marble stoppers in the neck filled with a fizzy lime drink. Goli means marble, hence the name of this very popular beverage.

Vendors push the marble stopper with their thumb to open the bottle. They then immediately pour the fizzy water into a glass while simultaneously squeezing the lime in. You can get nearly the same—but not identical—results by substituting seltzer. Black salt (kala namak) is an acquired taste, so add just a little at a time when making this drink.

| Mix all the ingredients and serve chilled over ice.

Holi Saffron Spiced Almond Milk [Thandai]

SERVES 4

1/2 cup slivered blanched almonds

2 tablespoons shelled unsalted pistachios

1/4 cup sugar

2 tablespoons poppy seeds

1 tablespoon fennel seeds

4 whole green cardamom pods

2 cups water

1 1/2 cups milk

Ice cubes, for serving

Holi celebrates the return of spring and is one of the largest and most inclusive religious festivals in India. It is the festival of colors—we throw colored powders in the air and shoot colored water at each other from pichkaris, kind of like super-size squirt guns. The colors symbolize the new growth of all living things.

We often traveled during the festival of Holi, and one of my favorite places to celebrate was in Dehradun with my cousins. Located in the foothills of the Himalayas, it is the most famous rice-growing region in India and home of the best basmati rice in the world. For me, the best part of the holiday was this saffron drink.

Pulverize the almonds and pistachios with the sugar in a food processor. Using a spice grinder, grind the poppy seeds, fennel seeds, and cardamom to a fine powder. Combine the two ground mixtures in a blender and gradually add the water with the motor running, followed by the milk. Strain the thandai through a fine-mesh strainer and chill. Serve over ice.

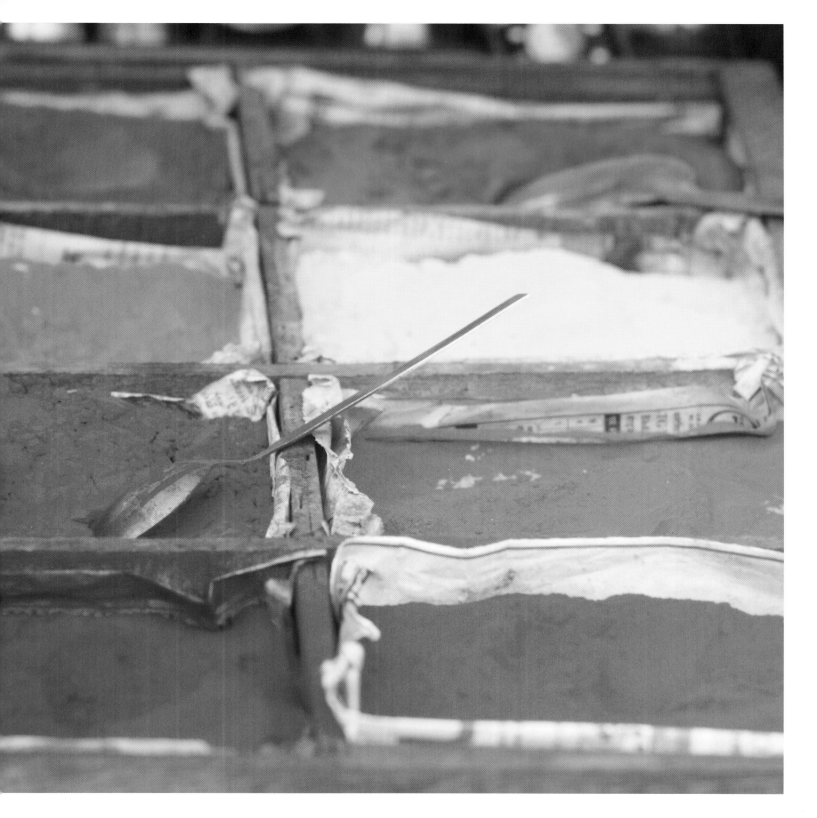

Resources

This list is intended to help you along with some of those harder-to-find ingredients. Here are some of my favorite stores for specialized ingredients including spices, legumes, grains, and vegetables.

Kalustyan's
123 Lexington Avenue
New York, NY
www.kalustyans.com
212- 685-3451
800-352-3451
212-683-8458 (fax)

Patel Brothers
Stores nationwide
www.patelbrothersusa.com
718-661-1112
718-661-2076 (fax)

Apna Bazar Cash and Carry
Stores in New York and New Jersey
apnabazarcashandcarry.com
718-565-5960

My Spice Sage
www.myspicesage.com
877-890-5244

Spice Corner
135 Lexington Ave.
New York, NY 10016
www.spicecorner29.com
212-689-5182
212-689-0067 (fax)

The Spice House
1512 North Wells Street
Chicago, IL 60610
(and elsewhere in Illinois and Wisconsin)
www.thespicehouse.com
312-274-0378
847-328-3711

Nepali Goods
Gundruk, jimbu, etc.
www.nepaligoods.com

Tibetan Tsampa
5337 Clinton Avenue
Richmond, CA 94805
www.tibetantsampa.com
510-230-8152

INDEX

CONVERSION CHART
US TO METRIC MEASUREMENTS

This book uses standard American measures: the 8-ounce cup and the tablespoon. One cup is equal to 16 level tablespoons, and 3 teaspoons are equal to 1 tablespoon. Measuring by cups makes it difficult to give weight equivalents; a cup of milk will weigh more than a cup of flour. Therefore, it is easiest to convert cup measurements to volume rather than weight. All measurements are rounded to the nearest whole number. The one exception is butter: butter is easier to measure by weight than volume.

1 stick butter:
(1/2 cup or 8 tablespoons) = 110 grams

To ensure the most accurate results, seek out a set of American measuring cups and spoons. Most major stores around the world sell American cup measures.

VOLUME

U.S.	Metric
1/4 teaspoon	1 ml
1/2 teaspoon	2.5 ml
3/4 teaspoon	4 ml
1 teaspoon	5 ml
2 teaspoons	10 ml
1 tablespoon	15 ml
2 tablespoons	30 ml
1/4 cup	59 ml
1/3 cup	79 ml
1/2 cup	118 ml
2/3 cup	158 ml
3/4 cup	178 ml
1 cup	237 ml
1 1/2 cups	355 ml
2 cups (1 pint)	473 ml
3 cups	710 ml
4 cups (1 quart)	.95 liter

WEIGHT

Most recipes call for things like chicken, lamb, and fish in terms of weight. Occasionally a can of food is called for in ounces. Convert to grams using the chart below.

U.S.	Metric
1/2 ounce	14 grams
1 ounce	28 grams
8 ounces (1/2 lb)	227 grams
12 ounces	340 grams
13.5 ounces	383 grams
14.5 ounces	411 grams
15 ounces	425 grams
15.5 ounces	439 grams
16 ounces (1 lb)	454 grams
28 ounces	794 grams

To convert ounces to grams, multiply the ounces by 28.35.

LENGTHS

U.S.	Metric
1 inch	2.54 cm

To convert from inches to centimeters, multiply inches by 2.54.

TEMPERATURE

Fahrenheit	Celsius
135°	58°
165°	74°
250°	121°
300°	149°
325°	163°
350°	177°
375°	190°
400°	204°
425°	218°

Information compiled from a variety of sources, including *The New Food Lover's Companion* by Sharon Tyler Herbst and Ron Herbst (Hauppauge, New York: Barron's, 2009) and *Jim Fobel's Big Flavors* by Jim Fobel (New York: Clarkson Potter, 1995).